PROTESTANTISM

IN AN

ECUMENICAL AGE

Its Root • Its Right • Its Task

by

Otto A. Piper

FORTRESS PRESS   PHILADELPHIA

MS, ~~Ecumenical movement~~
Protestantism — 20th century

PREFACE

Participation in the ecumenical movement in various capacities almost since its inception has led the author to feel that all too frequently the movement has followed the momentum given to it by its most active organizers, and that those leaders seldom had time and opportunity to examine the theological implications of the movement they were promoting. Such a development was almost inevitable as the free flow of the Spirit took on outward form in the World Council of Churches. Now that the task of organizing has been completed there should be more leisure for theological reflection and a willingness to let God's Spirit become master of the organization.

It is the author's contention that the enthusiasm of the early advocates and supporters of the ecumenical movement, and the industry, zeal, and efficiency of its organizers, has at times caused them to pay insufficient attention to its spiritual dynamic and to take things for granted which require and deserve critical assessment. Only by seeing both the movement itself and the existence of Protestantism in the light of holy history (*Heilsgeschichte*) can we hope to find the right synthesis of organizational effort and divine inspiration in our endeavors to make the unity of Christ's Body manifest.

Since such an approach to the ecumenical movement is concerned with principles rather than with the people who have played outstanding roles in it, names are mentioned here only sparingly. As the first generation of the ecumenical movement passes away, the author entertains the hope that the younger men and women who are about to take the place of the initiators will make this an occasion for critically scrutinizing and spiritually intensifying the work of the World Council of Churches and of the ecumenical movement which brought it into being.

A great deal of our investigation is devoted to the religious world outside of the World Council of Churches, in particular to the Roman Catholic church. It is obvious that there can be no true unity of the church of Christ if the existence of the Roman Catholic church is ignored, or if her participation in the ecumenical movement is precluded as a matter of principle. The more we try to realize a united church comprising all its branches, the greater the difficulties appear. Fortunately, however, there is also the encouraging fact that since the pontificate of John XXIII Protestants and Catholics are living in an atmosphere in which discussion of both the things that unite us and those that divide us has become possible.

The author takes this opportunity to express his profound gratitude to two former students of his, whose indefatigable love and careful attention to the minutiae of language no less than to the smooth flow of the argument have contributed substantially to polishing the style of this book. I am referring to Professor William Klassen of Biblical Seminary, New York, New York, and Professor Gerald C. Borchert of North American Baptist Seminary, Sioux Falls, North Dakota. This is one of the rare rewards of the scholar's life, that those whom he has guided on the road to scholarly accomplishment will repay him with their association in the common pursuit of the truth.

Otto A. Piper

Princeton, New Jersey
October, 1964

TABLE OF CONTENTS

PART TWO: PROTESTANTISM'S BASIC PROBLEM

Chapter III. THE PLACE OF PROTESTANTISM IN ECUMENICAL LIFE 83

Chapter IV. CONTEMPORARY PROTESTANTISM AND THE PROBLEM OF UNITY . 111

PART ONE

PROTESTANTISM
IN THE
MODERN WORLD

CHAPTER 1

WHAT IS PROTESTANTISM?

A. THE PROBLEM

Modern writers speak of Protestantism, the Protestant church, Protestant Ethics, and Protestant Culture as if the identity of Protestantism is beyond question. But what an elusive entity it is! What historical or sociological facts do we actually refer to when we designate a culture or an age as "Protestant"? Unlike their Roman Catholic brethren, Protestants have no external tie which holds them together. People who acknowledge the doctrinal and disciplinary authority of the Pope and the hierarchy are considered by Roman Catholics as belonging to the church, while people who refuse to recognize these authorities are considered outside the church even though they faithfully embrace all its dogmas. Are we to say then that the term "Protestant" designates all and every Christian outside of the Roman fold? But there are the Eastern Orthodox churches too. They tell us that in their view individuals as such do not count: Orthodoxy is formed only by churches, churches that are held together by their common allegiance to the dogmas and decrees of the ecumenical councils and by their common willingness not to advance theologically except through a new universal agreement reached by another ecumenical council. Attempts to bring about a rapprochement between the Orthodox churches and those of the Reformation have ended in failure because from the Orthodox viewpoint the Protestant churches were found theologically wanting.

Historically the designation "Protestant" was given to those German estates who, at the Diet of Spires in 1529, refused to accept the religious policy adopted by the majority and who not only "protested" against the majority action but also demonstrated their convictions publicly. However, the connotations of a designation which made good sense in the historical circumstances of the early sixteenth century are not necessarily appropriate to describe what we mean by the term in the second half of the twentieth century. Nevertheless, it is equally obvious that Tillich's bold attempt to broaden the meaning of the term Protestant by using it as a designation for every religious movement that arises in protest against mere traditions, be it in the midst of any of the Christian churches or in Judaism or secularism, has lost all but a functional connection with its original meaning.

Does history teach us how to use the term? We might think that all the established churches that sprang into being in the sixteenth century had a right to call themselves Protestant. But the matter is already doubtful when it comes to the Anglican church. For, unlike the Protestant Episcopal church, other member churches of the Anglican communion passionately refuse to be labeled Protestant. Conversely, not many members of the Lutheran or Reformed churches will deny the appellation Protestant to Anabaptists or Schwenkfelders, although they were never established churches. In view of the fact that a generally recognized criterion is lacking, where do we draw the line of demarcation between Protestant churches and other religious groups? Should we say that Unitarians, Jehovah's Witnesses, or Christian Scientists belong to Protestantism? One thing is certain: a definition of Protestantism cannot be based on those features which are common to all the religious groups or denominations variously classified as Protestant.

Another approach is suggested by the fact that the Calvinistic churches used to indicate their specific character by calling themselves "reformed." In the Middle Ages and down to the sixteenth century the term "reformation" did not designate, as it does today, an act by which existing conditions were improved, but rather the restoration of the original "form" which had been lost. There was little agreement, however, as to what constituted the original form of the church, and to what extent it had been lost. Consequently scholars refrained from applying the title "Protestant" to all the reform movements of the fifteenth and sixteenth centuries.

It will be advisable for us, therefore, to restrict our usage of the term Protestant to all those groups who directly and indirectly received their decisive stimulus from Luther's reformation. Application of the term to a wider circle than simply the Lutheran churches, however, is justified by its very origin. For the *protestatio* at the Diet of Spires was an act of solidarity. One of its purposes was to prevent a condemnation and subsequent suppression of Zwingli's reform. Lutheran princes thereby confessed that Zwingli's work shared a common origin with theirs. It matters little in this connection, whether or not a denomination wanted to follow the specific line of religion which Luther had adopted. Unlike Zwingli and Calvin though, and the Anabaptists who recognized their indebtedness to Luther, there are other Protestant groups such as Baptists, Quakers, and Disciples of Christ who have little in common with Luther except their complete reliance upon the Bible. Nevertheless they might never have come into being but for the fact that Luther had overthrown the authorities of the Roman Catholic church and had thereby created political conditions in which a "religion of the Book" was possible. Again, the Waldensians and the modern members of the *Unitas Fratrum* in Bohemia and Moravia are reckoned among the Protestants, in spite of the pre-Reformation origin of their denominations, because under the influence of the Reformation they radically changed their character in the sixteenth century. While originally they had been groups within the Catholic church intent upon remedying some of the abuses of that church, later they came to interpret their existence in the light of the

Reformation and thus established their spiritual life on an entirely new basis.

If it is advisable, as we have suggested, to refer the appellation "Protestant" to Luther's reformation, what then is the characteristic feature of that reformation? In accordance with a tendency that was soon to prevail in the Lutheran and Reformed churches, scholars have repeatedly attempted to characterize the Reformation in terms of certain theological doctrines. While not entirely wrong, such attempts nevertheless failed to grasp the depth of Luther's discovery and hence to ascertain what actually made him become the initiator of a new branch of Christianity. The origin of the Reformation does not lie in the introduction of a new doctrinal authority for faith and life (namely that of the Bible) to replace that of the ecclesiastical hierarchy. In his high regard for Scripture Luther was simply following the nominalistic tradition of his monastic order; some of his Catholic critics even cite this allegiance to nominalism as an explanation of his alleged exegetical errors. Luther's understanding of the Pauline doctrine of justification was likewise not without precedent in the long previous history of theological debate. Yet it would have remained as ineffectual in the sixteenth century as it is in the twentieth except for Luther's presentation of it in the light of his revolutionary spiritual experience. It is to this experience, therefore, that we must turn if we are to discover the very heart of the Reformation.

B. LUTHER'S REFORMATION EXPERIENCE

In the discussion of Luther's experience caution is required. Some of his admirers have attempted to explain his unique experience in terms of his peculiar personality. There can be no doubt, of course, that his new spiritual insight bears all the marks of the man himself. However, Luther himself emphasized that its uniqueness consisted in the fact that God had disclosed to him a way in which the presence of God in Christ could be experienced apart from the priestly work of the church. For Luther the significance of this disclosure lay in the fact that the light did not appear as a mystical experience destined exclusively for him personally, but as a possibility of life which God makes available to all human beings. Luther's basic experience differed from mere doctrine because it had grown out of a profound and radical question. The theologian, even when he professes new doctrines, proceeds from facts already known to him or from doctrines of whose truth he is already certain. The way of doctrinal truth proceeds from that which is firmly known to that which is less known or less verifiable. The circle of doctrine can thus be enlarged yet never transcended. Even where the theologian indulges in speculation he will go only as far as is consistent with his established knowledge, although he may be satisfied with probabilities. In the case of Luther things were different. From Augustine he had learned that the search for God begins with uneasiness (*inquietudo*). Thus the monk at Wittenberg started from a vital question which had originated in the doctrine of the church, yet for which the church did not provide a satisfactory answer. Judging from the fact that the question had been so carefully avoided in the past, one may even infer that the church felt incapable of offering the solution. Thus, even to raise the problem was, according to the terminology of the church, heresy and an attack on its teaching authority.

1. PERPLEXITY

The source of the Reformation is not to be found in a theological theorem but in the perplexity of a man's heart. Catholic scholars have attempted to delineate the genealogy of Luther's thought in medieval theology, and several Protestant theologians have followed them. There is an element of truth in such an approach, but so frequently it is overlooked that in his study of nominalism and Augustinianism, German mysticism and humanism, Luther finally ended in an impasse. With its topical method of treatment medieval theology had neatly dealt with God, man, and the universe as if they all were entities existing by themselves. But

Luther realized that the basic concern of Christianity and the church is with man in his relationship to both God and this world. Such an outlook was not alien to medieval Catholicism. Paradoxically, however, it was through the very emphasis it placed upon redemption that the medieval church greatly developed man's self-reliance. Man was thought of as being called by God to work out his own redemption. To be sure, that had to be done under the supervision of the church and with the assistance it granted through doctrine and sacraments, but at the same time man could take it for granted that by availing himself of these providentially offered resources he would eventually pilot his life into heaven. This placing of emphasis upon man's ability to work out his redemption served in turn to undermine the Catholic system. By laying so much stress on man's own activities the church actually fostered the mystical development in which the life of faith was sublimated and spiritualized.

The result was an inevitable tension between the life of faith and sacramental practice. When faith is thought of as the soul's awareness of its heavenly origin, the material nature of the sacraments arouses doubts as to their usefulness for salvation. The reason for doubt lies not so much in the moral indignity of the priest as in the apparent inappropriateness of external human actions to call forth spiritual effects. It was the mysticism of the fourteenth century that made Luther doubt the redemptive role of the Catholic church. This medieval mysticism was Christocentric. A high estimate of the value of the individual soul was thought to intensify the sense of gratitude for the Lord's redemptive work. How poor life would be, unless one had been brought back to one's heavenly origin; and how rich life would become, once the individual was enabled to realize the presence of God in his own life! This sense of personal value was further enhanced by the humanist movement with its extolling of the freedom of the heavenborn man and the resultant longing for an unlimited life.

However, over against the pantheistic tendency latent in

medieval mysticism and developed to full strength in humanism, Luther is doubly aware of the implications of the Christian doctrine of creation. Far from being his own master, man is in every respect conditioned by the God who made him; God uses even the cosmic forces of death, Satan, and sin to carry out his plans in this world. Thus the life of faith must be lived in a world that has turned against the will of the Creator. Nevertheless, the naive dualism of popular devotion was, in Luther's view, utterly inconsistent. Even though throughout his life he assigned a decisive role to the work of Satan and the cosmic forces, Luther never failed to emphasize their creaturely character. Here, precisely, lay his great problem. Obviously the cosmic forces would not be in existence and could not wield their power over man and this world apart from the Creator. Thus man is perplexed by the apparent contrast between God's redemptive will and his permissive will.

It has become customary to express Luther's basic question as, "How can I obtain a gracious God?" or "How may I receive God's mercy?" Consequently, his problem is interpreted as an obsession with sin, which in turn is explained in terms of the pathological fear and guilt caused by the stern discipline of his father. On the basis of this interpretation the scholar feels free to reject the whole Reformation and to substitute his own religious principles in its stead. But historical scholarship is unable to explain away the emphasis Luther placed upon God's forgiving grace. That Luther should dwell so powerfully on sin and guilt was not due to experiences of early childhood days, no matter how much they may have tinged his basic insight. Rather it was the stress the church laid upon man's moral activities, together with his study of Augustine, that led Luther to focus his attention upon the problem of sin.

This did not mean, however, that those theologians were right who saw Luther as concerned with moral problems only in the narrow sense of the term. At no juncture of his life was Luther's spiritual life geared toward moral perfection, nor did he ever consider the grace of God as a substitute for morality. If the outstanding feature of his spiritual life had been moral sensitivity, Luther would probably have become one of the saints of the Catholic church buried in his monastery, but he would certainly never have initiated a reformation of the church. What enabled him to transcend the moralistic outlook of the Catholic church was the stubbornness with which he clung to the centrality of God in the relation of God and man, thus enormously widening the perspective in which he saw his problem. It was not God the lawgiver or the God of the church only with whom he was confronted but also the maker of heaven and earth. Consequently, his perplexity arose from all the contradictions of life which as a human being he encountered everywhere in this world. This outlook explains the breadth of his concept of sin. Tradition had taught him that sin was disobedience to, and lack of compliance with, the commandments of God and the church. But Luther in his realism calls sin man's unwillingness to see the work of God in the conditions of this world and to accept his predicament as a divine assignment for service.

In keeping with Luther's view, the Augsburg Confession defines sin in terms of the absence of fear of and trust in God, not just feeling concupiscence. Even concupiscence, which had been related exclusively to moral life, is interpreted in a broader sense, namely, as self-assertion or desire to live as if the existence of God did not make any difference. In the Apology of the Augsburg Confession (Art. II, 8), Melanchthon elaborates his view by enumerating such manifestations of sin as ignoring God's activity in this world, despising God, lacking fear of and trust in God, hating God's judgment, despairing of grace, putting one's trust in the goods of this world, etc.

Such a comprehensive and realistic view of man's perplexity would not have been possible, however, had not Luther rejected the schoolmen's philosophical view of man. Luther's problem is concerned with the totality of man's existence in this world, whereas the Catholic church, adopting the Aristotelian view of man, started from the duality of body and soul (or mind). Accordingly, the body was considered mainly as an obstacle to the aspirations of the mind and soul; and man's problem was how to obey despite the incitements of the lusts of the body and how eventually to get the soul to heaven. In Luther's realism, however, the problem of man's life involves his whole bodily existence, both in relation to his neighbor and to the conditions of this world. Hence, the fact that in all his activities he is conditioned by the irrational forces of the universe, infinitely aggravates man's problem.

Luther's perplexity is eventually carried to an unbearable point by the consideration that sin, from which man is to be redeemed, would not be in existence but for the fact that God created man in such a way that sin was always a possibility in his life. From a purely rational viewpoint, there is no way by which the contrast between the work of God as Creator and his work as Redeemer can be reconciled. It is by the will of God that man is doomed to live in a world which by its destructiveness disregards his dignity as a child of God, a world that in every respect hems in his desire for unlimited existence. Above all, it is God himself who is responsible for the fact that freedom, the source of man's dignity, is also the cause of his misery as a sinner.

Luther's lectures on Romans are full of the terrifying paradoxes of divine omnipotence. Though delivered in 1515-16, they represent more than merely a passing phase of his theological development. In his monumental *Bondage of the Will* published in 1525, Luther emphasized, over against the facile and superficial views of Erasmus, the necessity to deal with human nature in its relation to God's work, rather than to regard it as a self-contained entity.

It is worth noting that the perplexity, in which the monk of Wittenberg found himself, was due to his resolute refusal to follow his humanist friends in their pantheistic leanings and to his faithful adherence to the Christian tradition. His agony was called forth by his determination to take his stand within the truth conveyed to him by the church. Yet, paradoxically, this very church, as a redemptive institution, proved unable to help him in his miserable predicament.

When the church's claims are confronted with the incomprehensible omnipotence of God, they seem to be unfounded. How can an earthly institution, exposed to the same fury of the cosmic forces as all human beings, pretend to have an infallible knowledge of God's will and to be free from error? Does not its contention to act on behalf of Christ here on earth disclose a tragic misunderstanding of the gravity of the dangers which beset human life? The church talked of incidental faults and shortcomings as though human beings could start existence with a clean slate; but is not man's problem that of historical existence? In our individual lives do we start as our own originators, as Nietzsche contended and as is implied in the Roman Catholic doctrine? Or do we, rather, enter life with a human nature ready-made and inherit all its capabilities and shortcomings?

We do not begin with a clean slate nor are we the masters of the universe. Although man is assured of his destination, namely, a life in communion with God, he discovers that actually he has to endure the pressure of the cosmic forces which seem to move him farther away from God every hour of his life. How then can man truly be himself? He is unable to accept life as it is, as if it were truly life, yet he cannot deny that there is a horrible correspondence between his own desires and the cosmic forces. To his dismay, man discovers that all the tendencies that mar life in this world are also present in his own will. In every respect he is part and parcel of the world in which he moves and acts. There is no place for the easy-going optimism which considered this world as the neutral raw material which man, by means of his innate goodness and the assistance of the church, is able to transform into a good world. The gloomy view of this world, so characteristic of sixteenth-century Protestantism, is not the result of a pathological mind. It merely expresses the depth to which the Reformers probed in their attempt to assay human existence.

2. THE GOD WHO SPEAKS

It is significant, however, that despite his gloomy view, Luther did not despair. He never gave up the hope that the church and its Christian tradition would lead him out of his perplexity into a new light. Troeltsch[1] notwithstanding, however, he did not expect the answer to his perplexity from a return to medieval theology. God himself was expected to provide the answer, since no creature could be considered capable of settling the dispute between man's divine destination and the oppressive power of the cosmic forces.

Eventually the answer came to Luther through the Holy Scripture, which the nominalistic tradition of the church had endeared to him, and which, as a theological professor, he was involved in teaching. The answer came, however, not through the exegesis of any passage which thus became relevant for his life, but rather through the discovery that God uses the Bible as a means of grace. The Bible had originally entered into his life as implementation of the church's authority, and thus as an infallible source of doctrine. In the midst of his perplexity, how-ever, when the inability of the church to provide a way of true life weighed so heavily on his heart, Luther realized that the Scripture does not derive its authority from the church. Rather, independent of any ecclesiastical teaching authority and disre-garding the theological tradition of the church, the biblical mes-sage authenticates itself in the believer's conscience by leading him out of his perplexity. The biblical word accomplished what no ecclesiastical doctrine or practice was capable of doing, thus demonstrating that the unbearable tension between man's divine destination and the hopeless predicament in which the cosmic

---

[1] Ernst Troeltsch, "Protestantisches Christentum und Kirche in der Neu-zeit," in Paul Hinneberg (ed.), *Die Kultur der Gegenwart* (2nd ed.; Berlin and Leipzig, 1909), pp. 433-54.

forces have placed him is ended for those who accept God's grace in Jesus Christ. Luther learned that his attempts to escape from his cosmic enslavement by his own efforts were presumptuous and would lead either to a superficial misinterpretation of the human predicament, or, once he realized the nature of the forces which confined him in his vexing situation, to despair.

3. FREEDOM

Whereas Luther stressed the freedom of God to act, in Catholicism man is seen as living in a firmly established order, compliance with which guarantees the degree of goodness or holiness a person possesses. The system will therefore determine what means the individual must use in order to progress in his Christian life. Grace is here understood as a divine energy dispensed by the church enabling the believer to do what is required for growth and perfection.

Luther learned from the Bible that grace is not an impersonal, supernatural power but rather the personal attitude that God takes toward the individual who in his perplexity puts his trust in his Creator. Since God's grace is condescending love, the individual can be sure that God will not abandon him, unless he abandons himself. Yet grace has no automatic effect; it does not by itself render the individual free, let alone good. But by means of grace man is enabled to believe in his destination, notwithstanding the fact that he constantly and painfully experiences the tyranny of the cosmic powers.

In the person of Jesus Christ the Bible confronts man not with doctrines but rather with the redemptive work of God himself. By persuading man's heart of that fact, the Bible manifests itself as the very word of God, that is to say, not as a record only of what God has once done, but rather as a means by which God himself speaks to the believer. Hence, the believer sees his life in an entirely new light. Luther began from his awareness of a God who dominated the believer's life by assigning to man a transcendental destination. Now in Christ's work man discovers a God who himself takes the initiative in man's redemption, and who by authenticating the truthfulness of the biblical message in the believer's heart makes him aware of the fact that Christ's work has been performed for the benefit of him to whom God is speaking.

Under the Catholic system the believer's relation to God had to be interpreted in such a way that man was under obligation to live his own life regardless of the obstacles which the cosmic powers put in his way. No wonder Luther experienced a sense of utter frustration. The new view of life presented to him in the Bible points to an existence where in spite of the temptations and afflictions caused by the forces of evil man sees God himself redemptively at work in his life. Christ's work of redemption is a divine activity which has taken place in the past, yet whose divine energy determines forever the subsequent course of history and the universe. Redemption is no longer to be understood, as in the Roman system, as a process in which the individual and the church are concomitantly engaged, the outcome of which is in doubt to the very last moment of the individual's life. Luther felt that according to the Roman view of redemption more is expected of both the individual and the church than they are able to accomplish in the presence of the cosmic forces. Luther insisted that all God demands of man is in keeping with man's ability. God wants man to believe that in Christ's ministry and death God manifests his love for mankind, and that in the Lord's resurrection man has the evidence of God's ability to keep the cosmic powers under control. By relying entirely on God the believer will experience the fact that human aspiration for an unlimited existence is no longer doomed to failure. If he will only believe that the work of Christ was performed for his redemption from the cosmic forces, the power of Christ will also be his. Sin will then be sin forgiven, a power no longer able by its aftereffects to poison his life. Death will no longer frustrate his life, because in what he does by faith, the energies of the life of the risen Lord are at work, and he is therefore sure

15

that beyond this life the resurrection is waiting for him. While it is true that the powers of enmity, want, and destruction are still doing their dreadful chore in this world, the believer is nevertheless at the same time able to discover the universe in the beauty of a world which is in harmony with God and thus to be enjoyed.

This view of life explains the emphasis Luther places upon the believer's freedom, yet also the uncompromising ruthlessness with which he rejected the demands made by the rebellious peasants in the name of evangelical freedom. Freedom, as Luther understands it, is not a congenital gift of man. The freedom of choice with which man is endowed must operate in a world dominated by the cosmic forces, and hence is nothing more than the ability to choose one's ruler. For that very reason, true freedom is possible only as a gift of God. Through faith in Christ the individual is enabled to abide in harmony with God. Hence the believer is free in self-determination to embrace the goal for which God has destined him. Because God took the initiative, the goal of man's life is not the result of his own planning. Likewise, on each step of the way to his goal the individual remains dependent on the insight and the strength that comes from Christ.

Notwithstanding its divine origin and constant dependence on Christ, this freedom is nevertheless genuine freedom. As a divinely granted privilege it entitles the believer to reject all interference with it, for instance, on the part of the church or philosophy. It should be kept in mind, however, that Luther's protest against the Roman church is not directed against its functions as teacher, educator, physician, and judge of the faithful but against its use of these services as means by which the believers are to be held under its tutelage. Likewise, while the cosmic powers seek to determine the choice of the mode by which faith may express itself—the expression of faith will always bear the marks of the individual's nature and be conditioned by his resources and the historical circumstances—they are unable against his will to determine or condition the choice of his goal.

Unlike the Catholic view, which conceives of faith as obedient acceptance of all the teachings of the church, the faith derived from the New Testament is readiness to receive the new opportunity of life offered by Christ. Faith is not the end of danger and oppression. On the contrary, the believer will realize that he must live by the righteousness of God in a world in which the same evil powers are at work which operate in his heart. The true life cannot, therefore, be regarded as a perfect life. It is rather that life which in the given circumstances is possible to the individual, that is to say, a life in which—in spite of his dejections, doubts, and wrongdoings, his rebellion against fate— he never completely loses sight of the triumph which God has won through Christ over the powers of evil. Man cannot keep this triumph in view, however, without acknowledging that it is his own fault that his predicament is so hopeless. Paradoxically, the grace of God breaks the will of the self yet without thereby destroying the ego. The death of his self-seeking will coincide with the emergence of a new will which operates in harmony with God's redemptive work.

The assertion that the faith which Luther had thus discovered in the Scripture was Christocentric does not simply mean that in Luther's system of thought Christ occupied the central place whereas, for example, in other systems that position is assigned to creation or eschatology. Rather, for Luther the work of Christ had become the central fact of his own life. Thereby both the ego and the church are demoted from their central position. They are not annihilated, however, but seen as existing for Christ's sake. The existence of the ego for the sake of Christ explains the significance which vocation and service assume in the individual's life, as contrasted with the idea of meritorious works in Catholicism. The church and all her resources, in turn, are seen in a new perspective. Inasmuch as the church is a human organization, no ecclesiastical work can bring about man's redemption. But since Christ is at work in it, its activities and resources are means of grace through which the individual is acquainted with, and assured of, God's redemptive work.

4. THE MEANS OF GRACE

The preceding discussion of freedom may suggest mystical elements. While in the beginning of his career Luther felt a strong attraction to mysticism, his decisive experience taught him that without drastic modifications mysticism does not agree with the nature of faith. Whereas Luther's perplexity was caused by experiencing his need of redemption, mysticism does not postulate that need as an objective one since the individual partakes of the divine substance in one way or another. Only in a subjective sense can it be said that the uninitiated individual is in need because he is unaware of his divine dignity. On account of the sufficiency of his existence, the mystic has no need of the visible fellowship of the church and its resources; and if he remains an obedient member of the church, he does so for reasons not implied in his mystical experience. This fact suffices to show that Luther's basic experience cannot be considered the outcome of his mystical leanings. He never entertained any doubts concerning the necessity of the fellowship of the church and its resources.

It was possible for a man with Luther's experience to remain within the Catholic church only by means of a radical transformation of the traditional view of the church. Luther insists, for instance, on the necessity of the sacraments, although he reduces their number from seven to two. But unlike the medieval church, he does not ascribe to them any participation in divine nature or energy. Even the vehemence with which he defends the real presence of the Body of Christ in, with, and under the elements of the Lord's Supper, must not mislead us into assuming that he believed in some kind of transubstantiation. The elements are and remain earthly substances, but they are the means or vehicles through which God personally assures the believer of his gracious will. The elements are not efficacious *ex opere operato* as Rome taught. Rather, they presuppose faith, and hence also the perplexity of the believer, who receives them as the divine answer to his doubting question. Only thus is it possible for Luther to coordinate sacraments and Scripture, an unheard-of combination in the Catholic church. In either case, sacraments or Scripture, it is the present God who by means of them communicates efficaciously with the believer, and in either case it is not the human use which determines their value and significance but rather the fact that God himself has chosen them. When later generations of theologians tried to ascertain whether or not the Bible was the word of God *extra usum* (apart from its use) they only manifested their incapacity to understand Luther's concept of means of grace. Such a question makes as little sense as asking what light is like by itself, that is to say, apart from an object which is thereby illumined. Of course God speaks through the Bible even to people who do not anticipate such communication, and it becomes God's word, not by man's faith but by God's act of speaking. Apart from faith, God's word cannot be perceived, and therefore it can be said that for those who do not have faith the Bible is nothing but a historical document. Those who are without faith are themselves at fault, however. They are like people who find foreign money only to throw it away because they are not able to read it.

Although one discerns a certain formal analogy between the place the Bible occupies in Luther's experience and the place that had formerly been occupied by the teaching authorities of the church, the Bible is not simply substituted for the teaching authorities, because it does not operate as a teaching authority but as a means of grace. Certainly, Luther allows that the Bible conveys noetic insights which can be expressed by the use of propositions, but this is an inference drawn from its original effect. As a means of grace the Bible, first of all, calls forth the certainty of faith.

If the Bible is a means of grace calling forth the certainty of faith, you cannot prove faith by way of syllogisms based upon the Bible. Biblical texts can only be used as pointers to the new attitude of faith which has been brought about in the believer through the Bible. Luther's understanding of the means of grace did full justice to the biblical view of God. As Creator he is not a part or a function of this world, nor is he its life, its mind, or its source. Rather, even though everything in this world is conditioned by him, he always remains hidden behind the things of this world and thus is completely beyond the reach of man. In the Catholic practice of the sacraments, that absolute transcendence had been lost; God's presence is thought of as being conditioned by the ritual performed by the ministering priest. Yet Luther experienced that the Creator is not so transcendental and beyond human knowing that earthly facts could only serve as symbols hinting at the Creator's work. If such were the case, man's relation to God would be something that could not be experienced at all—not even as the relation of the creature to his creator—but only postulated as a notion of one's mind. It is, in fact, by manifesting himself through the means of grace that God makes himself known in his redemptive activities and their effects, although he himself remains hidden in his capacity as their transcendental agent.

Where the means of grace are not so understood, people either fall back into a Catholic way of thinking which is contrary to biblical faith or fail completely to derive spiritual benefits from them, noticing only their earthly nature. In the former case, the Bible is used as an infallible standard of doctrine, and supranatural effects are ascribed to the elements of the sacraments. In the latter case, the Bible is read as a historical document or a piece of literature only, and the sacraments lose all significance because they are interpreted as mere rites or symbolical representations of doctrines. Since according to this view the sacraments merely illustrate doctrines that have been established otherwise, they are denied any specific effect. In the former case, membership in the church is considered as an absolute prerequisite of redemption, since the visible church claims to be the source of redemption.

Conversely, where only the earthly side is stressed, the fellowship of the church has lost all significance, and faith degenerates into mere subjectivism. All attempts, however, to reduce Luther's own theology to a doctrine of the word is contrary to his actual teaching and practice.

In summary, faith, as Luther understood it, starts from a state of perplexity which is not purely secular but rooted in Christianity. Faith presupposes a knowledge of the basic tenets of the Christian faith and contact with, if not membership in, the fellowship of Christians. The fact that all the Reformers of the sixteenth century had originally been members of the Roman Catholic church indicates that this prerequisite of faith can be met by any Christian church. The turning away from the older forms of Christianity to Protestantism was initiated by the doubt resulting from the relationship between the divine destination of the individual, on the one hand, and his perplexing predicament in a world which is the prey of cosmic forces on the other. Apart from this vital inquietude the Protestant answer to the question of faith cannot be appreciated. The perplexing doubt is overcome when the individual experiences God's speaking to him through the means of grace and when he is ready to build his life upon nothing but the manifestations of God's grace, above all upon the work of Christ.

Faith, as Luther understood it, combines in a unique way objectivism and subjectivism. The subjective element is found above all in the fact that the individual becomes aware of the perplexing character of his existence as a human being, in his accepting Scripture and sacraments as God's means of dealing with him in a personal way, and in his readiness to trust exclusively in God's grace thus manifested. The objective element lies in the realization that God, although pure subject, is only indirectly known in this world through that by which he is manifested. Although God's creatorship and purpose underlie every detail of this world, knowledge of God by means of the general course of this world is misleading because of the evil results of the operation of the cosmic forces. Were it not for the fellow-ship of the church, as well as word and sacraments, the believer would have to content himself mainly with a negative theology unable to resolve his perplexity and doubt. As in all of life, the subjective and objective aspects of faith are correlated. Even the doubt related to faith would never arise if the individual were not aware of the relationship in which he stands to God. In turn, the means of grace, though existing independently of the individual's faith, are nevertheless intended for the spiritual bene-fit of the individual. Apart from faith, their existence is empty.

C. THE STORY OF PROTESTANTISM

Having surveyed the nature of Luther's experience, we cannot understand Protestantism without looking at its subsequent development.

Protestantism as we know it has its roots in Luther's own spiritual experience. It sprang into being through the writings in which he bore witness to that experience and indicated the significance it had for the various aspects of the relationship which man as a citizen of this world has to God. The historical consequence of Luther's work as a reformer, however, was not confined to the formation of the Lutheran churches. Various denominations and groups bear witness to the fundamental sig-nificance which his experience had for the spiritual life of mankind.

The multiplicity of religious communities found in Protes-tantism is due, in the first place, to the fact that the complex relationship of objective and subjective elements in Luther's experience left ample room for more than one single emphasis. This complexity is obvious in a comparison of Calvin with Luther. Calvin is in full agreement with the Wittenberg Reformer on the basic principle that the meaning of man's life depends exclusively on the grace of God. Both of them interpret the work of Christ as a redemptive act by which man is not only delivered from the tyranny of the cosmic forces but also set free for a new life here on earth. But while Luther originally advocated comprehensive social reforms, he shifted his emphasis remarkably after 1525 by adopting a conservative attitude. The Lutheran message that molded subsequent history dwells so intensely upon the miracle of divine forgiveness that the individual, while by faith defying the cosmic forces, nevertheless receives little incentive to manifest the new life of faith in his dealing with this world. Luther describes life in the home and in the order as the two principal spheres in which faith becomes articulate.

Calvin's experience led him in a different direction. He focused his attention upon the fact that in faith man is endowed with the power of the Holy Spirit. Consequently, faith shows its obedience in an activity which aims at defeating the cosmic forces and transforming the whole world. For Luther the most characteristic attitudes of faith are defiance of Satan, confidence, and love, whereas in Calvin the emphasis falls upon humility, service, and fortitude.

Similarly, the functional view of the means of grace leads inevitably to divergent doctrines. For instance, why have sacraments in addition to the word? With George Fox, such considerations led to the complete repudiation of the sacraments, and similar positions account for the practical neglect of the sacraments in many Protestant churches.

Another factor that is responsible for the multiplication of denominations in Protestantism is the effect historical conditions have upon spiritual vision. While man's spiritual predicament is basically the same everywhere, the way in which faith manifests itself in one's spiritual life is inevitably conditioned by factors such as one's level of education, racial characteristics, and the historical situation in which one lives. It is not surprising, therefore, that whenever outward circumstances offer an opportunity, new types of spiritual life emerge from a given group. The absence of coercive power, characteristic of the Protestant churches, and the additional freedom resulting from the separation of church and state have greatly fostered the existence of numerous denominations and groups, particularly in the Anglo-Saxon countries.

It is important, nevertheless, to distinguish between two types of multiplication in the history of Protestantism. The one type which accounts for the greater number of small Protestant groups and sects is a result of human weakness, e.g., ambition, vanity, narrow-mindedness, inability to endure differences of viewpoint, and unteachability. Accordingly, the outward freedom enjoyed by Protestantism is exploited for splits and schisms. Closely related to this tendency is the trust placed in private revelations. Ever since the days of Luther people have attracted followers by pretending that they were in a particular way commissioned or illumined by God.[2] The possibility of private revelations or the subjective sincerity of people claiming to receive them should not be denied. But their claims to be true guides of the Christian flock, and their denunciation of the clergy would sound more convincing if they were anxious to lead people into the whole truth concerning the human predicament instead of spinning indefinitely around the one illumination given to them.

A second and legitimate reason for the multiplication of denominations is found in the very nature of faith as understood by Luther. While historical circumstances explain the specific character of new denominations, they do not form the reason for their emergence. What inevitably produces new denominations in Protestantism is the tension between faith and institutions. Since the religious community is gathered around the means of grace, that is to say, the tangible way in which God manifests his grace, it necessarily becomes an organized institution. Once this happens, however, there is the temptation to treat the institution and its resources as an end in itself rather than as the place on earth where the life of faith is to be practiced. Fortunately, God remains in control of the means of grace, and thus the

---

[2] The history of the Mormon church is typical in this respect. Cf. *Joseph Smith Tells His Own Story* (n.d.).

institutional character never prevails so completely as to obliterate the true nature of faith. God's grace, shown in his speaking
to the believer, is the reason for the revivals and reform movements which periodically agitate the church.

In some instances, however, experiences whose depth approxi-
mates that of Luther led to the formation of new denominations.
The coming into existence of Mennonites, Quakers, Baptists, and
Methodists, or more recently of the Holiness and Pentecostal
movements cannot be regarded as random events but rather as
evidence that God still speaks to his church. Historically speaking, the emergence of these groups results from the power of
Luther's experience asserting itself afresh in the midst of Protestantism. This recurrence explains why the new denominations,
at least in their inception, are not geared to winning outsiders
for the faith but to the formation of new groups within Protestantism. In such developments we see the work of the Holy
Spirit. Emphases of spiritual life, seemingly of no special significance for the majority of the members of an existing denomination but considered wholesome by a minority, are thereby made
articulate.

D. THE CONTEMPORARY SITUATION

1. PROTESTANTISM IN SEARCH OF ITSELF

Our brief portrayal of the story of Protestantism has shown that
the history of Protestantism has been primarily a spiritual history.
Since it took its start from man's total life in his world, Protestantism was bound to influence in every respect the sphere in
which its members moved. Nevertheless, it was definitely a
mistake to write Protestant history as though it were primarily
an aspect of cultural or economic history. When Troeltsch dates
the beginnings of Neo-Protestantism in the eighteenth century,
he is wrong theologically, although he notices correctly Protestantism's relation to contemporary culture and civilization. The
Catholic Counter-Reformation stands in striking contrast with

Protestantism in that it aims to continue the theological tradition of the Middle Ages, in which the church is the center of all social life including culture. The Baroque style is rightly associated with the spirit of the Counter-Reformation, being a typical Catholic style, primarily religious in character and hence, even in its secular applications, more appealing to Catholics than to Protestants. But it is also the last style inspired by Christians. As the Counter-Reformation lost momentum, the Baroque style went out of existence. The new styles of the late seventeenth and eighteenth centuries have a purely secular origin. Far from giving expression to an idea, they merely represent the taste and pleasures of the courts and nobility in that last period of their sway over social life.

Ernst Troeltsch has correctly observed that, from its inception down to the end of the eighteenth century, Protestantism was rather reactionary in its relation to culture.[3] It was mainly engaged in preserving the heritage of tradition. Similarly, Max Weber's attempt to credit Protestantism with the rise of modern capitalism was based upon a misreading of the record.[4] Capitalism as a new form of economic life flourished in the Catholic cities of Northern Italy and Flanders no less than in Protestant Holland or England. Moreover, it was in the countries of Calvinistic persuasion rather than in Lutheran countries that Protestants were predominantly engaged in economic activities, especially in trade. The contribution that Protestantism made to the life of the nations is not found in the cultural sphere as much as in the new ethos it brought. It has created such types as the Huguenot, the Swiss, and the Prussian, and unmistakably has left its marks upon the American national character.

In the Europe of the sixteenth and seventeenth centuries the political field was dominated by the conflicts between the Catholic and the Protestant powers. But in this area, too, people were

---

[3] *Op. cit.*
[4] Max Weber, *The Sociology of Religion*, trans. E. Fischkoff (Boston, 1963).

fighting for political power rather than for the triumph of the truth. The fact that their clashes took place on confessional lines was inevitable as long as the Catholic church attempted to crush the Reformation and to regain her secular power by the use of arms. That process reached its end with the Treaty of Westphalia in 1648, which established the principle of religious toleration. Indeed it would be hard to point out the differences between Catholic and Protestant powers in the political and military field. The emancipation of culture from ecclesiastical control, which began with the humanistic and Renaissance movements, continued successfully, and both Protestants and Catholics eventually realized their inability to stop it. Modern Christendom first acquiesced in the idea of a secular culture and eventually endorsed it. Thus the political, economic, and cultural history is only indirectly affected by the presence of Protestantism. The real history of Protestantism took place in the fields of dogmatics and ecclesiastical institutions. In these areas Protestants were preoccupied with discovering their identity and giving it appropriate expression.

This development differed strikingly from that of contemporaneous Catholicism. The Roman church in that period began with the assumption that it knew exactly what it was like and what it stood for, and that at the Council of Trent all the issues that had been called into question by the Reformers had been definitely settled to the satisfaction of all good Catholics. Protestantism, in turn, since it did not start from dogmas but rather from an experience, had no alternative but to find out what was implied in the experience of faith in the light of subsequent spiritual and historical events. No wonder, then, that the early history of Protestantism presents a picture of divergent and hotly polemical theological views, and that splits and new denominations continuously came into being. But no less characteristic of the spiritual character of Protestant history is the way in which the new issues were taken up by the whole of Protestantism. They were not simply ignored as is often the case

27

with rival schools in philosophy. This discussion of new theological issues in which all the Protestant churches engaged simultaneously is evidence that the various Protestant groups could not help but remember their common origin.

When Adolf Harnack in his *History of Dogma* contended that Protestantism by the nature of the case could have no dogma, he laid bare one of the significant features of the history of doctrine in Protestantism.[5] Unlike the Roman Catholic church, in which the dogmas form a solid edifice from which no stone can be removed and in which all have lasting validity, Protestantism, at least in the eyes of Catholic observers, is in constant flux. In a sense this is true, yet it does not mean, as Catholic critics are inclined to believe, that Protestants are never sure of what they believe. Rather this process is an indication of the way the Holy Spirit guides the church. There is a permanent dialectical relationship between Protestantism's basic experience, on the one hand, and the various spiritual problems emerging from the historical situation, on the other. Protestant theology has classics, that is to say, works which by virtue of their excellent method or the profoundness of their thought repay careful study, but not even Calvin's *Institutes* or Luther's *Works* could occupy the place of authority that the Catholic church has assigned to Thomas Aquinas. Similarly, Heinrich Schmid[6] and Heinrich Heppe[7] had no difficulty in compiling the basic ideas shared by the theologians of Lutheran and Reformed orthodoxy respectively. But such compilations serve purely historical interests. One could never say, "You must believe all this in order to be considered a Protestant." Hence in the Protestant church it will never be possible to compile a work like Denzinger's *Enchiridion Symbolorum*, a collection of dogmatic statements made by popes

---

[5] Adolf Harnack, *History of Dogma*, trans. Neil Buchanan, from 3rd German ed. (Boston, 1895-1900; repr. 1958), VII, 168-274.

[6] Heinrich Schmid, *The Doctrinal Theology of the Evangelical Lutheran Church*, trans. C. A. Hay and H. E. Jacobs (3rd ed.; Minneapolis: Augsburg Publishing House, 1961).

[7] Heinrich Heppe, *Die Dogmatik der evangelisch-reformierten Kirche* (Elberfeld, 1861, rev. ed. by Ernst Bizer [Neukirchen Kreis Moers, 1935]).

and councils during the history of the church which is binding upon all Catholic theologians.

Since Protestantism was to assume its place in historical life, it could not help seeking an organizational form by means of which it would be capable both of giving expression to its nature as a spiritual institution and of operating without false compromise in this world. The scope of possibilities was foreshadowed by the contrast between Zwingli's city-church, on the one hand, and the very loose associations of the early Anabaptists in Zurich, on the other. Yet there was no ideal model from which all Protestant groups could start, and as a result a great diversity of church polities came into existence. The task of forming a fellowship of believers which would bear witness to the gospel as they had apprehended it by faith, was the same throughout the ages; but even within the same denomination various forms of institutional life proved to be helpful and appropriate at various times.

Theoretically the coexistence of several rival theologies and types of church life does not seem to present any special problem. People frequently point to the coexistence of political parties in a democracy. That comparison overlooks the fact, however, that the democratic parties consider their aims to be relative and therefore compatible. It is only when a political party thinks it has taken hold of an absolute political ideal, that it becomes fanatical and seeks to suppress all dissent and opposition. In Protestant church life both methods have been tried. In many circles the support of the ecumenical movement is based upon the conviction that it matters little which denomination one joins, because all of them have apprehended a relative truth or only a fragment of the truth. The zeal of the sixteenth-century church leaders who burned, imprisoned, or exiled all dissenters, belongs in the opposite camp, found in our day in the lust for power and fanatical hatred of those self-appointed prophets who would gladly exterminate that part of Protestantism which refuses to acclaim their leadership. History, however, has shown that the effective discharge of Protestantism's task is not attached to any given form. Different circumstances and needs and different types of spiritual experience demand adaptation and hence lead to multiplicity.

The diversity of Protestantism becomes a vexing problem, however, when the task assigned to a group is tied up with the redemption of people. Where is the border line to be drawn between absoluteness and relativity? The answer could be found only by relating the doctrine and institution of the church to the basic experience of the Reformation. The Reformation was an event within the spiritual history of Christianity, not a new origin. By the nature of the case it was therefore prevented from becoming a universal movement and was foreordained to remain a particular process. That is to say, Luther's specific experience was inevitably tied up with his person and could not express itself as an abstract general truth. Yet Luther never claimed to have a revelation entitling him to found a new religion. He bore his testimony within the church and to the church, whose head and principle of unity remained Christ. Consequently Luther refrained from assigning absolute validity to his message. The lordship of Christ left room for other interpretations of the significance the grace of God has for man's relation to God. Theoretically, the history of Protestantism might have been similar to the genesis of the different monastic orders in the Catholic church. But in its attempt to safeguard the oneness of the church within the diversity of experiences, Protestantism was beset by a special problem. If it had been an entirely new development, Protestantism would probably have grown in a manner similar to the history of the early church in the late first and the second centuries: the diverse types would simply have coexisted side by side.

As a movement *within* the church, however, Protestantism's right of existence was constantly challenged by the church of Rome. As a result, doctrine was placed at the side of the Scripture. Rome would not content herself with the reference to an experience in which God had spoken; she demanded proof that the biblical texts appealed to by the Protestants had this and no other meaning. The result of this demand was the Augsburg Confession, upon which theologians established a type of doctrine, namely, Lutheran orthodox dogmatics. For the same reason, the Reformed church had to inaugurate a parallel development. Thus the necessity to have a theology was inherent in Protestantism itself. Evidence that it would have taken place even if there had been no Counter-Reformation can be seen in the Anabaptist movement, where likewise an orthodox system of thought and ethics grew up. The reason was not only that Protestants and Catholics disagreed on the interpretation of Scripture, but also that the basic Protestant experience when analyzed and expressed in theoretical terms, proved that Scripture left ample room for diversity of exegesis. Thus even Luther and Calvin were unable to agree fully on the doctrine of the Lord's Supper, notwithstanding Luther's admission of the congenial character of Calvin's intention in the understanding of the sacrament. Among their followers the disagreement degenerated into theological controversies in which minute differences were blown up to gigantic size.

We would not do justice to the development of Protestant creeds, however, if we saw in it only the *rabies theologica*, about which Melanchthon already had reason to complain. The cause of intolerance is to be found in the theologian's realization that he is dealing with God's saving truth, and that salvation is so precious that every effort must be made to safeguard it. The theologians were entirely right when they made every effort to present the saving truth in such a manner that those who embraced it could be certain of their salvation. Where these theologians erred was in their failure to differentiate between the infinite content of the work of the God-man on the one hand, and the inevitable limitations of the human mind on the other. They failed to realize that in theology a certain position can be true without thereby invalidating other positions. Yet since this pluralism of truth is not identical with relativism, it is imperative for the theologian to examine most carefully the relation of his own theology to the Christ of the gospel. For this reason the theologian must endeavor to state the reasons for his position and at the same time insist that others demonstrate the acceptability of their views despite objections raised against them.

Of course, one could imagine a history of Protestantism, in which the various types of experience showed complete toleration for each other, because doctrine was considered a merely human attempt to give expression to the word of God. But the Anabaptists and Schwenckfeld no less than Luther and Calvin were obviously so deeply rooted in medieval modes of thinking, that doctrine was soon placed beside the word of God, and eventually above it. Once this trend had started institutionalism was on its way. As long as Protestantism placed the emphasis upon the speaking of God, no room was left for differentiation among the believers. All of them were considered equally close to God. While the ministry was not abrogated in the Protestant churches, the pastor no longer was endowed with the prerogatives of the priestly order. With his special training he was able to act as teacher and guide in the congregation, but he was not thought of as possessing deeper spiritual understanding than the lay people.

When the emphasis shifted to doctrine, however, the learned theologian alone was in a position to decide the nature of faith, and accordingly the organized church, rather than the testimony of the believer, became the center of Protestant faith. This development would have led to complete and permanent stagnation except for the fact that the Bible retained its dominant position in Protestantism. Hence one of the factors in the dialectic of Protestant history is the claim made for the ecclesiastical institutions. In that dialectic the tendency to make the impersonal organization and its activities prevail is tempered by the fire of a living faith.

Nevertheless, the history of Protestantism is not merely an

alternation between these two tendencies. Modern Protestantism, although an outcome of the Reformation, is by no means any longer identical with its sixteenth- and seventeenth-century predecessors. Increasingly it has become aware of its own nature as a spiritual process and thus has been able to dissociate itself from its historical implementations. In the century of Luther, for instance, it was still natural that the Protestant churches should identify themselves with their nation, its culture and history, with the scholarship and the education of their age, and with the social order in which they lived. But gradually, and often painfully, they realized that with such an outlook the concern for their environment and its preservation threatened to assume the same degree of significance as the believer's relation to God.

Since man's problem as conceived by the Reformers is the problem of a life lived in this world, yet in relation to God, the detachment from the believers' historical environment could not mean that Protestantism must enter into a process of increased egocentrism and internalization of religion, as it was occasionally interpreted, but rather that a new concept of relationship had to be forged. The historical conditions, originally considered as the believer's home, in which he could cultivate his spiritual life, were reinterpreted as a challenge to service, which could be effectively answered only when the believer was aware of the fundamental difference between God's action, on the one hand, and that which he and other people did, on the other.

It seems that the realization that Christians are a peculiar people different from the rest of mankind, yet that they must live in this world in order to render their specific contribution to their fellowmen, has come with intense urgency to our generation. We realize that the differentiation of the church from the world is counteracted by the realism and this-worldliness of Protestantism. With the experience of God speaking to man and using the means of grace as media of communication, the medieval distinction between the spheres of the natural and the supranatural has lost its significance. There is nothing in this world except what belongs to this world. The church itself is human in character. Yet in and through things of this world and by human beings who are part of this world, God manifests himself and carries on his redemptive work. Thus man can enjoy this world and discover divine meaning in its history.

This belief in the goodness of this world can, however, easily degenerate into ascribing to the historical process itself a redemptive function. Thus, for instance, the idealistic philosophies, by ascribing to man an innate religious faculty, would postulate that the existence of the church was the necessary outcome of human history, because thus alone could the religious side of culture be supplied. Such speculations sound both naive and phony to our age. At a time when the value of the cultural life of mankind has become questionable and life seems to be a mere scramble for survival, a religion that would satisfy only cultural needs seems terrifically out of place.

It is true that the change of outlook has been forced upon us with an unexpected abruptness. By the end of the last century the church felt comfortably at home in this world, and the theological controversies could be regarded as evidences of the church's vitality. Conservative divines would fight and denounce their liberal colleagues, who in turn would repay with the same currency. But neither lifted his eyes to the world outside their fences until in the conflagration of two world wars and a worldwide social revolution their cozy homes, too, burned down. Things have now moved to the other extreme. Protestant leaders all over the world are hypercritical of Protestantism itself, and busy themselves in discovering an unassailable position outside of the historical world. Another large number attempts with an unprecedented zest and energy to silence these denunciations by means of literary production, multiplicity of conferences and generous relief work. The question must be raised, however, how far this new ecclesiastical activity and productivity is motivated by the basic doubt inherent in the Protestant faith, and how far by listening to the speaking of God.

2. THE FATEFUL CHALLENGE

We have attempted to portray the contemporary picture of Protestantism as it emerges from within. This self-searching has caused Protestantism to reflect on the place it has assigned to doctrine, to look afresh at the way it defines the church-world problem and the place it has within the larger church.

In addition, Protestantism faces a fateful challenge from outside its ranks. If nothing else could be said about the future of Protestantism, one thing is certain. It has entered into a phase of its history in which its continued existence is even more in doubt than it was during the dreadful years of the Counter-Reformation. Then the flame of its spiritual zeal was still shining brightly, as evidenced by the quality of its devotional literature and hymns and by the boldness of its martyrs. Modern Protestantism is so permeated by a spirit of skepticism and defeatism that some of its theological leaders are prepared to write it off completely. If we are to believe those critics, Protestantism is definitely doomed and the history of mankind has already entered the post-Protestant age. This gloomy picture seems to be justified by the actual predicament of modern Protestantism. After a long period of uninterrupted advance it now finds itself assailed from all sides, with no effective methods yet developed to cope with this situation. Although conditions vary from country to country and are—at least on the surface—least disturbing in the United States, there is no reason for optimism. The very fact that Protestantism has spread over the whole world is the reason why losses and dangers now in one area will likewise affect all other areas. There is also reason to ask whether the appearance of vitality which Protestantism presents in this country is not to a large extent merely statistical. The external forces which threaten modern Protestantism to a special degree are militant atheism, Islam, Roman Catholicism, and secularism.

a) *Militant Atheism*

The atheism which Protestantism encounters today in Communistic propaganda may be considerably cruder than the ironical and witty atheism of the eighteenth century, but its appeal is not, therefore, less powerful. While the former atheistic propaganda confined itself to the educated classes and accordingly attacked the consistency of the doctrinal system of Protestantism and the truthfulness of the historical records of the Bible, it has completely changed its front since it has directed its appeal to the masses. Since this propaganda addresses itself to primitive people, many of whom are still practicing the lowest forms of pagan religion, the denunciation of alleged superstitious elements in Christianity can play but a subordinate role. The main attack is turned against the close connection of Protestantism and capitalism. Belief in God is accordingly interpreted as a capitalistic trick intended to keep the oppressed masses in subjection and to suppress their urge to deliver themselves by their own efforts.

The appeal this propaganda makes upon the millions of distressed people in Asia and Africa should not be underrated. The Communistic media of mass communication reach immense crowds to whom the missionary is unable to present the truth of the gospel. In addition, the missionary finds it increasingly difficult to refute that propaganda because the facts are undeniable. Ridiculous though it is to present the missionaries as the stooges of capitalism, the missionary is unable to deny the charge that it was through members of the "Christian" nations that colonialism and capitalism have subjected Africa and Asia to themselves. As a result the missionary today encounters a hostility toward his message even in those "new countries" which have no Communistic leanings. No matter what progress Protestantism may make in the future among the people of the Western world, Communistic propaganda of atheism has effectively curbed its progress on the "foreign field." There it becomes necessary for Christianity to dissociate itself not only from the political and economic interests of the Western nations, but from those same tendencies in the nations of Asia and Africa as well. The propaganda of militant atheism has laid bare one of the dangerous consequences of Protestantism's this-worldliness. Imperceptibly the acceptance of this world as made by God and presented to the believers as their field of service, has changed into conformity with this world. In turn the people of Asia and Africa look to the Western world for help in their struggle for better education and a higher standard of living. It is exceedingly difficult for the messenger of the gospel to deny the fact that God's word is not of direct practical usefulness, because it is true that to those who accept it, material benefits will also eventually accrue.

b) *Islamic Propaganda*

A second threat to Protestantism has unexpectedly arisen in Islamic propaganda. No other religion had as consistently, stubbornly, and contemptuously refused to have any contacts with Christianity as Islam. Although this fact had been well known ever since Christians had made attempts to proclaim the gospel to Moslems, it came, nevertheless, as quite a surprise even to experts that Islam again began an offensive after centuries of complete stagnation. But there can be no doubt that the new pan-Arabism with its material and spiritual center in Egypt has given Islam a new lease on life. It uses the religious teachings of Islam as its most effective weapon in its fight against the Western world among the non-Arabic nations of Africa. What makes the Mohammedan religion so attractive to the African nations is the extreme simplicity of its doctrine and worship and its uncomplicated and lenient ethics. Whereas Protestant dogmatics require a subtle and complicated adjustment in order to appeal to the native mind in Asia or Africa, hardly any transformation is necessary in the case of Islam.

Still more important for the advance of Islam is the clever way in which Egypt merges religious propaganda with political objectives. In its desire to win the new decolonized countries of Africa as allies, the Islamic propaganda caters to the native resentment against their former colonial overlords. The most powerful argument, the principle of full equality and the absence of racial prejudice in Islam, hits the missionary activity of the Protestants more effectively than that of the Catholics. Since the latter has usually addressed itself to whole native groups it has been able to preserve the tribal organization. Consequently the fight for independence was carried on by the whole tribe without prejudice to its Christian foundation. Protestant missionary work has, on the whole, followed the individualistic pattern of the Western Protestantism much more than has Catholicism, and thus has alienated the Christian converts from their tribes. It is no wonder that the native Protestant Christians should feel more directly the status of inequality assigned to them both in the missionary activity and in social intercourse with the white people. The fact that the Protestant churches of South Africa should have identified themselves with the apartheid policy of their government has naturally been exploited by the Islamic propaganda as a particularly effective weapon against Protestantism. In our judgment the advance of Islam, while it will not be able to lure many of the native Christians away, will nevertheless be a powerful roadblock for the Protestant mission. Whereas the missionary formerly was received as a friend and benefactor, in the future he will have to overcome serious prejudices without being able to whitewash the Western nations from the charge of race prejudice.

c) *The Catholic Church*

Relations between Protestantism and Catholicism have been of a rather contradictory nature in modern times. With the stabilizing of Protestant and Catholic political power around 1650 the Protestant and Catholic churches lived side by side without taking much cognizance of each other. Recognizing itself as a branch of Christ's church, to which the Catholic church too belonged, Protestantism has never entertained the desire to destroy the Catholic church. At a time when Rome's power had arrived at an all-time low in the eighteenth century, it was characteristic of the Protestant attitude, that Protestant churches did not join the militant rationalists in their fierce attempt to exterminate Catholicism. By the end of the nineteenth century Protestants and Catholics had come so close to each other that Catholic theologians in Germany, France, and Great Britain took an increasing interest in Protestant theology, particularly in the biblical field. Notwithstanding the fact that the stern antimodernist measures succeeded in silencing this movement for some time, the interest not only continued but grew more powerful and has recently reached also the Mediterranean countries. It is no exaggeration to say that, at present, Catholic and Protestant biblical scholarship works together closely on a basis of complete reciprocity.

Nevertheless, this is but one aspect of the relationship between the churches. The new dogma of the corporeal assumption of Mary and the uninhibited proclamation of the Virgin as coredemptrix show that at least one powerful section of the Roman Catholic church is making a clean break with the Protestant position. Conversely, the significance of such groups of the *Una Sancta* and similar movements which are devoted to the theological rapprochement of the churches should not be overrated. In no respect do they represent the official attitude of their respective churches or the sentiments of substantial portions of the believers.

Yet there is another change in Rome's attitude which cannot fail to stir up serious apprehensions on the part of Protestants. The church of Rome, which in the course of the eighteenth and nineteenth centuries had constantly lost power, has finally made a comeback and has recently entered into a new phase of Counter-Reformation. According to all the evidence this new quest for power is directed by a leadership which shows extraordinary vision, intelligence, and determination. The center of gravity of this new assault lies in the United States; but its activities are skillfully seconded by Adenauer's Christian Democratic Union in Germany; and by the Catholic political parties in other European countries. Whereas the territory of the United States of America was colonized almost exclusively by Protestant immigrants, the need for industrial labor has in the last hundred years attracted large numbers from Ireland, Eastern Europe, the Mediterranean countries, and Puerto Rico, that is to say, a predominantly Roman Catholic population. Although originally economically poor and unorganized, many of them have recently risen to prosperity and political power thanks to their organization by the labor unions and the skillful guidance of the Catholic clergy. The aim is not primarily to make converts from Protestantism, though the Paulist Fathers and the Knights of Columbus do not neglect this objective. The main goal is the acquisition and accumulation of political and economic power in the hands of the clergy and the Catholic millions.

Since this comeback is not manifestly directed against Protestantism as a religion, the seriousness of the situation is commonly underrated by Protestants. Of course, in a country whose national character and political institutions have been thoroughly molded by the Protestant ethos, people will hardly suspect that their political and social institutions might be used for the formation of an entirely different political system and a Catholic way of life. Protestantism is in no way prepared for this turn of events. Not only are organizations such as the National Council of Churches utterly unfit to give leadership in this new competitive situation; a political counteraction also is out of the question, because Protestants support both political parties, and there is no Protestant headquarters from which a Protestant strategy could be directed. The most serious shortcoming in the Protestant camp, however, is the widespread spiritual indifference. The numerical increase of the membership of the leading Protestant denominations in the United States cannot conceal the fact that for the majority of Protestants spiritual life is confined to Sunday worship and a general ethos of decency, and consequently Protestantism lacks the power and determination to mold the individual's professional life and his outlook on political and international affairs.

Of course, the Catholic church is not as powerful everywhere as it is in the United States, Germany, Belgium, and Spain. In all probability its weakest position is in Central and South America. A pitiful scarcity of priests, and the social and cultural indifference of the clergy, no less than popular superstition and ignorance, have alienated the masses of Latin America from the church, and with an unexpected enthusiasm they have turned a friendly ear to Protestant missionaries. In the crudest way the Roman church organized its resistance in Columbia by availing itself of the traditional methods of arson, murder, banditry, and arbitrary police action. In doing so it has succeeded in drastically reducing the number of Protestants in the rural parts of Columbia and in seriously disorganizing the missionary activities all over that country. One cannot be sure that the protective measures taken by the present government of that country will survive a change of government. While conditions in the rest of Central and South America are not likely to develop along the Columbian pattern, there can be no doubt that the tempo of Protestant advance among our neighbors in the South will slow down considerably in the near future, because in the face of her losses the Catholic church has become aware of her responsibility and is beginning to reform in a radical way.

Reports in the secular press may create the impression that with the Second Vatican Council, the relationship between Protestantism and Roman Catholicism has radically changed. The truth is that with the pontificate of Pope John XXIII, encounters between Protestant and Catholic churchmen and theologians took place in a warmer and more amiable atmosphere than has ever been the case since the days of the Reformation. Catholic bishops officially attend Protestant meetings, and officially invited Protestant observers at the Vatican Council are full of praise for the extraordinary consideration with which they are treated and the frankness with which a number of Catholic bishops and theologians speak to them about their problems.

All this is certainly good, and it is most gratifying that Paul VI, the successor to the "ecumenical pope," is methodically continuing the "liberal" policy of his predecessor. This is a very effective way to stimulate dialogue between the churches. But it is obvious that in its official utterances the Vatican carefully avoids terms that might be interpreted as implying that the Protestants are also members of the infallible church of which Rome is the head. Theologically, the Vatican Council has not adopted any doctrine that would lessen the opposition to the Protestant confessions of faith. While individual bishops and professors may have made utterances which could be understood as doctrinal rapprochement, the Council has been eager to preserve the traditional position. There were even manifest tendencies to accentuate the differences in soteriology. Above all, the desire of more liberal theologians to let the bishops share in the prerogatives of the Bishop of Rome has met with stubborn resistance on the part of the very influential Curia. Hence the friendliness which the Roman Catholic church shows toward the Protestants leaves the theological and ecclesiastical position unchanged.

d) *Secularism*

The most dangerous threat confronting the Protestant churches in our time, however, is the spread of secularism. As distinct from atheism, secularism does not fight religion, but rather considers it an unnecessary, purely mental experience. The basic axiom of secularism is the principle that man's life in this world has full meaning in itself and that this world provides all the resources necessary to render man happy. As a result, secularism practices a complete divorce between religion and the rest of life. The rapid upsurge of natural science and technology seemingly supports this attitude, because no religion is required of one who wants to excel in these activities. In turn, it is on the basis of this development that modern man has been enabled to enjoy the amenities of life to an extent never known even by the richest and most powerful people of the past. However, on this road the inner life of the individual loses all contact with his fellowman or the world in which he lives, as is most conspicuously manifested in existentialism and abstract art.

Secularism has made wide inroads into Protestantism, which was exposed to it through the public school and the media of mass communication, which are controlled by interests that profit from exploiting this mentality for commercial purposes. As a result, the spiritual life in Protestantism is eroded in large circles to a dangerous degree. The sacraments are interpreted as symbols of natural life, and religion is appreciated merely as a means to secular ends, for instance, for the preservation of Western culture and national life, or as a shortcut to peace of mind. Since this attitude is based upon a purely functional view of God it makes no difference what a person believes. It is no longer God who brings redemption to man, but rather man who becomes his own redeemer by adopting a religious symbol. By such an approach, the nature of faith as discovered by the Reformers is completely perverted. Whereas Luther began with the doubts called forth by man's relation to God, now people start from their relation to this world. Hence God, who in his omnipotent dealing with this world appeared incomprehensible to man, has eventually become an instrument which man utilizes for the satisfaction of his earthly needs. The social conformism, which is the inevitable outcome of modern man's egotistic individualism, affects his religious life too, and manifests itself as indifferentism. Why do we have so many denominations, people ask, since we are all Christians? And why do we send missionaries to foreign countries, when one religion is as good as the other?

Strangely enough, this attitude can pose as ecumenical interest or as the religion of the Spirit. But we must not be deluded by its pose. There is a world of difference between such indifferentism and the striving for that metahistorical and spiritual unity that transcends the historical particularities of the denominations, and enables people to worship God in common notwithstanding all that separates them in their organizational life and their ways of worship. Similarly it is one thing to hold that all religions are basically one and symbolize man's fears or ideals, as does the secularist, and another thing to scrutinize another religion in order to find the point of contact in it, and then to show to the devotee of that religion how God offers him infinitely more in Christ.

Secularism disguises itself occasionally as active interest in the problems of the world, and it blames the non-secular Christian as being other-worldly and callous in a world of injustice and suffering. Granted that there are "biblical" Christians who lack interest in and sympathy for the needs of this world. But the secularist approach to social ethics is superior to the gospel in appearance only. It is based upon the conviction that man is living in a neutral world over which he has control and which in his wisdom he can mold so that it will yield a maximum of beneficial results. Biblical faith is aware of the fact that man and this world are in a hopeless predicament unless God comes to their rescue. To be sure, Christians should be concerned with the needs of their fellowmen, but they should be even more concerned with giving the right kind of help. The secular approach does not yield any real help; people's needs are only shifted from one area to another. The postwar "German miracle," for instance, far from resulting in a diminution of crime, a rise in cultural interests, and increased concern for other people's needs, is accompanied by a terrifying and rapid increase in delinquency, vulgarity, and egotistic self-centeredness. Likewise concomitant with the affluence of the American people is the steady rise in mental illness. While the Christian faith knows of effective remedies for the world's ills, they are withheld from the world whenever Christians are merely anxious to be and to act like everybody else rather than contributing their specific gift.

CHAPTER II

THE RENEWAL OF PROTESTANTISM

A. THE NEW IMAGE OF PROTESTANTISM

The question, "What is Protestantism?" was posed in the previous chapter. The answer, it was seen, must be arrived at in the context of the fourfold challenge confronting contemporary Protestantism. Ultimately, however, we concluded that the question cannot be answered apart from a serious study of the history of Protestantism and especially a study in depth of Luther's own experience. There are indications of renewal in Protestantism and it is our aim to sketch the new image of Protestantism and look at some new manifestations in its total life.

1. THE LUTHER RENAISSANCE

The critical situation in which Protestantism undoubtedly finds itself in our age, has not been accepted everywhere in a purely passive way. It has, rather, been viewed in many places as a challenge to re-examine the traditional image of Protestantism. The nineteenth century had marked the apex of religious atomization. The proliferation of new sects and denominations was paralleled in theology by a craving for originality. The unity of Protestantism, if felt as a problem at all, had become a transcendental task or a Platonic idea, while in actual life individualism and subjectivism triumphed. No wonder that for many of its adherents, Protestantism was defined only in negative terms, for instance, as anti-Romanism or anti-churchliness.

Of course, it would be a serious exaggeration if we denied

the widespread impact which outstanding evangelical theologians made upon the Protestant churches of the nineteenth century, and the unifying role they played between Lutherans and Reformed on the continent and between the Church of England and the Free Churches in Britain, or the various denominations in the United States of America. But wholesome as the influence was of these theologians upon the lives of those who followed them, their theology was not able to stem the advance of subjectivism and secularism in contemporary Protestantism.

More recently, however, two factors have contributed to the restoration of the Protestant image: the so-called Luther Renaissance and the rediscovery of biblical realism. Of course, Luther's works have been studied in all ages, and biographies of Luther have inspired and encouraged Protestants in good and evil days. A radical change occurred, however, when R. Seeberg, Karl Holl, Heinrich Boehmer, Werner Elert, and Carl Stange, all following the example of Theodosius Harnack, exposed the fundamental methodical errors of their predecessors in Luther research.[1] The Lutheran churches had been so sure that they were the faithful disciples of "Father Luther" that they did not even consider the possibility that changes might have occurred between the days of Luther and those of Lutheran orthodoxy, not to mention the neo-Lutheranism of the nineteenth century. Very naively they read their later systems into Luther's own works with the result that everything in Luther which could not be used as a proof text for their systems was conveniently ignored. The arbitrariness of such a method of historical research

---

[1] Reinhold Seeberg, *Die Lehre Luthers* ("Lehrbuch der Dogmengeschicte" IV, 1 [2nd ed.; Leipzig, 1917]); Karl Holl, *Gesammelte Aufsätze zur Kirchengeschichte. Band 1: Luther* (Tübingen, 1921); Heinrich Boehmer, *Road to Reformation: Martin Luther to the Year 1521*, trans. J. W. Dobertein and T. G. Tappert (Philadelphia: Muhlenberg Press, 1946); Werner Elert, *Morphologie des Luthertums* (2 Vols.; Munich, 1931-32), trans. W. A. Hansen, *The Structure of Lutheranism* (St. Louis: Concordia Publishing House, 1962); Carl Stange, *Die Anfänge der Theologie Luthers* ("Studien der Lutherakademie, N. F. 5"; Berlin, 1957); Theodosius Harnack, *Luthers Theologie* (2 Vols.; 1862; neue Ausgabe: Munich, 1927).

came to light when scholars devoted their attention to the early stages of Luther's thinking, and particularly when the rediscovery of Luther's notes on the Epistle to the Romans (1515-16) revealed thoughts which differed strikingly from those of his later years.

The enthusiasm caused by this new image of Luther led to exaggerations; some theologians, for instance, were quite willing to jettison the traditional image of Luther and to canonize the "young Luther." In the meantime it has become obvious that, notwithstanding its spiritual verve, the commentary on Romans is nevertheless a document of transition from Luther's discovery of Augustine's mysticism to the position of the Reformation. Nevertheless once scholars had realized that the historical Luther was not identical with the system of Lutheran orthodoxy, his other works were studied with fresh eyes. The principal result of those investigations was the discovery that Luther was not so much a leader in systematic theology as a reformer, and that his goal in life was not that of adding a new *summa* to those of the schoolmen but rather to lead people to a correct understanding of God's grace and its implications. This shift of emphasis from theological concepts and systems to the grace of God as apprehended by faith resulted in giving Protestant theology a new theocentric perspective.

While, in its beginnings, the new Luther research had been inclined to stress exclusively the subjective element in faith, it soon became obvious that by faith Luther meant the believer's response to God's revelation. This emphasis radically transformed the concept of Protestant theology. In the nineteenth and early twentieth centuries academic theology was based upon the external authority of the Bible or the confessions of faith by a good number of theologians, while in other circles it was an attempt to amalgamate in a subjective manner a philosophy of religion with Protestant tradition, with the result that the volume of tradition was increasingly reduced or philosophically reinterpreted. It came as quite a surprise to the students of Luther to notice that in his theology he combined a strictly subjective view of faith with the acceptance of a divine revelation which no man had a right to alter.

It is not by chance that the study of Calvin and Zwingli has not been pursued in modern Protestantism with the same zeal and enthusiasm as characterized the new Luther research. Scholars soon realized that in discovering Luther's view they had hit upon the formative principle of the whole of Protestantism, which offered not only the clue to the whole history of the Reformation, but also promised to restore the purity of Protestant theology. While, as a result of the Luther Renaissance, Protestant theology has been enabled to adopt an entirely new perspective, this discovery, nevertheless, was not by itself sufficient to give Protestant theology a new beginning. A good deal of the Luther research has been merely historical, implying that Luther himself became the absolute authority in theology. This attitude is most conspicuous with regard to the problem of revelation. Just as conservative theology of the past had onesidedly concentrated upon the principle of the infallibility of the Bible without showing much interest in its message, so the emphasis which Luther had placed upon revelation received a disproportionate amount of attention. Much thought was devoted to defining the nature of revelation as contrasted with the natural powers of the human mind, while relatively little attention was paid to the word which God in his revelation is speaking to the believer.

2. Biblical Realism

Significant as these developments in Luther research are for the renewal of life in Protestantism, of greatest significance for theological development in recent Protestantism is the radical change which has taken place in biblical scholarship. Quite unexpectedly the study of the Bible took a turn toward a new type of biblical theology. Right down to World War I students of the Bible were preoccupied with historical and philological problems. The quest of the historical Jesus kept the best minds busy, the objective of the quest being to find a Jesus who would be acceptable to the modern mind and modern scholarship, as contrasted with the Christ whom the Primitive church proclaimed. Similarly the motive behind the nineteenth-century biblical theologies in the field of the Old Testament was a purely historical one, which was perhaps even more outspoken than in the New Testament. Nevertheless the aim of these works was either to vindicate the traditional position of Protestant conservative theology, or to prove by means of historical investigation that the liberal concept of religion had its roots in the historical teachings of Jesus. In neither case was there an intimation of the radical challenge implied in the revealed character of the Scripture, which was so constitutive for Luther's concept of faith.

The complete change that has since occurred in the field of biblical studies is most conspicuous in the re-evaluation of the biblical record. Many of the features of the Bible which previous scholarship threw out as antiquated, historically dated, or superstitious, or "debunked" as residues of more primitive modes of thought and carry-overs from Judaism or Hellenism, such as eschatology, miracles, the church, the Son of man concept, etc., are now taken seriously by the student of the Bible. This change is due to the rediscovery of biblical realism, that is to say, to the realization that the biblical writers were not so much interested in developing a system of religious notions as in bearing witness to facts of experience and to the significance of these facts for our redemption. The biblical writers expressed their testimony in the language of their day, and their own nature and experience tinged their witness. But they wrote about objective facts, nevertheless, whose facticity confronts the modern reader no less than it confronted the writers themselves. What makes the Bible relevant is not, therefore, the religion of its authors—which is but the frame of reference within which they speak—but rather the object of their religion: God acting redemptively, particularly in Jesus Christ.

Viewing the biblical writers as witnesses results in a new understanding of faith which provides a new perspective for exegesis. The biblical scholar no longer contents himself with holding a consistent theory of redemption. Rather he expects the biblical revelation to show him what this world and his own life mean in their relation to God. Redemption is thereby transferred from the realm of theological speculation to a concrete experience. The Bible assumes a fundamental difference in a man's life between sinfulness and new birth. The Holy Spirit, formerly the stepchild of systematic theology, is restored to his central position in Christian experience. Similarly, scholars became aware of the dominating influence that Greek philosophy and mentality have exercised upon the thought of the church, and how the meaning of the biblical message has been obscured through this influence. The problem of man was treated as though he were merely mind or soul and his physical existence in this world did not matter. But the reason why man, as the Bible describes him, is so perplexed about his predicament lies in the fact that he is a being of flesh and blood, and as such so harrassed by the cosmic forces that he cannot find comfort in the prospect of a pleasant future and a life free of conflicts as long as that prospect concerns only his soul.

Most revolutionary is the new treatment of biblical eschatology. With its emphasis placed upon redemption through justification, Protestant orthodox theology had completely neglected the eschatological teaching of the New Testament. The doctrine of the Last Things was confined to the description of life after death. Of course, this theology rightly frowned upon the predilection for apocalypticism encountered in small Protestant conventicles and sects because thereby the doctrine of the Last Things had lost all connection with the redemptive work of Christ. But unfortunately these excesses of apocalypticism made the theologians of the churches unwilling to reconsider eschatology's place in the gospel. Eventually, however, guided by biblical realism, scholars discovered that Irenaeus and more recently the school of *Heilsgeschichte* (holy history, or history of redemption) were on the right track in emphasizing the purposiveness of God's activity. Hence, notwithstanding its all-sufficiency, the work of Christ has a temporal aspect. God has made him Lord in order that he might subdue all of God's enemies so that finally God will be all in all. Seen in this light the eschatological passages of the New Testament no longer sound as strange and absurd to our time as they did to previous generations. Rather the New Testament reminds us of the paradoxical position in which we find ourselves, living between the accomplished work of redemption, on the one hand, and the complete victory of Christ, on the other.

3. THE FUNCTION OF THEOLOGY

As a consequence of the shift of interest from systematic theology to biblical theology the whole theological enterprise underwent a re-evaluation. Because the Protestant churches were not in a position to establish a teaching authority in their midst that could match that of the episcopacy and the Pope in the Catholic church, their concept of theology still followed the Roman pattern for a considerable time. The claim was upheld that whatever inferences were derived by clear and consistent reasoning from the Bible would share in its absolute authority, and that there was but one system of theology that could come into being in this manner. No wonder that each of the Protestant churches claimed to have the secret of this avenue to infallibility. This approach to theology was in principle identical with that of the Catholic church in that the Bible was regarded as an infallible textbook of theology, and that the progress of theology was expected from the scholarly efforts of the theologians. Things appeared in an entirely different light when, following Luther, the believer's perplexity again formed the starting point of theology and the theologian therefore relied on the revelation God grants him in and through the Scriptures. In that case it became obvious that orthodox theology's claim to be infallible was ill-founded since it relied on dubious sources such as the logical ability and the biblical scholarship of the theologians.

As a human activity theology stands under the law of diversity like everything earthly. The oneness of revelation when reflected in human thought appears in a multiplicity of theologies. Theological study is not thereby rendered worthless, for it rests on a solid objective foundation, which is God speaking through the Bible. But by its diversity, theology gives expression to the fact that it differs essentially from revelation and must never take its place, even though it is an adequate interpretation of revelation. Thus understood, theology has a real claim, since it no longer rests upon the sole authority of the theologian. Yet the individual theologian is able no longer while fighting other theologies to pose as the lone advocate of faith against the representatives of error and falsehood.

The ecumenical movement would never have been possible apart from this new view of the relationship of revelation and theology. Characteristic of this development is the way in which leading theologians of our age assess their own work. Karl Barth, e.g., by starting from the dialectical relationship in which the theological systems of Protestantism stand to each other, did not offer his own theology as a new system to replace all of them but rather as a mere corrective of contemporary theology. That this intention was well taken is obvious. Although few theologians have completely adopted Barth's system for themselves, practically all of his Protestant colleagues, and not a few Catholics, have recognized their indebtedness to his timely rejoinder. He has broken the ban of subjectivism in Protestant circles and the fetters of scholasticism in Catholic theology. Similarly, a study of Rudolf Bultmann shows that his main concern is not with inducing people to adopt his system of biblical theology. He wants to deliver Protestantism from the stranglehold of historicism. While he may not have been as successful as Barth in his theological venture—mainly because together with historicism he throws out the historical work of Jesus—his call to an existential interpretation of the Bible has found an echo in the most diverse corners. This response is obviously due to the fact that he treats the New Testament as a work destined to engender faith rather than as a textbook of theology. Even Paul Tillich, who certainly is anxious to propagate his ideas as modern man's true philosophy of religion, is, nevertheless, free from dogmatism. His aim is to call forth in Christians the courage to live in a new and changed world without giving up the gospel.[2]

The modern theology of revelation has become humble in comparison with that of previous generations. Its representatives are overwhelmed by the enormous scope of their task. How can the human mind ever succeed in expressing God's redemptive purpose and work in a valid manner once the "infinite qualitative difference between the Creator and the creatures" (Kierkegaard) stands at the beginning of all theology? It is only as it sees itself as an aspect of the continuous witness that the church bears to God's revelation, that theology is able to carry on its work without losing heart. No wonder that the modern theologian dissociates himself from his nineteenth-century colleagues who wanted to be original at any price. The contemporary theologian contents himself with serving the church. Those who complain that no great theologian has yet arisen in the present generation completely misunderstand the radical change that has occurred in Protestant theology since World War I. While theological interest is hardly flagging, and some of the best brains of Protestantism are engaged in theology, they do not take delight in shocking their contemporaries by propounding new and unheard-of views but rather are eagerly engaged in interpreting the believer's predicament—that is to say, a condition shared by both the theological author and his readers.

One should not be overly surprised that such attempts are

---

[2] Paul Tillich, *The Courage to Be* (New Haven: Yale University Press, 1952); *The New Being* (New York: Charles Scribner's Sons, 1955).

primarily analytical in character and do not provide new theological ideas. Willingness to probe the very depth of our perplexity is more in agreement with the nature of faith than are
bold assertions that brand new answers have been discovered.
For the same reason only the advocates of the *status quo* in
theology can find comfort in the fact that no Barthian or
Brunnerian school of theology has sprung up, and that Bultmann
is being taken to task by his own disciples. This development
does not mean that the influence of the "grand old men" is
waning; rather it indicates that precisely because they are taken
so seriously, their approach to the theological problem, and not
their theological statements, is to be perpetuated. Instead of
forming schools and simply adopting the views of masters, the
younger theologians are critical and prefer a certain eclecticism.
They rightly realize that such an approach is the most effective
way to teach an otherwise complacent generation of church
people that there is a challenge implied in God's revelation.

The case of Paul Tillich is particularly instructive in this
connection. What he calls the principle of correlation is an
ingenious device designed to apply to theological methodology
Luther's understanding of faith and its transition from perplexity
to certainty. Man asks questions and God provides the answer,
is the way Tillich formulates his principle. In rebuttal of criticisms, according to which man would in that case always receive the kind of answer he is waiting for, Tillich has rightly
insisted that the question would not be a real question if man
knew the answer in advance. That Tillich has had no real fol-
lower in the field of systematic theology is not due to a rejection
of the principle of correlation but rather to the fact that Tillich's
thought moves on a philosophical level, even when he wants to
discuss theology. Since, according to his thinking, life's basic
question arises from man's relation to the universe, rather than
from man's living in a universe in which he is confronted by God,
the answer too is inevitably a philosophical one, notwithstanding
Tillich's religious interests. Tillich fails to distinguish between

the philosopher's question which arises from man's natural
ignorance about which facts are relevant for a meaningful life,
on the one hand, and the believer's perplexity which is due to
his inability to handle the cosmic forces whose superior power
threatens his relation to God, on the other. The philosopher
asks his question because he feels humiliated in his ignorance,
aspiring as he does for complete control of his life; whereas the
believer is groping for light because in his perplexity he is
threatened by the seemingly unlimited power of the cosmic
forces. In turn there is a difference of essence between the kind
of answer with which the philosopher will be satisfied, and the
answer required as a result of the believer's perplexity. The
believer needs assurance concerning the limits which God will
set to the menacing cosmic forces; he needs an answer which
will provide hope, confidence, and comfort. In Tillich's system
the answer is conceived of on the philosophical level as is seen
from the fact that it is couched in ontological terms. He does
not proceed beyond the analysis of what *is* toward the discovery
of an impending redemption. The divine, or ultimate reality, is
accepted in its determinative role, whereas by faith man transcends the universe and receives God's grace. Hence it is obvious
that the schematism of question and answer which underlies Tillich's principle of correlation is of real value for theological
methodology, but also that in order to be helpful for theological
problems it must be modified. The question must be concerned
with the specific perplexity of the believer, not with the general
problem of human existence. The answer in turn is not to be
sought in the relation in which human life stands to the general
order of being, but rather in the fact that God enters the individual's life and speaks to him concerning his salvation.

4. Theology and Non-revealed Knowledge

The new trend in Protestant theology just described has helped to
clarify the relationship of theology to other branches of scientific
thought, in particular to philosophy and science. It is well known

that Luther considered it his mission to deliver theology from the fetters of philosophy, and Schleiermacher, Ritschl, and Barth have defined the task of theology in a manner largely reminiscent of Luther. These men have frequently and severely been scolded for such an attitude by those who insisted that theology was basically philosophical in character. It cannot be denied that irrationalism and even obscurantism have occasionally been introduced into the church in the name of the gospel; nevertheless, a view which depreciates philosophy has not been shared by the theological leaders of Protestantism, and the theologians who insisted on the primacy of revelation were far from advocating an abandonment of rational thought. They only contended that man is unable to discover the answer to his question of perplexity by a rational scrutiny of this world. Man depends for his answer on God's self-disclosure.

In this respect the modern trend in theology differs greatly from the common understanding of systematic theology in the nineteenth century. It was held that in order to be valid, theology must be elaborated in a scientific way, and the only useful method seemed to be to transform the theological tradition into philosophy, or at least to supplement it by philosophy. Thus it is not surprising that even Ritschl, who, more than anybody else, was opposed to the sway Greek philosophical thought held over traditional theology, finally placed a philosophical view of man into the center of theology in lieu of the traditional metaphysical notion of God. The new emphasis assigned to revelation does not rule out the usefulness of philosophy. But theologians now begin to realize that the philosophical question is not identical with the question of faith, notwithstanding the service that philosophy renders to the clarification of faith's question. Since the believer who asks the question is not a mere mind or soul detached from this world but a person who is perplexed about his relationship to God as he lives in this world, realistic types of philosophy in particular aid him because they help him to ascertain the place he occupies in this world; for they treat man as part and parcel thereof.

In one respect the relationship of theology to philosophy has become more intimate now than it was in the nineteenth century, because then the various adaptations attempted required that either philosophy or theology had to surrender its specific character. Consequently there was a constant suspicion on either side lest by such a treatment one might lose its purity. The new theology recognizes that the philosophical question is a constitutive part of the theological problem. At the same time, however, the distance between theology and philosophy has grown enormously. No direct transition can be effected from the philosophical to the theological question. The mere substitution of a theological term for a philosophical one will not do, as is most obvious in Bultmann's use of "existentialism." Rather it is necessary to modify the philosophical question by relating it to the specific perplexity of faith. Modern man, who feels unable to find satisfaction in a secularized world of his own making, is still seeking himself. The question of faith, however, is the question of a man who seeks God in his life because, to his own sorrow, he has realized that the traditional forms of faith have no direct bearing on his hopeless predicament.

In a similar way the attitude of theology toward science has changed. As late as the seventeenth century, theology considered itself the queen of all knowledge, and it was taken for granted that natural science depended on the Bible and theology. With the self-assertion of the natural sciences, however, theology and science came into conflict because unwittingly Christian doctrine had been wedded to an antiquated model of the world. Since modern science had the observable facts on its side, the outcome of this conflict seemed to be so undoubtedly in favor of science that, more recently, theology attempted a kind of reconciliation on the basis of mutual compatibility. The results of these apologetics left both sides unhappy. When, to mention one instance, the Virgin Birth is explained as an instance of biological parthenogenesis, as it is found in a number of animal species, the scientist is no longer able to contend that such an event is impossible. But, at the same time, the Virgin Birth of Jesus ceases to have any theological significance because it would be a mere freak of nature rather than the result of a divine plan.

Consequently, modern theology, by following the lead of biblical realism, will not use the data of science as evidences of the truthfulness of the biblical record but rather as the starting point for the definition of the perplexity of faith. The treatment of the unconscious mind is an instructive point in case. There is hardly a single theologian who still shares the older apologetic view that man's unconscious life is the source of revelation. Modern psychoanalysis has opened an abyss in man's heart to our generation and thereby has helped to shake the nineteenth-century belief in the innate goodness of man. Man's unconscious defiance of the objective moral law and the influence which the cosmic forces have upon human nature have now been laid bare by Freud and Jung. Yet modern theology rightly points out that man's sinfulness is not located in the depth dimension of the human mind, although it also manifests itself in that sphere. Sin has to do with man's relation to God, and it is the self as such that is destined for such relation, not a faculty of the mind or only a specific layer of existence. Thus sin resides in the very center of man's existence, determining his conscious no less than his unconscious life. Sin is the presumptuousness of the self which wants to live its own life irrespective of whether or not God exists.

Such a manner of dealing with the data of modern psychology is characteristic of modern theology's attitude toward science. The former warfare between science and theology is over wherever the purely descriptive character of science is realized. Science is not able to explain existence; it must confine itself to description. Connecting things in a causal way does not explain a process. While such a procedure may tell us which materials and which antecedents and environmental factors contributed to bringing about a phenomenon, it does not tell us, for instance, why it is that a given material has specific effects when brought together with another material. Of course, theology is not capable of explaining the details of the material world either. But over against the scientist, who has to state helplessly that things just happen to be so, the theologian can at least point out that the redemptive purpose of the Creator is the ground of order in this world, and that things must be what they are and operate as they do because thus alone can they serve the general goal for which the world exists. Thus Christians share with non-Christians the general ignorance concerning the meaning of the actual events in this world. But while the scientist has only the choice between an attitude of fatalistic agnosticism on the one hand, and the provisional adoption of a working hypothesis on the other, the theologian has good reason for finding his situation bearable, because he has been made sure of a firm ground and an unchanging goal of this world, notwithstanding his doubt concerning the specific functions which the various aspects of his life have in this world.

In the past, failure to make a clear distinction between metaphysics and theology created the impression that the theologian knew the answer to every problem in either field. With the modern differentiation between theology and science, the theologian—and the believer as well—must reckon with an area of dim twilight, in which neither theological scholarship nor scientific scholarship is really at home. The realm in which the theologian can move with certainty, because it has been illumined by God's revelation, is that of man's destination. However great the menace of the cosmic powers may be, Christ's resurrection assures the theologian that they are under control, and thus the believer can be certain that his faith will not be defeated no matter how great and manifold his failures may be. In turn the scientist can operate with the assurance that the means of knowledge at man's disposal are sufficient to find out what this world is like and what man is in relation to this world. Technology is the proof that scientific knowledge implies objective truth because it yields practical results.

God's revelation, inasmuch as it deals with man's predicament in this world, confirms the existence and power of the cosmic forces. While it unveils their limitations, it does not unmask them as mere appearances nor as powerless. Christ himself does not claim to have annihilated the powers but merely established his right to reign over them. Thus while the believer is assured of the fact that no force in this world will ever be able to separate him from the love of God in Christ, he also knows that for the rest of his life he has to live under the constant menace of the cosmic powers. God does not even tell him in advance by what means he will curb these powers as they operate upon the individual's life or what way of action he has in mind to lead him to victory. In other words, the believer is never completely lifted out of his perplexity. Its terror has been overcome as far as his ultimate future is concerned, but the apparent meaninglessness and incomprehensibility of his existence continue to vex him in the particulars of his life. Faith therefore remains "belief in spite of unbelief," or perhaps better, faith is harassed continually by acts of unbelief and doubt in spite of the heart's assurance of salvation.

Similarly this twilight covers a considerable area of the field investigated by philosophy and science. Obviously it is impossible to find final meaning and purpose in the nature of things, for true meaning and purpose depend on an ultimate reality. Theology provides an ultimate in God's redemptive activity. But since God's revelation is concerned primarily with man's redemption, the rest of this world is illumined only indirectly by revelation. A Christian philosophy of nature, desirable as it is, can only be sketched out in the most fragmentary way because by the nature of the case it must confine itself to that narrow area of man's life in this world which is simultaneously illumined by scientific knowledge and God's revelation. In the philosophy of history, matters are considerably more satisfactory because the redemptive work of God takes place in a historical process of holy history. But even here neither revelation nor historical science help us to answer the question: What will happen next in history? or, What is the specific meaning of the present historical situation? Thus it is quite natural that now and then Christians should tremble at the thought of impending events. Yet faith cannot be shaken by despair, for that would imply the denial that God is in control of history.

5. PROTESTANT ETHICS

In Protestant ethics one notices the same influence of biblical realism and the belief in God's revelation. The starting point is God's saving activity in this world, with special reference to its eschatological perspective. What the believer ought to do depends not only on what God has done for him and is still doing, but also on the goal that God pursues with mankind. In ethics no less than in systematic theology the dividing line between the new method and traditional ways cuts across all denominational lines. This is the more remarkable because all denominations originally developed their specific ethos. This kinship has not entirely disappeared, yet it manifests itself mainly in the choice of specific ethical goals and ways of action, whereas it is the general outlook and the function of ethics that have undergone a change in connection with the new method.

For one thing, it is realized that the intensity of response to God's revelation varies greatly from individual to individual. The former tendency toward doctrinal uniformity resulted in the adoption of a denominational ethos which roughly corresponded to the response of the average believer. It was as distant from moral indifference as it was from enthusiasm and radicalism, and, for that reason, rather dull and pedestrian. Significant for this outlook was the treatment of the Sermon on the Mount. Its commandments were emasculated by interpreting them either as being meant only for the life to come, or as destined by their rigorous demands to call forth in the believer a sense of guilt, while their application to practical life was commonly denied. Those who by the impact of revelation felt impelled to a more rigorous concept of ethics joined small groups such as the Mennonites or Quakers.

Now matters have radically changed. It is realized that the impact of revelation does not and cannot require a uniform response. Furthermore, as the teleological character of God's revelation is apprehended, it becomes obvious that dullness and lack of enthusiasm are not of the essence of Protestant ethics. If God moves mankind on toward his destined goal, the believer's attitude must in turn be an enthusiastic response. Consequently the venture of faith and the Christian experiment, far from being heretical, are advances of faith to be commended.

Moreover, Protestant ethics is about to overcome an erroneous procedure borrowed from the ethics of rationalism, namely, the belief that the ethical life of the believer consists in carrying out a program of action. There is nothing wrong with programs when a certain practical goal is to be realized. For greatest possible efficiency a plan must then be drawn up, and the most appropriate means for its execution have to be chosen. But the action of faith is a response to God's revelation. Thus what matters is not so much the work which is being done or aspired for, because its choice depends on the urgency of practical needs, but rather the frame of reference in which the believer must act. The success of his actions should not concern the believer, for the goodness of our deeds does not depend upon their size or quantity but rather on our attitude toward this world manifested in our accomplishments and plans. Nothing is good or evil by itself, and thus the response of faith must consist in treating it according to the destination which God has given it. The principal error in identifying the moral duties with a program of action lies in the fact that the executor of a program is tempted to overlook the obligations which his everyday work and his daily environment have placed upon him. The results of our actions must not be our concern. We may leave that to God. As long as we are willing to serve him, our actions can be used by him for the realization of his plans.

This new understanding of Protestant ethics has not developed with equal speed in every region of life. Hence one should not be surprised to discover that in certain areas, for instance, the handling of money, traditional views are commonly found, while in others the transition to a new ethos is obvious. The realm of political ethics is one of these areas of change, and the reason may be that political life, more than any other thing, affects people's traditional ways. In the democratic countries Christians no less than non-Christians are made aware of democracy's fight for survival, whereas in other countries dictatorial demands affect the individual's freedom to such an extent that it can be doubted whether or not Christian action is possible. The time is past when on account of the middle-of-the-road attitude of Protestant ethics the political status quo was regarded as the will of God, and change as such was considered the work of the devil. We are now living in an age where political change seems to be the rule, and thus the Christian attitude cannot be equated simply with counter revolution or the defense of the status quo, notwithstanding the fact that the Roman Catholic church and many conservative Protestants lean politically in those directions.

While it is true to say that God is a God of order and therefore anarchy is contrary to the will of God, the diverse forms of political life are the work of human beings. It is not feasible, along with the ancient writers and their modern followers, to hold that one form of government is in itself superior to others. The value of a form of government depends on its implementation by the people concerned, as well as on the historical situation and the qualifications of the ruling group. The superficial way in which "democracy" is often talked about in the United States, completely ignores the fact that there is a world of difference among American, British, French, and Scandinavian brands of democracy, let alone the democracy of the "people's republics." Hence the Christian finds himself in a paradoxical situation in political life. He realizes that he has no right to sabotage the existing order and that he is called by God to live a Christian life within it, but also that he has the right, and at times even the obligation, to refuse obedience, or else he resists God's will.

Conversely, since the actual political order is the work of man, the Christian is free to embrace any kind of political regime, provided he is convinced that it serves the interests of the nation. In our age the issue has become a burning one with regard to socialism and communism. There is no doubt but that the way in which the Roman Catholic church and some Protestants identify Christianity with the interests of the upper economic classes or the capitalistic order has no basis in God's revelation. Fighting an economic issue in the name of God would require not only omniscience but also complete freedom from sin. We have no right to deny membership in the church of Christ to the Christians of Eastern Europe or China who have identified themselves politically with the Communistic regime while they disavow the materialistic philosophy of Marxism. Political life too, as all ethical life, belongs to the twilight zone of faith. We can agree on the nature of the facts of social life, when employing experience and science to guide us in that area. We must agree by faith on the goal set for us in this world, namely, to act in accordance with God's will and thus place his interests above our own. But there will inevitably be divergence of views concerning the manner in which our readiness to serve God and the neighbor is to be implemented.

Such an attitude does not lead to sheer subjectivism in Christian living. On the contrary, it is in keeping with the rediscovery of biblical realism that Protestant ethics is showing a new interest in "natural law," that is, in the features of human nature and the nature of this world which determine human action. Yet the Protestant view differs characteristically from that of Roman Catholicism and naturalism. The Catholic view is static by nature. In the Middle Ages the Christian civilization of Western Europe was taken as the starting point and its common features, or its underlying principles, were considered "natural law." The latter served thereby to stabilize the existing order. Modern Catholicism has not principally abandoned this view, as can be learned from Maritain's presentation, for instance.[3] Everything that is found in the social order of the Catholic countries, or that is considered a profitable means to establish or maintain that order, is therein labeled as "natural law."

Over against this static outlook modern naturalism has adopted a teleological view. The goal of life is seen in the preservation of life, or in happiness, and therefore all those constant features in man and nature that are conducive to man's happiness are endowed with a legitimate claim to be satisfied. Such an approach provides greater flexibility than the Catholic view, which is inevitably driven to espousing the type of order in which the church occupies a dominant position. Modern naturalism, on the other hand, may shift from one extreme to the other. The Italian writer Alberto Moravia,[4] for instance, who first glorified sex as the supreme source of happiness, is now able to describe the sexual urge as the source of futility in human life.

In search of a solid basis of ethics, modern Protestantism accepts clues offered by sociology, as, for instance, the reference to those constant elements and dynamics in social life which serve the preservation of the social group and thus the sustenance and development of the life of the people gathered therein. But since life here on earth is not an end in itself, the moral principles of social life cannot be derived directly from the sociological data. To do so was the error of Lutheran theologians who interpreted the doctrine of the "orders of creation" in a naturalistic way, which led to the belief in the autonomy (*Eigengesetzlichkeit*) of the social order. Rather in the light of revelation it is seen that the social life serves as the means by which the life of

---

[3] Jacques Maritain, *The Rights of Man and Natural Law*, trans. Doris C. Anson (New York: Charles Scribner's Sons, 1943).

[4] *The Empty Canvas*, trans. Angus Davidson (New York: Farrar and Strauss, 1961).

faith is rendered possible here on earth. This implies in turn that in a group which includes Christian members, their life of faith will constantly modify the social life of the whole group. The fact that in our day we seem to have little use for the Social Gospel, for instance, does not detract from the value it had in its day. Nevertheless, being an answer to the perplexity of an earlier generation, it automatically fails to give guidance in our day.

This correlation between social needs and divine demands is particularly clearly seen in the Protestant churches' attitude toward war. The existence of the political order, the nation's sovereignty and its ability and willingness to fight for its continued existence are generally acknowledged as necessities resulting from the fact that we are living in a world in which nations and political power are indispensable for the preservation of life because sin constantly interferes with order. Inevitably, therefore, situations will arise in which a nation has to go to war or be swallowed up by an aggressive neighbor. The Protestant churches have never felt able to propagate the abolition of war because such a demand rests upon a humanistic delusion. Man is not good and peaceable by nature, and thus there is no hope that the power of the peace-loving people could totally contain the aggressive minority.

But Protestant theology has refused to glorify war as a desirable phenomenon in national or international life; war is considered an outright evil, and it would never occur but for the fact that God is angry with a sinful mankind. What separates Quakers, Mennonites, and other historic peace churches from the rest of Protestantism, is not a different evaluation of war. They all agree in condemning war as a horrible thing. The divergence has to do with the practical attitude to be taken toward war. Unlike the peace churches, which consider the refusal to bear arms one effective means of combatting the warlike spirit, the other denominations doubt the effectiveness and consistency of that gesture. The peace churches place the emphasis upon the practice of mutual help and reconciliation as means by which the Spirit of Christ is to become effective in mankind.

B. NEW MANIFESTATIONS OF PROTESTANT LIFE

1. REFOCUSING THE IMAGE OF THE CHURCH

The twofold thrust of outside attacks and the rediscovery of Protestantism's root has had a visible effect upon the life of the Protestant churches and denominations. The religious individualism which dominated the Protestantism of the nineteenth century engendered general indifference toward the forms in which Protestantism lived. In the field of worship one could notice an antiquarian return to the liturgies of the sixteenth and seventeenth centuries. Church architecture, in part, imitated medieval styles which, if taken seriously, would amount to a denial of the Reformation's protest against the Middle Ages, and, in part, such imitation was dictated by purely practical considerations. Nobody expected the church to become articulate in public affairs or cultural life, and the numerous criticisms and attacks levelled against the church represented individual views even when they emanated from Protestant Christians.

All this has changed in recent times. Hand in hand with the new understanding of revelation as God's actual speaking goes a new appreciation of the institutional life of the church. Its function is no longer confined to the education of the young or otherwise immature Christians, while the mature ones may dispense with it. Rather the church is the instrument through which the redemptive work of Christ becomes articulate in the life of mankind. By emphasizing its instrumental role the Protestant church differentiates itself from the church of Rome which pretends, as the Body of Christ, to be the dispenser of his grace. Recognizing their instrumental function the Protestant churches have become aware of the human nature of their forms of organization and their pattern of action to which must never be ascribed absolute authority. The forms may legitimately vary from place to place, and they must be adapted to the historical circumstances and needs of their members. Nevertheless, churches are not able to serve Christ unless they have a certain polity, a form of organization, and a specific way of activity. Thus the manifestations of Protestant life cannot be left to the subjective preferences of the individual believer. The believer must act in such a way as to achieve the task that Christ has chosen for himself in this world.

On this basis a new image of the church emerges. No room is left for such nineteenth-century antitheses as: Experience or church? Religious sentiment or dogma? Personal faith or sacramental devotion? Inner light or Bible? Rather the inwardness of faith and the outward manifestations of God's grace are only two aspects of the believer's relation to God. Any separation of the inward from the outward would vitiate the life of faith. The result is a new joy in the existence of the church and a new desire to make its outward manifestations express its God-given task. The edge of self-criticism is not thereby blunted. The ecumenical motto "Let the church be the church!" implies the painful recognition that for a long period the church has not been what it ought to be and even at present may not have reached its destination. Far too frequently in the past the church has been subservient to ends which had little if anything to do with its spiritual function. Its task is to make manifest through its organization and actions that in its midst the mystery of Christ's redemptive work is performed in this world. In Protestantism, the church is now anxious to show that the life of faith is the response to the light of revelation which illumines the basic question of perplexity.

Probably nowhere else is this new understanding of the church as conspicuous as on the mission field. As long as the denominations coexisted in the Western world they were anxious to preserve their identity over against each other. That was an attitude called forth by the specific circumstances of spiritual history which had made their coming necessary. From the new understanding of their instrumental function they learned that the spiritual situation on the mission field is not identical with that which brought the Western denominations into existence, and therefore the specific form by which they present the gospel is of limited significance and usefulness only. Consequently, the emergence of the "younger churches" has ushered in an entirely new phase in the relationship between the denominations of the Western world and the people to whom the missionaries were dispatched. More is involved than an administrative change when the leadership of the churches in Asia and Africa passes into the hands of indigenous Christians. As a result of this step, the "younger churches" cease to be a mere appendix of the sending churches. The degree of their independence from their mission boards is seen in their liberty to join other denominations or to merge into a new church which, within the limits of Protestant tradition, is free to shape its polity, its forms of worship, and its confession of faith, in accordance with its own experiences and needs. The Church of South India is at present the most striking example of such a development.

2. Activation of the Laity

Alongside the various ways in which the church is being redefined, and equally significant, is the increasing participation of the laity in the life of the church. Notwithstanding the emphasis placed upon the "priesthood of all believers," the churches of the Reformation continued to assign a place of special and far-reaching spiritual authority to the minister. In some denominations attempts were made in subsequent centuries to remedy that inconsistency, yet, if for no other reason, practical needs rendered it necessary to grant an outstanding position to spiritual leaders. Practically it meant that with a few exceptions the Protestant denominations would doom the spiritual life of the majority of their lay members to a purely passive state. Yet such a role was tantamount to the denial of the Protestant principle according to which God is speaking directly to all the believers.

No wonder, therefore, that in the history of Protestantism, movements arose in which the laity gave evidence of its spiritual abilities. How amazingly great these abilities are has come to light recently in emergency situations, for instance in Mozambique, where during the last war Protestant missionaries were not allowed to work except along the coast, or in Northeast India, where there was a serious shortage of missionaries. In both countries the indigenous Christians began independently to engage in evangelism, and the success of their work far surpassed all that the missionaries had accomplished.

What was the spontaneous response to an emergency in those countries became a matter of principle in Japan's No-Church Movement. A large proportion of the laymen, particularly among the intellectuals in Japan, rejects the church as an institution and congregational worship conducted by ministers. Instead, small groups meet for Bible study and prayer. The movement grows by means of personal invitation. Even those critics who hold that this movement has veered too far toward subjectivism recognize that it serves as a timely and urgently needed protest against a development in Protestantism in which the predominant place assigned to the minister had obscured the meaning of the universal priesthood of the believers. Efforts are not lacking to activate the laity within the framework of the organized church. One thinks of the widespread tendency in American Protestantism to divide the congregation into small groups which take care of the various functions of the church, and even more so of the Sunday school, which lies entirely in the hands of lay people. While these activities move in conventional grooves, the Evangelism-in-Depth action in Central America has mobilized ministers and laity for a comprehensive evangelistic campaign which reaches the non-Protestants in their homes and on the job.

The historical significance of this activation of the laity must not be underrated. Of course, the laity, even in Protestantism, will need expert guidance for the study and proclamation of the

Bible. This guidance is necessary, not for spiritual reasons, but because of the historical character of the Bible and, in particular, the strangeness of its language and the mentality of its authors. The layman does not need the pastor for the spiritual comprehension of the Scripture; in that respect a layman may greatly excel his minister. The activation of the laity is thought of so highly because in it Protestantism attains the realization of its nature in the social sphere. The members of the church learn that it is both their privilege and their obligation to bear witness to the presence of Christ in his Body.

3. THE CHURCH IN THE WORLD

Along with the emergence of lay involvement in the church, mention should also be made of the rise of a new sense of naturalness and secularity in the Protestant churches. The Reformers had rightly seen that the Roman concept of the church as the only sovereign body in the world, on whose authority all the other social groups depended, rested upon a misconception both of God's work in creation and of the work of Christ. The church is called upon to serve the whole of mankind and therefore must live in the midst of the people. This was the original meaning of the idea of national churches in the ancient church, and it still survives both in Orthodoxy and in Protestantism. National churches were not conceived of as established churches dependent on the political authorities but rather as independent bodies free for self-chosen service yet coextensive with a nation. In the Protestant perspective, the church was no longer to call people away into its own realm—as does the Catholic church—but meet them where they were. It was unfortunate that the Protestant groups which sprang up in protest against the establishment were forced by political pressure to become sectarian. They were denied the right to have a share in the life of the nation directly and thus had to devote themselves primarily to the spiritual interest of their members. This condition, in turn, prompted them to develop negative ethical standards by which they wanted to show

how radically they differed from the "world," for instance, by strictly rejecting alcoholic beverages, card games, dancing, and so on. Perhaps even more unfortunate was the fact that the seemingly stricter spiritual life of these groups induced many congregations in the larger denominations to adopt similar views.

The change is manifest in our days, however. Not everybody will interpret the present situation in the manner suggested occasionally by Bonhoeffer. He speaks of the world as having come of age and thus no longer being in need of the church. Some of his followers understood him to be thereby advocating the dissolution of the institutional churches. From my own contacts with Bonhoeffer this interpretation seems to be far off the mark. What he had in mind was in all probability a historical situation in which the organized church would be completely smashed by her enemies. In that case Christianity would have no choice but to carry on its mission in the world as an integral function of purely secular activities. In its history Protestant Christianity would have pentrated the life of its members sufficiently to make of them evangelists who would apply the gospel to their daily life and who would be able to dispense with the formal worship and methodical education of the church. Things have never gone that far, however. Bonhoeffer's idea was conceived only as a pattern for the life of an imprisoned pastor who, though cut off from the institutional life of his church, was nevertheless bent upon continuing his ministry.

Yet underlying Bonhoeffer's suggestion was the realization that the specific character of Christian life does not lie in the things from which the believer refrains or abstains. Rather, as the example of Jesus shows, it is to be lived as a life which fully participates in the activities of the rest of mankind even while differing in its general outlook and goal. Christians are called by God to serve the world in which they live, in such a way that through the nature of that service they confront the world with the gospel. The task of Christian living is thereby rendered easier than before in one respect, yet more difficult in another.

It is easier in that the Christian can participate in all the vocational and social activities of his environment, yet it requires a very delicate and sensitive conscience on the part of the Christian to tell him how far he can go with those outside, and above all, how he can use the common life as an opportunity to serve them. Modern Protestantism is in the midst of a radical transition. Aroused from the slumber of a comfortable ecclesiastical complacency, it is ready again to assume its obligation toward a world whose stupendous need has suddenly come to universal attention.

Indicative of that change is the Protestant youth work. In striking contrast with the aloofness and the inferiority feelings of Christian youth organizations only two generations ago, Protestant youth behaves now in a natural way, as indicated, for instance, by the coeducational character of its organizations, the nature of its recreations, and its cooperation with non-Christian and secular organizations. Such worldliness implies the danger and temptation, of course, of simply becoming an undistinguishable part of the secular world instead of working as leaven within it. Proclaiming programs of social and international ethics alone will not do. The world can never reach a higher level of moral goodness than that attained by the church, and thus it is only through a new way of life that the church can hope to render a real service to the world. The Christian settlement movement and Christian work camps are signposts which make the new way manifest. But most promising in this respect is the endeavor of various vocational groups to find out in common deliberation how their faith is able to manifest itself in their daily life. The German Evangelical Academies have provided helpful leadership for this desire for "service through participation."

Another area in which the new understanding of Protestantism manifests itself is in modern church architecture. The nineteenth century was notorious for its lack of style in church buildings. A church was simply a building in which the congregation gathered on Sundays. According to the mentality of the pastor and his elders, building a new church meant either the unreflective imitation of medieval styles irrespective of the practical needs of the congregation, or the predominance of utilitarian considerations disregarding all esthetic standards. Fortunately a new type of church architecture has now come to life. Two of its most characteristic features are the formation of a new style which indicates that the building is destined for adoration, meditation, and fellowship, and the desire to combine sanctuary and educational wing in an architectural unit, thus underscoring the rightful place of the laity in the house of God.

4. THE GERMAN CHURCH CONFLICT

No event in recent church history has left a deeper imprint upon the whole of Protestantism than the German Church Conflict. In its beginnings it seemed to be hardly more than a theological protest, namely, raising the charge of heresy against Hitler and his followers by a handful of courageous German ministers. When Hitler claimed that his National Socialism was "positive Christianity" these men pointed out that the alleged biblical foundation of the Nazi views did not exist, that Paul did not represent Jewish mentality, and that Jesus could not be interpreted as a political and social revolutionary advocating the use of violence and furnishing ammunition for anti-Semitism. Nor did the Nazis have a right to enlist Luther as a comrade-in-arms, notwithstanding his bitter denunciation of Judaism.

When Hitler came to power in 1933 he took measures against the church which had the appearance of legality because the German Protestant churches, though disestablished in 1918, nevertheless enjoyed special political privileges as "public corporations" and depended largely on the financial support of the state. Hence a cynical head of state could easily manipulate them for his own purposes. This Hitler attempted, though eventually he failed. For what had started as a fight against a heresy, suddenly became an effort to rediscover the true nature of the church as distinct from the state. There was no precedent for such a distinction, and, above all, the official leadership of the church lacked spiritual vision so completely that it took much self-scrutiny and spiritual growth until the objective of the fight clearly emerged. Even Karl Barth, who for many eventually became the symbol of this combat for the right of the church, was of the opinion in 1933 that faith, being man's inward life, could in no way be endangered by the church politics of the Nazis.

The Declaration of Barmen in 1934 was evidence, however, that a small group of ministers and laymen had taken cognizance of the fundamental difference between the church, on the one hand, and the state and other social groups, on the other. From 1934 until 1945 two church bodies existed side by side. The official churches made all kinds of attempts to find a *modus vivendi* with the Nazi regime, and if not approving of its teachings and violent actions, at least not showing signs of disapproval. The Confessing Church, in turn, was a secret organization that refused to acknowledge the legality of the legislative and administrative acts of the officially recognized churches. Since the theological faculties had been muzzled or made themselves instruments of the Nazi philosophy, the Confessing Church had to set up its own clandestine seminaries, moving them from one place to another to evade the Secret Police. But above all it was through their undaunted preaching and teaching that the ministers of the Confessing Church, notwithstanding persecution and martyrdom, became the spiritual conscience of German Protestantism.

It is no exaggeration to say that, except for Socialists and Communists, the men of the Confessing Church formed the only group that resisted the Nazis with determination and clarity of vision. Nevertheless, the significance of their resistance did not lie in their opposition to the political regime—although that was the facet of their work that was given principal publicity abroad —but rather in the fact that like the Reformers they put God in the center of their faith and thus felt impelled to take a public stand both against the arrogance and presumptuousness of the Nazis and against the acquiescence of their brethren who wanted to accommodate themselves to the Nazi regime. Is it by chance that in the homeland of the Reformation the Protestant church finally understood that the church's task is to bear witness to the sovereignty of God? In any case there was an undeniable inner connection between the Luther Renaissance and the men of the Confessing Church who by their resistance aroused Protestantism all over the world. As Bishop Berggrav publicly stated, it was this aspect of the fight of the Confessing Church which made it possible for the Lutheran church of Norway to become the center of resistance against the Nazi occupation. Moreover, it was the example set by the German Protestants that moved Protestants everywhere to rethink the practical implications of the church's task to bear witness to the gospel. The notion of witness itself was not a new one. It had played a considerable role in the modern revival movements. But the German Church Conflict showed that what is needed is not so much a witness borne to one's own conversion and convictions but rather to the sovereign God who vindicates the cause of his people in spite of its weakness.

5. The Ecumenical Movement

Finally, mention should be made of the way in which the new understanding of Protestantism manifests itself in the ecumenical movement. We pointed out that the medieval emphasis upon pure doctrine survived in the Reformation churches, and that in consequence the Reformers failed to give expression to the one-ness of the church within the diversity of its theological manifestations. Yet it was not by chance that Protestant leaders became the principal promoters of the world-wide movement for Christian unity, and the very way in which that unity has been steadfastly interpreted as diversity in unity goes back to a typically Protestant view of the church. Hence the ecumenical movement is not confined to the cooperation of the official heads of the member churches united in the World Council of Churches. Much more important is the far-reaching and intense exchange of ideas, experiences, and leaders, and the practical cooperation in relief, supply of literature, and training of ministers that is now going on at various levels of organization and often outside all official ecclesiastical relationship. Significant also is the fact that there are denominational seminaries in which a large proportion of the student body comes from other denominations. Yet no attempt is made to win them over to the theological views of the host denomination. There is obviously enough common ground in their Protestant convictions to exclude proselyting.

The ecumenical movement is greatly indebted to biblical realism. The denominations have come to realize that notwithstanding their numerous and deep differences and divergencies they have a common ground in Christ's activity in his Body. The conviction has increasingly gained ground: we must cooperate and take a common stand in spite of all that separates us. The most moving and impressive manifestation of this new spirit has been the services of intercommunion celebrated during ecumenical gatherings. Evidently denominationalism is undergoing a radical transformation. In spite of the apprehensions in certain quarters, the recent formation of world organizations of the greater denominations has not become an obstacle for the ecumenical movement. Obviously the denominational confessions of faith are no longer considered weapons by which to fight other denominations but rallying points within each denomination. By means of a deepened understanding of its nature, each denomination is enabled to make its specific contribution to the other denominations and to the ecumenical movement.

Most strikingly, the new understanding of faith and the church has come to expression in the churches' changed attitude toward nationalism. The positivistic-pragmatic view of the church which dominated Protestantism right down to World War I has yielded the field to the apprehension of its spiritual task. What a contrast between the "holy nationalism" of the Protestant churches during and shortly after the First World War, and the concern for the peace of the world manifested in the Protestant churches all over the world during the second! Whereas as late as 1925 French and German church leaders refused even to sit together in one ecumenical assembly, in 1945 the church representatives of the hostile nations hurried to meet right after the termination of hostilities in order to discuss problems of relief, rehabilitation, and intimate cooperation. Significantly the Church World Service branch of the World Council of Churches did not confine its charitable activities to the member churches but distributed its materials and funds all over the world to the people in need, irrespective of their religious affiliations.

Another evidence of the fact that the Protestant churches are no longer thinking of themselves as ends in themselves but rather as being called to serve the cause of Christ in transforming this world, is given in the little publicized yet highly important activity of the Commission of the Churches on International Affairs (CCIA), which, in its efforts to reconcile conflicting parties and to counsel moderation, works in close cooperation with the United Nations and the governments of the whole world. In all these activities the Protestant churches manifest their deepened understanding of faith, which has turned from mere inwardness to service.

Seen against the background of world events, all these manifestations of a new understanding of faith may seem to be parochial and inconspicuous. It is true that they have not ushered in a social revolution or a completely new international order. Cynics may even say that the mentality of church officials has undergone no change. Nevertheless, apprehended within the context of Protestantism and seen as symptoms of an important transformation, the significance of these changes can hardly be overrated. By itself the new understanding of faith as taught by the Reformers is a scholarly discovery of considerable historical interest, but without spiritual significance. All the above-mentioned manifestations of new spiritual life are indications, however, that new insights have come to the various Protestant churches, and thus point to a renewal of Protestantism through the spirit of the Reformation.

Characteristically, these manifestations of new life are not confined to any particular denomination in Protestantism but rather cut across all of them. Yet they do not replace or transform the denominational characteristics. On the contrary, they make them stand out in bold relief. This is an indication that they have their common roots in the native soil of Protestantism, that is to say, in the Reformation. In this we see the historical significance of the present phase of Protestantism. In the bewildering multiplicity of its denominations, Protestantism is again finding itself at home in the experience of the Reformation and thus taking the second step in its history, an advance toward a Protestant form of the church.

PART TWO

PROTESTANTISM'S
BASIC PROBLEM

CHAPTER III

THE PLACE OF PROTESTANTISM
IN ECUMENICAL LIFE

A. PROTESTANTISM IN SEARCH FOR ITS PLACE

1. ASKING A NEW QUESTION

Our survey has shown that modern Protestantism, while assailed from many sides, shows a remarkable vitality, and so an optimistic prospect for its future seems to be justified in spite of the prophecies of gloom on the part of some critics. But the ecumenical movement has raised an entirely new question: What right does Protestantism have as a church within the *Una Sancta*, or the Body of Christ? Most paradoxically the right of the Protestant churches had been handled in the age of the Reformation as a problem of constitutional law without regard to the fact that the Reformation itself originated in spiritual and theological questions. The power of the Pope had been so weakened by the Reformation that it was left to the political rulers to decide what religion should be followed by their subjects. Once the legal right to existence had been thus settled, Protestantism began to take its existence for granted.

Now unexpectedly and unanticipated by the early advocates of church union, the question has become a theological one. Is there such a thing as a Protestant church qualified to join with the Orthodox church, and perhaps even with Rome? This question will retain its full weight, irrespective of the way in which Protestants participate in the ecumenical movement. Even if

Protestant leaders should be willing to merge all Protestant denominations into one vast ecclesiastical organization, the very existence of a World Council of Churches devoted to the task of giving expression to the oneness of the church implies the question: Does Protestantism have a right to consider itself as a church in the same sense as Rome and Eastern Orthodoxy do? Mere numerical oneness would alter the sociological nature of Protestantism but would not suffice to make it a church. If the World Council of Churches had been brought into being for the mere purpose of common action in the pursuit of Christian objectives and interests, the problem would be mainly an organizational one, viz.: What form of cooperation is best for efficient and effective action?

From the very outset, however, the Faith and Order movement has been an integral facet of ecumenical activities, and while not as accentuated in the work of the World Council of Churches as is the advocacy of joint political, social, and cultural activities, it has been strong enough to prevent the latter tendencies from monopolizing the Council's work. But it seems that Protestantism has not yet become aware of the new situation into which it has been brought by its participation in the ecumenical movement. One of the most notable results of the Faith and Order Conference held in Lausanne in 1927 was the quest for a theological understanding of the church. Prior to that date very few Protestant studies of the theological nature of the church had been made, and with the prevailing individualism it obviously had never occurred to Protestant theologians to search the Bible for a scriptural doctrine of the church.

Things have changed radically recently. Protestantism can boast now of a number of outstanding studies preoccupied with the church's nature and task according to the New Testament. Strangely, however, these studies have had only limited influence upon ecumenical thought. One would expect questions to be raised like: Is Protestantism in agreement with the scriptural view of the church? And if that question were answered in the affirmative, should we not ask ourselves and our friends in the Anglican Communion and the Eastern Orthodox churches, whether their churches fulfilled that requirement too, and whether or not they were willing to recognize that Protestantism was according to Scripture? Above all, nearly everybody is agreed that the church cannot be truly one as long as Rome stands apart from the rest of the churches. But the Roman Catholic church holds a doctrine which differs essentially not only from that held by the other church bodies but also, if the modern Protestant studies are approximating the truth, from the church of the New Testament. Yet how certain can we be that our interpretation of the pertinent New Testament material is not a reading of Protestant prejudices into the text? And if we could prove to our own satisfaction that our exegesis was correct, how would we proceed in moving the other church bodies to accept our views? Is it realistic to expect them to undergo a reformation and to become churches of our type?

It is disappointing that in the recent literature on the church these important questions are never raised. Earlier Protestant treatments of the doctrine of the church were apologetic or polemical in character. Thereby they at least indicated awareness of the problem implied in the existence of Protestantism even though they started from the axiom that the author's church did comply with the requirements Christ had laid down for his church. With the advent of the ecumenical movement, however, the tone has changed. The earlier investigations were dominated by their author's denominational viewpoint. This applies even to Troeltsch's famous study of *Protestant Christianity and Church* (1906).[1] While seemingly concerned with all the Protestant denominations, the author finally reaches the conclusion that real Protestantism, or Neo-Protestantism as he called it, is found only among the theologians of the German Establishment.

---

[1] Troeltsch, "Protestantisches Christentum und Kirche in der Neuzeit," in Paul Hinneberg (ed.), *Die Kultur der Gegenwart* (2nd ed.; Berlin and Leipzig, 1909), p. 14, n. 1.

The studies called forth by the ecumenical movement all contrast with the former parochialism. Lately we have had quite a number of books and articles on the nature of Protestantism, which list with more or less accuracy the common doctrines and practices found in the various Protestant bodies and the religious attitude characteristic of each of them. A striking feature of these studies is the absence of apologetic undertones. In spite of the fact that the Protestant denominations are now confronted with the quest for the unity of the church, the existence of Protestantism is simply taken for granted. Since, in its overwhelming majority, the Protestant bodies are members of the World Council of Churches, it is obviously held that this fact is sufficient proof that Protestantism occupies a legitimate place within Christianity. But to what extent is this assumption justified?

2. THE PROTESTANT NATURE OF THE ECUMENICAL MOVEMENT

Let us begin with an undeniable fact. The ecumenical movement has its roots in Protestantism. It presupposes a Protestant view of the Christian faith and the church. That some Anglo-Catholics have been very active in the Faith and Order movement is a historical fact. But in joining a movement that appealed to all the existing churches, even those Anglo-Catholics abandoned their former tactics. Consistent with their view of the church, they had started negotiations between the Church of England, understood as a Catholic church without pope, on the one hand, and Rome or Eastern Orthodox churches, on the other. Yet their participation in the World Council of Churches—reluctant as it is—is obviously motivated by their desire to avail themselves of the many and informal contacts with the Orthodox churches rather than by an espousal of the World Council's proper objectives. Historically it is probably correct to say that the main impetus of the ecumenical movement came originally from Calvinistic churches, who unexpectedly found a powerful ally in the Swedish Archbishop Söderblom. The resulting collaboration of Protestants with non-Protestants has aroused suspicion in certain Protestant groups, which tends to weaken the ecumenical significance the majority of Protestant denominations ascribe to their membership in the World Council of Churches. The fact that churches comprising thirty-five to forty per cent of American Protestantism have for theological or other reasons refused to join the World Council of Churches (thus far the most notable outcome of the ecumenical movement), is an indication that a serious division still prevails within the Protestant camp. For, unlike the opposition to the World Council which resulted from the unscrupulous agitations of certain American "apostles of discord," those Protestant bodies feel unable to join the international organization because to them it appears a betrayal of the Protestant view of the church.

The affiliation of a number of Eastern Orthodox churches with the World Council of Churches is highly welcome because it is a symptom of their willingness finally to give up their aloofness and to establish contacts with non-Orthodox churches. Nevertheless, the theological significance of their affiliation should not be overrated. It is a well-known fact that the Orthodox churches are not full members of the World Council in the sense in which the Protestant denominations are. Consistent with their doctrine of the church they refrain from voting on matters concerned with theology and church polity. Their participation in the World Council is avowedly in the first place for practical purposes, although the fact is obvious that their participation has borne remarkable spiritual fruits both in their own spiritual life and that of their Protestant partners. The loose connection in which the Orthodox churches stand with the World Council is in itself a challenge to the complacent Protestant assumption that the Protestant concept of the church, and the concept of church unity based upon it, is theologically legitimate.

The ignoring of Rome's contention that she is the only true church was facilitated in the early years of Protestantism by two facts. On the one hand the Reformers believed they had good reason to denounce the Catholic church as an apostate church, and on the other hand the new Protestant churches enjoyed political privileges which precluded competition between Rome and Protestantism in the same territory. Though merely tolerated under the Edict of Nantes, the French Reformed church continued its polemics against Rome throughout the seventeenth century on the basis of the Reformation, and Rome likewise never changed her viewpoint though a few new arguments were proffered. Since the political power of the state could be invoked by the Protestant leaders to persecute and suppress the *Schwärmer*, who were the theological advocates of a different type of churchhood, there was no need for examining one's own concept of the church. The "free churches" or "sects" were denied the right to challenge the established churches. The "free churches" in turn felt confirmed in their own views, including those on churchhood, by the very persecution they suffered. Such a fate seemed to be the divine sign and approval of their being the true church.

The ecclesiastical history of the North American colonies shows to what extent the theological right of existence was identified with political power. When such identification proved to be politically inexpedient, toleration was granted on the basis of irrelevancy. All kinds of denominations and religions were admitted provided they were not politically harmful or indecent. In the same manner the political protection granted to the established churches explains why debates on the Catholic view of the church remained purely academic. The policy of toleration, which had been gradually adopted in the seventeenth century, had no immediate influence upon theology, particularly the doctrine of the church. The Protestants were no longer afraid of the efficacy of Catholic propaganda, and their only concern was with the growing political power of Catholicism. In this respect too, however, the ecumenical movement has created a new situation.

It was natural that an organization like the World Council of Churches, created for the purpose of fostering the unity of the church, would not only challenge the Protestants' contention to be a church but would also raise the question, What kind of unity shall it be? The question was not a new one. Leibniz had already encountered it in his negotiations with the French Catholics in the seventeenth century. Although they had been willing to make great concessions to the Protestants in matters of doctrine, they were adamant in their insistence on the authority and power of the bishops. The Anglicans, in turn, who at the beginning of this century were most eager to have ecclesiastical unity, were able in their negotiations with the Orthodox Church of Romania to reach a measure of mutual cooperation on the basis of apostolic succession. But when they approached Cardinal Mercier at the Malines Conversations (1921-25) they were told that the Vatican could not consider apostolic succession a sufficient basis for unity. Recognition of the spiritual and doctrinal primacy of the Pope would be the prerequisite of any serious discussion of church unity. Thus the Protestant churches were forewarned that church unity, far from being accomplished by organizational measures, was basically a theological issue, one which could not be settled onesidedly on the terms of the Protestant partners or by means of a compromise in church polity. In the meantime Rome, although watching the ecumenical movement very closely and with keen interest, has nevertheless, until recently, quite categorically declined to have any official dealings with it. It is true that this policy has recently been changed. Roman Catholic observers have been delegated to various Protestant conferences and meetings. But this does not mean that Rome considers the World Council of Churches, or its constituent parts, as organs of the *Una Sancta* as understood by Canon Law and Dogma. Of course, the Vatican cannot ignore the importance of the fact that for the first time in history Protestantism has been able to speak and act with a united voice. With a World Council of Churches in existence, Rome is no longer confronted with isolated bodies of Protestants. Whatever happens to the Protestants of Spain or Columbia or Angola has now become a concern for the whole body of Protestant churches assembled in the World Council.

The joining of practically all of the Orthodox churches since the New Delhi meeting of 1962 has greatly increased the interest the Vatican takes in the World Council. It is obvious that Rome earnestly desires to heal the rift which has divided the Eastern and the Western churches for so many centuries.

3. The Unity We Need

The World Council of Churches is in a sense the brain child of Protestantism and thus a challenge to the other churches. But it is obvious that the unity envisaged cannot be the unity Protestants would seek if they were the only church. It must rather be the unity which results from the theological nature of the whole church of Christ. Seen from this angle the World Council is a rather strange entity full of tensions and paradoxes. Officially the Anglican churches have always been among the warmest supporters of the ecumenical movement. Yet it is no secret that many priests and laymen within the Anglican Communion resent the participation of their church. It is equally well known that Anglo-Catholic influence exerted upon the delegates of that denomination has in some instances proved to be a powerful obstacle to a Protestant-inspired action or declaration.

Still more ambiguous is the participation of the Orthodox churches. It is obvious that membership in the World Council means a lot to them because it proves to be practically useful in matters of church politics, relief, publicity, personal contact among theological and ecclesiastical leaders, and even in international relations. Yet their cautious affiliation is evidence of the reservations they have concerning full partnership with Protestant churches—which in their eyes are heretical. It will be helpful to remind ourselves that the *Confession of Dositheus* of 1672, which is accepted by all the Eastern Orthodox churches, rejects the Calvinists as outright heretics and speaks of the "madness" of Luther.[2] Their condemnation of the Protestant heresy is not as devastating as Rome's, as their membership in the World Council indicates. But while they do not consider Protestants outright unbelievers, Protestants are certainly bad Christians in their eyes. The Orthodox leaders are willing to admit that theologically there is some common ground held by them and some Protestants, but since for them theology is not a mere agglomeration of doctrines but rather an integral body of dogma, the mutual theological agreement on particular doctrines is only of small practical consequence. In a way it would be easier for Protestantism to reach doctrinal agreements on disputed matters with Rome than with the Orthodox churches; for in Western Catholicism each doctrine is a self-contained rational unit, whereas in the East it is an integral part of the whole organism of dogma. In the eyes of the Orthodox teachers any theological conclusion established upon the Protestant understanding of faith is from the outset vitiated by the heretical features contained therein. Thus, while Orthodox membership in the World Council of Churches enables them to have practical cooperation and common defense against secular oppression, there is no possibility of concerted action in the theological or evangelistic field.

4. THE BIG OBSTACLE

Of course, everything in this world is subject to change, even rigid churches. It is not absolutely impossible that Anglo-Catholics will take a positive stand on the Thirty-Nine Articles and will be willing to be numbered among the Protestants rather than pretending to form a separate family in Christendom. It may not even be utopian to hope that as a result of continued contact and exchange with Protestants the Eastern Orthodox churches will drop the charge of heresy against Protestantism. By such developments the churches united in the World Council

---

[2] Jon Michalcesu, *Die Bekenntnisse und die wichtigsten Glaubenszeugnisse der griechisch-orientalischen Kirche* (Leipzig, 1904), p. 129.

would attain a considerable degree of spiritual oneness. Nevertheless, even then the formidable barrier to real unity would be the church of Rome. This is the case no matter whether or not the World Council is officially or unofficially in touch with the Vatican. For the question of what constitutes church unity cannot be answered one-sidedly by a single church or group of churches. The answer must be obtained by the agreement of all those groups who consider themselves members of the Body of Christ.

Rome's position in matters of church unity has been stated in an unambiguous manner as early as 1864 in the encyclical *Apostolicae Sedi* [*sic*].[3] In it, Pius IX inveighs vehemently against those who hold that the Greek Orthodox, the Roman, and the Anglican churches have equal rights to call themselves "catholic" and to practice intercommunion, notwithstanding doctrinal differences. There can be no communion between Rome and schismatics, let alone heretics. They cannot even pray in common for the unity or reunion of the churches. "There is no other Catholic Church than the one which being built upon that unique Peter rises in the oneness of faith and love." In the same spirit the First Vatican Council of 1870 never tired of emphasizing the absolute uniqueness of the church of Rome.[4] On account of its superior dignity (*propter potentiorem principalitatem*)[5] it has in all times been necessary for believers all over the world to find their unity in her. For that unity is the basis of salvation. The encyclical *Satis Cognitum* (1896) proclaims in an unmistakable manner that "those who do not go to that church [namely Rome] go astray because they deviate from the will and commandment of Christ the Lord, and leaving the route to salvation they proceed toward their ruin." [6] Pius X only re-

---

[3] H. Denzinger and C. Bannwart, *Enchiridion Symbolorum* (14th ed.; Freiburg, 1922), nos. 1685-87.

[4] *Ibid.*, nos. 1781-1840.

[5] *Ibid.*, no. 1824.

[6] *Ibid.*, nos. 1954-62.

peated what had been an axiom for his predecessors when he said that "there can be no holiness where people disagree with the Pope."

Of course the fact is well known that in Central Europe the common danger of National Socialism and communism has led recently to a certain measure of practical collaboration between Protestant and Catholic clergy. It is also gratifying that in the planning of the new Roman Catholic Council, Agostino Cardinal Bea extended an invitation to the non-Roman churches "to join in the common pursuit of their aims" irrespective of their denominational basis. Such happenings notwithstanding, the theological attitude of the Vatican has not changed.

Is it not characteristic that in its very invitation the church of Rome presumed that the theological and practical goals of the Second Vatican Council must be pursued also by those outside of the Roman church? For the church of Rome, the Protestants remain heretics outside the church of Christ, and they are loved as brothers who have gone astray yet are to be brought back to the fold of the papal church.

It is certainly true that the Roman Catholic evaluation of Protestant theology is flexible. Soon after World War I, Father Przywara of the Society of Jesus, writing on Protestant theology, was unable to see in it anything but natural theology and subjectivism, and he stated expressly that, notwithstanding his strong emphasis on the word of God, even Karl Barth was in no way an exception to the rule.[7] In our day, however, Barth has become a best seller among the Catholic clergy, and biblical scholars in the Catholic church openly express their indebtedness to Protestant scholarship. It should be kept in mind, however, that the increased flexibility which now characterizes Catholic theology is free within narrow limits only. For it is counterbalanced by the inflexible rigidity with which the Vatican insists on the absolute primacy of the Bishop of Rome.

---

[7] Erich Przywara, "Protestantismus," *Die Religion in Geschichte und Gegenwart*, 2nd end., IV, cols. 1600-02.

Very significantly, the Curia made it plain, for instance, that in the case of birth control no single bishop or theologian had a right to proclaim personal views. This was a matter to be decided exclusively by the Holy Father.

Yet while we painfully realize the seemingly insurmountable obstacles which Rome puts into the way of church union, we have no right to flag in our zeal for that goal. Unfortunately, many Protestants are prone to brush aside as presumptuous the Roman Catholic dogma of the oneness and integral unity of the church, as well as Rome's claim that that unity is guaranteed by the historical continuity of its episcopate and the primacy of the Pope. But even if it were possible to dismiss so easily the theological accretions of the centuries, the claims made by Rome and the Eastern Orthodox churches should at least be accepted as a challenge to the Protestant position. In ecclesiastical matters the argument of antiquity weighs heavily in the eyes of those who believe in Christ as the head of the church and the divine promises given to it. From the very outset Protestantism has had to struggle with the fact that the older churches had already been in existence for nearly fifteen hundred years when the Reformation began. By refusing to accept any compromise on their respective views of the church, these two great Christian bodies practically contend that in their eyes Protestantism has no right to exist. Perhaps it is not as easy as we think to vindicate Protestantism's very right to exist, and, inasmuch as we have a well-founded claim, our right of existence may demand a heart-searching rethinking of our position.

The Protestant view of the church has been formed in the heat of controversy and conflict, and little has been done in the centuries following the Reformation to change that perspective. But in an ecumenical age the doctrine of the church more than any other doctrine must be rethought in an attempt to discover the common ground in which unity is feasible. The task ahead of us is not one of adopting the Orthodox, Roman, or Anglo-Catholic view of the church. For each of these bodies contends to have become what it is as the result of a historical necessity, which renders impossible the attempt to identify unity with uniformity. This is the basic axiom of ecumenicity, no matter whether the advocates of a fast and facile solution recommend surrender of the other churches to one type, or suggest a basis which would be formed of elements found in all of the component bodies. It is obvious that no church will be able to retain completely its basic characteristics in a united church. But equally obvious should be the fact that no church or denomination can be required to drop completely its identity, provided it is able to show that its particular nature is rooted in the spiritual nature of the church. Historical, sociological, cultural, or anthropological reasons may have greatly contributed to the molding of a denomination; but being contingent factors, they are unfit to prove the necessity of a specific type of church. Purely rational arguments are equally insufficient. The appeal to them ignores the fact that here on earth the church belongs to the realm of history and thus is inevitably subjected to change. Since the claim of Protestantism cannot be based upon the factors and circumstances by which it was brought into being, the possibility should be investigated of finding its title to existence in the course of the historical process. But prior to proceeding to such an investigation, let us, on the basis of these considerations, review the reasons which Protestantism has thus far presented to justify its existence.

B. HISTORICAL SURVEY OF PROTESTANT SELF-VINDICATION

1. The Apostasy of the "Catholic" Churches

If for no other reason, the churches of the Reformation had to vindicate their right of existence in order to receive political recognition. The arguments presented by the church leaders of the early sixteenth century moved on two different, though closely related, lines. First, they denied the right of the Curia to speak in the name of the church. Rome, they said, had lost the continuity with the Ancient Church, and the Protestant churches are the ones who have restored it. In the most outspoken manner this view was represented in the Reformed Confession of Eger-Debrecin of 1561, which, following Calvin, points out that the Reformed faith is in agreement with the Church Fathers and the ancient ecumenical councils (*consensus antiquitatis*). In the Lutheran church the so-called Magdeburg Centuries upheld the view that since the days of Constantine the church had lost its innocence and purity and that the Reformers had "reformed" the church, that is to say, restored its original formative principle. Thus Protestantism was not an innovation but rather represented the truth of the church which, after having been concealed for a long while, had been brought to light again.

Other theologians developed the argument from history in terms of spiritual life. Melanchthon refers to the Reformers as men to whom God had given the grace of understanding the Scriptures in a church that had abandoned God, and Luther speaks of the Protestants as the "holy believers," the sheep who finally are listening to their shepherd's voice.[8] Similarly Calvin untiringly points out that a new outpouring of the Holy Spirit has taken place in Protestantism. The argument from history has proved to possess little convincing power, however. When the moment at which the "great apostasy" took place was identified with Constantine's granting recognition and political privileges to the church, Protestantism exposed itself to the unanswerable question: What difference is there between the union of state and church under Constantine, on the one hand, and the established churches of Protestantism, on the other?

2. PRIMACY OF SCRIPTURE

A second argument of the Reformation age was considerably more powerful than that drawn from history. It invoked the authority of Holy Scripture which allegedly had been especially

---

[8] Texts quoted in Ernst Walter Zeeden, *Martin Luther und die Reformation im Urteil des deutschen Luthertums* (2 vols.; Freiburg, 1950-52,) II, 1-11.

slighted by the doctrine of Tradition in the medieval church. Thus the bishops had usurped the place which rightly belongs to God. The Protestant theologians pointed out that, instead of being scolded for having introduced innovations, Luther should be praised for having discovered the Bible's divine claim. By disregarding it Rome had grievously sinned and blasphemously placed human doctrines and commandments on a par with God's own word. The Protestants would therefore contend that they form the true church because in their congregations the pure word is preached and the sacraments are administered in the right way. On this point we notice full agreement between Calvin and the Augsburg Confession, and throughout the age of Protestant orthodoxy this argument formed the common basis of Reformed and Lutheran theology. Likewise it dominated the theological controversy in England down to the seventeenth century.

The providential significance ascribed by the Protestants to Luther's rediscovery of the Bible found its theological expression in the fact that the doctrine of Scripture was treated at the beginning of their systematic presentations of theology. Far from being just one of the topics which the churches teach, the dogma of the Scripture forms the basic axiom from which all other topics in theology are deduced. This fact should not be over-looked by those who for good reason take the orthodox theologians of the sixteenth and seventeenth centuries to task for their theory of the infallibility of the Bible. The orthodox theologians recognized the fact that the authority of the Bible is founded upon its being given by God, not upon its infallibility. Notwith-standing the fact that the nominalists had already made a great deal of the doctrine of biblical infallibility, Luther opposed their use of the Bible. For its value is not to be found in its being an infallible document of past revelation, as was held by Lyra, Gerson, Faber Stapulensis, and Erasmus, but rather in its being God's word. Through its words Christ himself speaks to us (*Deus loquens*). Those who, while reading the Scriptures, listen to Christ speaking, receive a divinely wrought assurance of salvation.

Calvin's mature view of Scripture differed somewhat from Luther's. To the Genevan Reformer, Christ is the source of all revealed truth, and his revelations are written down in the Bible (*Deus dixit*). The sinlessness of the Savior is the guarantee of its truthfulness. This view, if taken in isolation, would come very close to that of the nominalists. However, the fact must not be overlooked that in referring to the Bible, Calvin invariably appeals to the work of the Holy Spirit. By leading us to the Scripture and opening it to us, the Spirit bears his inner witness, that is to say, he makes us sure of the reliability of the content of Scripture. By moving the reader or hearer to take all its details seriously, the Spirit enables people to learn how the Bible applies to their own lives. Thus the Protestant theologians of the seventeenth century were undisturbed in their belief that Protestantism had a right to exist. Since the Reformers had discovered in the revealed Scriptures the only true way in which God can be encountered, faith for them did not rest on ecclesiastical dogmas, as in the Roman church, but rather on the direct experience of God's saving power.

3. Infallibility

While with the passing of years Protestantism simply took its existence for granted, its intrinsic development was to a large extent a process in which the very foundation on which it had been established was disregarded. Thus we notice, for instance, in the theology of Protestantism an increasing inability to appreciate fully the *sola Scriptura* principle of the Reformers. Gradually it had come to mean for the Protestants, as for their Catholic adversaries, belief in a divinely given and infallible book. Yet in this later development the contradistinction between revelation and reason was practically obliterated. Whereas the Reformers considered themselves recipients of divine revelation, their successors were satisfied with having a document from whose infallible text rational conclusions could be drawn for the formulation of theological doctrines. With this new perspective the inspiration was but an incidental feature. The Bible would have served the same purpose apart from its divine origin only if one could be sure of its infallibility. In dealing with Rome this development had serious consequences because the theologian could no longer appeal to the self-authentication of the Bible over against the authority of Rome. The infallibility of the Bible had to be proven, and that was not an easy task. The Catholic theologians were quick in pointing out that the numerous textual variants of the Bible, no less than the contradictory accounts, made the claim of infallibility appear spurious. Even worse was the fact that the Protestant exegetes were unable to agree among themselves on the true interpretation of the Bible. Quite obviously the infallibility of the text did not guarantee an infallible interpretation, and thus the very truth of the Bible was jeopardized. The Protestant theologian was pushed into the embarrassing situation of a man who had to commend the value of God's message by defending the cogency and accuracy of the logical deductions which he drew from the Bible. Hence it was the authority of the theologian in the fields of erudition and scholarship, rather than the divine authority of revelation, which would decide whether one's exegesis was right.

The harmful consequences of this substitution were not immediately noticed, and its effects upon the whole history of Protestantism have only recently come to light. Rome could conveniently counter the argument that biblical exegesis was apt to lead to diversity and controversy, by pointing out that the teaching office of the church would easily detect error and stop it. Protestant orthodoxy chose a smiliar device by canonizing Luther and Calvin, or by curbing the exegete's subjectivism by the authority of confessions of faith. Yet as a result, biblical interpretation was limited to what had been taught by the leaders of the Reformation or what had been agreed upon by the ecclesiastical authorities. The time was bound to come when exegetes would reject such confessionally bound exegesis because it meant the intrusion of a historical document between the Bible and the interpreter. During the eighteenth century this process of rejection took place simultaneously in pietism and rationalism, and with similar consequences notwithstanding their considerable theological disagreements. The rationalistic interpreters of the Bible contended—rightly from their viewpoint—that with their insistence upon a scientific interpretation of the Bible they were far from undermining the authority of the Bible; they were only objecting to a literalistic understanding of the text because such an understanding would involve contradictions between various statements of the Bible, and the existence of these contradictions would be incompatible with the pretended infallibility of the Bible. In the nineteenth century basically the same reasoning formed the starting point of the so-called higher criticism of the Bible. This fact explains the seemingly paradoxical situation in modern biblical exegesis. Even though some scholars pursue modern biblical criticism so intensively that little of the Bible has been left intact, even the radical critics are, in general, anxious to be teachers of the church—because in their own way they too accept the authority of the Bible. Obviously they believe that by their critical approach alone can the truthfulness and the divine origin of the Bible be preserved.

Pietism, including Methodism and revivalism, on the other hand, while preserving the integrity of the Bible in theory, nevertheless engaged in an eclectic use of Scripture because the spiritual interest of the pietists was focused exclusively on personal redemption and the practice of devotional life. Thus, in both opposing camps alike, the original appeal to the Scriptures meant, in practical effect, an increasing truncation of the Bible. The growing neglect of the Old Testament, so typical of the modern Protestant churches, originated in this pietistic tendency. This is not the place to ascertain the extent to which this new approach to the Bible had been a necessary or wholesome development. The point to keep in mind is that the changes in the view of

Scripture resulted in hopelessly weakening the Protestant position in its confrontation with Catholicism. Whereas Rome continued to stress the authority of the whole Bible and believed in its divine origin, Protestantism had only portions of the Scripture left, and the authority of the Scriptures obviously depended no longer on their divine origin but rather on the "sound judgment" of the individual theologian. Exegetes are more or less intuitively aware of the precariousness of their position. The complete lack of historical basis would deprive their interpretation of its normative character. Thus the more the authority of the Scripture as a whole disintegrates, the more stubbornly scholars cling to the historical authority of the remainder. In turn Paul, or the Synoptic Gospels, or Mark, or eventually the "original kerygma," will form what is considered the assured historical nucleus of biblical proclamation.

4. The New Concept of Faith

Luther emphasized that one of the principal sources of misunderstanding the gospel was the wrong concept of faith held by the Catholic church. To him, the new discovery of the Bible as the word of God resulted in a new view of faith as the mode of receiving God's revelation. According to Catholic doctrine, faith is the obedient assent that the individual gives to the statements contained in the Bible and the doctrines and commandments proclaimed by the church. In view of the excessive quantity of the materials presented to the individual's faith, it is furthermore stated that for salvation an "implicit faith" is sufficient, that is to say, the willingness to accept as true everything that the church sets forth for belief and not to doubt the church's ability to proclaim the whole saving truth.

Over against such a view, Luther and Calvin were anxious to emphasize the personal character of faith. The relevancy of the Bible does not lie in its truthfulness as such but rather in the fact that by speaking through the Bible God assures the individual

that the salvation announced therein is destined for him personally. God reveals himself thereby as *Deus pro nobis*, i.e., the God
who is concerned with our salvation. Thus faith cannot be confined to accepting the biblical message as true; it also implies
trust in God's redemptive will (*fiducia*). Faith has not thereby
become a kind of wishful thinking. The Reformers refer frequently to the fact that the objectivity of faith lies in its receptivity. Man would be foolish if in his perplexity he would seek
comfort in a figment of his own invention. Rather it is the
grace of God offered to us which prompts us to adopt this
attitude of confidence and trust toward God; or, to use Calvin's
language, it is the Holy Spirit who convinces us of God's redemptive will concerning ourselves. Having become aware of God's
gracious dealing with him, the believer gives up every claim of
being somebody in relation to God or of being able to attain a
worthwhile life apart from the divine initiative. In short, he is
certain that whatever God may do with him will be right.

It is only in this relationship of saving faith with the God of
Scripture that the Reformers' insistence on "by faith alone"
makes sense. They were right in pointing out that, seen in this
light, the Roman Catholic understanding of faith was insufficient
for salvation because it was man's own work. Even the things
to be believed in, including the Bible, were presented to the
Catholic upon the church's authority. While this may have been
an oversimplification of the Catholic view, the Protestant position nevertheless proved to be superior because it ascribed to
God the initiative in the work of salvation and thus made redemption independent of the intensity of one's spiritual life. Conversely, the original Protestant view is distorted by Catholic
polemicists who contend that the identification of faith and
confidence or trust showed that faith for the Protestants was
sheer subjectivism. Melanchthon at numerous places pointed out
that the difference in the two views of faith was to be found in
the fact that the Catholics were satisfied with a "historical faith,"

i.e., mere acceptance of doctrines as true, whereas for the Protestants that was only the prerequisite of saving faith.[9]

But this original view of faith did not prevail throughout the history of Protestantism. While the element of trust was not completely lost in the concept of faith taught in Protestant orthodoxy, the one-sided emphasis placed upon doctrine and on the infallibility of the biblical document resulted in a view of faith that came dangerously close to the Catholic view. Trust in God was to follow the acceptance of theological propositions and was no longer man's response to God's direct dealing with him. For Catholic theologians it was easy to point out that the doctrines to be believed varied from one denomination to another. Protestantism lacked a generally recognized teaching office that was able to fix what ought to be believed. How then could a person be certain of his salvation if he were taught one thing by Lutheran theologians and another by Calvinist or Anglican divines? The fury with which the contending theologies were defended was hardly apt to reassure the layman that he was by definition capable of finding his way to God's grace through the word of Scripture.

Unfortunately, neither the Enlightenment nor pietism was able to rectify the Protestant situation in this respect. Rationalism suggested that a universally valid philosophy be substituted for the irreconcilable theological opinions. Even though it boasted of having discovered that truth, the philosophy of the eighteenth century was more divided on such basic issues as God's nature and relation to this world, the possibility of knowing God, and the application of the knowledge of God to practical life, than had been the theologians whose disagreements the rationalists treated with so much indignation. But inasmuch as the Protestant theologians succumbed to the lure of rationalism, they rightly fell under the condemnation of the Catholic colleagues, who

---

[9] *Apology of the Augsburg Confession*, IV, 48-60: *Quid sit fides justificans.*

charged them with having given up belief in the revealed origin of the Christian religion.

The issue at stake was not confined to the epistemological problem of the relationship of reason and revelation. In the age of rationalism God is dethroned. He has ceased to be the sovereign God, who in his freedom chooses the way in which he addresses man and who may determine by himself who is deemed worthy to receive his message. Symptomatic of the radical change that has taken place is the abandonment of the idea of judgment. The God of rationalism is not a God who is to be feared because he has power to send man to hell forever, but rather a God who must leave it to the philosopher and theologian to decide what he is supposed to be and in which area he is to work. Faith accordingly is not saving faith; it is transformed into personal religion.

Pietism as a movement arose in protest against Protestant orthodoxy and endeavored to return to Luther. Scripture was emphasized over against the predominance of the theological system and the stress placed on right doctrine. Similarly the faith required was again the trust put in God's word and the assurance that in his grace God wanted to be "my God." At a time when Catholicism had reached an all-time low, pietism allied with the kindred movements of the Moravians and Wesleyans in the eighteenth century to advocate the cause of Christianity, and by doing so created a new sense of oneness across the denominations. Yet, notwithstanding the fact that biblical realism originated in this movement, pietism was not capable of successfully defending Protestantism's right of existence over against Rome. The reason for this inability is found in the emphasis pietism laid on the subjective side of faith.

In order to articulate the personal element of faith, so central in the Reformers' view, pietism and related movements stressed the emotional aspect of faith, especially the struggle of repentance, the love of Jesus, and the joy of one's salvation. While none of these features is alien to the New Testament, the perspective in which they were seen and the one-sided emphasis placed upon them implied a shift from a faith which is response to the divine initiative to a faith altogether of man's own making. For practical purposes, that was a return to the Roman Catholic view of faith, especially its development in the seventeenth century, and the question, "Why not become Catholic again?" was justified. The obstacle to such a step was evident: these movements lacked a theological idea of the church. The groups which they founded were based upon the emotional and spiritual maturity of their members, and the congregational life and its organization depended on this psychological factor. The aloofness in which these groups held themselves from the other Christians was therefore inevitable.

The trend that manifested itself first in pietism was bound to lead to a religion of subjectivity. Both pietism and rationalism show an intrinsic tension between the emphasis placed upon the subjective side of faith, on the one hand, and history, on the other. Neither movement was willing completely to drop the authoritative role of the Bible. The inevitable consequence was that faith was not completely its own master; it implied an objective relationship to the Bible as a historical document and to the completed work of Christ. In pietism this tension resulted in an unclear vacillation between an emotional piety, on the one hand, and a residual orthodoxy, on the other. While the intellectualism and the excessive evaluation of systematic thinking found in the orthodox theology were rejected, the doctrines related to personal salvation, in particular the sinlessness of Christ, his redemptive death, and his love of the sinner, were presented in bold relief. Rationalistic theology, in order to retain its place in the church, took recourse to a philosophy or theology of history. Christianity can be envisaged as the final outcome of a theological education of mankind (Lessing), as the work of the wisest of all men, who had apprehended the truth more appropriately than any other sage (Locke), or as the historical integration of all human wisdom and goodness (Herder).

However, while in all these instances Christianity is the outcome of a rational necessity in history, the end product is by no means identical with historical Christianity as represented by the Protestant churches or the church of Rome. In a strange manner pietists and rationalists became bedfellows in that both of them considered themselves the only true Christians. The problem of church unity mysteriously evaporated because this "spiritual aristocracy" eliminated everyone except themselves from being worthy to be called Christian. The trouble with this view is that of necessity it has to be applied in retrospect too. Since the two schools or groups did not exist in past centuries, their self-evaluation would imply that there had never been any true Christians prior to the eighteenth century—obviously a rather absurd idea.

It was left to Schleiermacher's ingenuity to offer a satisfactory way out of this dilemma. By defining religion as the sentiment of absolute dependence he combined subjectivity and objectivity in a marvelous manner. Religion is absolutely subjective in that it is man's awareness of the divine. Man must not turn to something outside of himself in order to be religious. On the contrary, the more he goes into himself, forgetting the world in which he lives, the purer is his religion. Religion is not an activity or a response of man, but rather his very nature. The Bible is not useless, but its value for religion consists merely in making one's religious feelings articulate. However, this subjectivity of religion does not mean that it is a mere figment of his mind. There would be no religion if man were not aware of that by which he is absolutely conditioned. According to Schleiermacher all past thinking about religion was basically mistaken because it considered God and man as two entities subsisting side by side in mutual independence. In fact, however, man is a being that is rooted in God and for that very reason cannot help feeling his dependence on him. God is as close to the ego as that ego is to itself.

Prior to Schleiermacher, Kant had already held a similar idea.

But by concentrating on the moral life of man he had taken so narrow a view of religion that most of the so-called religious phenomena were thereby excluded. Schleiermacher's view, on the other hand, embraced not only the whole of Christian religion but all the religions of mankind. Christianity occupies the highest place among them as the result of a modification of the religious faculty, which has been brought about by a historical event, namely, the redemption brought by Jesus Christ. Nevertheless, unless Christianity is to be understood as a purely contingent event, the coming of Jesus must be interpreted as necessarily being implied in the original relationship of God and man. As a result, Christianity is the highest of all the religions but at the same time differs only in degree from the rest. The unity of the church has thus become merely a matter of expediency. Since, objectively, all Christians are one in their common dependence on the redemption brought by Christ, there should be no reason why they should not give outward expression to their intrinsic unity. Plausible as such a view sounds for those who share Schleiermacher's view, it is highly unsatisfactory to most Christians. For it implies that the differences between Catholicism and Protestantism, or among the various Protestant denominations, have been caused by contingent historical stimuli, while the churches are one in fact. The differences can therefore easily be ignored, removed, or rendered inoperative once their contingent character has been realized. However, this philosophical glossing over of the problem of diversity clashes with the actual facts. Denominations would not subsist in history except for their conviction that their existence had been necessitated either by a radical change in man's predicament or by an aspect of faith which had heretofore been overlooked or insufficiently satisfied, and which God wanted emphasized.

The seeming inconsistencies in Schleiermacher's view of history prompted Ritschl and, especially, Troeltsch to apply a new philosophy of history to Protestantism's understanding of its role. Ritschl combined Kant's moral emphasis with the idea of a divine purpose. Hence he saw the basic error of classical Protestantism in the interest it showed in dogmatics. According to Ritschl, Luther's great discovery is in his shift from the *fides quae creditur*, i.e., the assent given to theological propositions, to the *fides qua creditur*, i.e., man's trust in God's love in Christ. Man is not only prompted by his innate moral sense to move to increasingly higher levels of morality, but is also, through Christ, assigned for a divine destination. Through a moral life of active love he is to transform nature into culture. This goal has been reached in principle in the Christian religion and fully realized in Protestantism. Yet Ritschl, too, takes it for granted that Protestantism in all its denominations is basically identical with what he considers the essence of Protestantism, so that theological and ecclesiastical differences can be ignored. Roman Catholicism, in turn, in his judgment is placed at a lower level of historical development, and what separates it from Protestantism is an inferior view of ethics. It is obvious that Ritschl was unable to solve the dilemma left by Schleiermacher. Troeltsch discerns the superiority of Protestantism over Catholicism in particular in two respects. Protestantism, he held, is that branch of Christianity in which the whole realm of culture and life has been permeated by religion; and Protestantism alone, by the emphasis it gives to grace and faith, has succeeded in developing an idea of personal life which is directly related to the absolute. Thus Protestantism emerges both as the most advanced world view and the highest religion of the modern age.

According to Troeltsch, however, the very distinction of Protestantism is its undoing. Like all world views and all religions, it is the outcome of the never-ceasing activity of the mind, that is to say, the cosmic forces by which man is rendered human and excels over all the other creatures. Troeltsch shared the optimism which has characterized modern thought since the days of rationalism. Everything is well with man as he is. What evils are encountered in life are due to circumstances which he has not yet fully mastered but over which he will eventually triumph. Hence he needs no redemption and no redeemer. Likewise the idea of a final judgment is to be understood as merely designating the fact that each generation is accountable to the mind. History itself is judgment in that everything perishes that is not in agreement with the postulates of the mind.

This immanent urge of the mind, however, which constantly makes it surpass whatever stage has been reached in history, is fatal to Protestantism. Although we may not know of any higher type of religion than the Neo-Protestantism espoused by Troeltsch we have to reckon with new developments and must be open to their coming. While Troeltsch is ready condescendingly to acknowledge the positive elements in other forms of Protestantism, and perhaps even in Catholicism, it would have been difficult for him to proceed from that basis to some kind of church unity. For recognizing the others as being on a par with his own position would imply a denial of the transcending urge of the mind. One wonders therefore how Wilfred Monod, whose thought in some respects moved on the same line, was able to be one of the most active and energetic proponents of the ecumenical movement. Monod laid particular stress on the fact that religion is that process in human history in which the Spirit becomes articulate and triumphs over materialistic and ritualistic tendencies.[10] Thus in God's history Protestantism stands highest since it is the permanent protest of the Spirit, and, in particular, Roman Catholicism stands condemned as the enemy of the Spirit. That Monod should have been an ardent advocate of church unity is due to the central place he assigned in his ecumenical thinking to the idea of the Body of Christ and the universal lordship of Christ. As a result he thought of the church of the future as an organism held together exclusively by the Spirit and thus in no need of special institutions or organization. The problem which the French theologian's enthusiasm overlooked was how to overcome the suspicion felt by the various

[10] Wilfred Monod, *Du Protestantisme* (Paris, 1928).

churches and denominations against each other. The more dedicated a church is to its way, the greater will be its fear that the others might not be members of the Body of Christ. Yet the unity of the church cannot be given outward expression unless each group is certain of, and willing to recognize, the fact that the others too have a legitimate place in the fellowship of Christ.

CHAPTER IV

CONTEMPORARY PROTESTANTISM AND THE PROBLEM OF UNITY

A. MOVEMENTS THREATENING UNITY

In the previous chapter we have surveyed the place of Protestantism in ecumenical life. As Protestantism searches for its place it has been forced to ask new questions as new developments within the church have made the old questions and answers obsolete. Our historical survey of Protestant self-vindication indicated that various answers had been given to the question of the place of Protestantism.

We now turn our attention to the contemporary scene to see how contemporary Protestantism addresses itself to the subject of church unity. First, attention will center on the factors that threaten church unity, such as subjectivism, biblical criticism, fundamentalism, and confessionalism. Then the true basis for unity as developed from the vital center of Protestantism, spiritual vision, the church, the Bible and Luther's vocation will be portrayed.

1. Subjectivism

In the eyes of the Vatican the most embarrassing obstacles to closer relations, let alone to union, with Protestantism are the prevailing subjectivism and the kind of higher criticism of the Bible which seem to be characteristic of modern Protestantism. Conversely, there are large circles in contemporary Protestantism who consider these features their inalienable rights, which they are unwilling to surrender under any circumstances.

No doubt, for many Protestants, faith has become mere religion, that is to say, a state of mind in which they develop thoughts and sentiments concerning the ultimate fate of man. While few of them entirely reject the help which the Bible can render in such a condition, they nevertheless interpret the principle of free examination to mean that a Protestant Christian has a right to decide by himself how much of the Bible he considers relevant for his own spiritual life. While the devotional value of certain biblical passages is not denied—although often placed upon the same level with other religious literature—the average modern Protestant refuses to ascribe binding authority to the Bible. Obviously this attitude developed from the emphasis which the Reformers placed on the personal character of faith. But what an enormous difference between the Reformers' concept of faith and the modern religion of subjectivity! As understood by the Reformers, faith is entirely centered in God, whereas the modern Protestant religion is centered in the individual. The Reformers spoke of an attitude in which the individual as a person feels called by God's good news and hence gives up every claim of being somebody: rather he trusts himself entirely to what God in his grace will make of him. In this encounter God confronts the individual as the sovereign Lord, who elects people in his freedom and who on account of his absolute power has to be sought where he wants to be found. Seemingly it was Kierkegaard who called Protestant Christianity back to a new appraisal of subjectivity. But he was merely protesting against a view of faith in which the individual believed in doctrines without being personally concerned. Kierkegaard made enough of the sovereignty of God, however, to indicate that for him subjectivity did not mean mere subjectivism.

A large section of Protestantism, however, seems to be unaware of the fact that the believer is confronted by a sovereign God. Rather God, or "the Divine," is understood as being the principle, cause, or apex of the world in which we live, and man is thought to have a natural or innate knowledge of God. Because he is by his nature related to God's work in this world, the modern Protestant holds that he has a right to decide which books or passages of the Bible are relevant to him, and that he has an a priori knowledge of what is true in the Bible and what is not. Not so with the Reformers. They were taught by experience that God is never in our power, and that it is the encounter with God in Christ which decides what is relevant or worthless in life. Far from taking it for granted that man has a natural knowledge of God, they realized that there is nothing more mysterious than God's redemptive will and that man unaided by the biblical revelation is utterly confounded by the appearances of this world, provided he has the courage to take the earthly reality seriously.

It would seem to us that the modern Protestant subjectivist grossly overrates his abilities and resources. In his self-confidence he will ask, Am I not capable of having the same kind of experience that Luther or Athanasius had? Is not a man on the side of God worth more than the rest of mankind? Let us not forget, however, that Athanasius in defying the whole host of secular powers was certain that he had Christ's church standing behind him to support his position. Similarly when Luther exclaimed, "Here I stand, I can do no other," he was far from establishing his position on a purely subjective conviction. Rather he was prepared to defy the emperor and the Curia because he was confident that the God who had addressed him through the New Testament was the Father of Jesus Christ, not the "God of the philosophers and scientists" or an "ultimate reality" labelled God, and that he was thus surrounded by God's people. Removed from the Christ of the Bible, the modern subjectivist is in the company of the humanists, even though he may use a Christian vocabulary. There is nothing specifically Christian in his message.

Here lies one of the most dangerous hazards for the ecumenical movement. This doctrinal indifferentism makes it easy for its representatives to advocate church mergers because apparently none of the specific features of a denomination has a deeper meaning or is to be considered the result of a spiritual necessity.

Yet, while it may be possible in this way to mold big bodies for the cultivation of religious interests, its members will thereby be deprived of spiritual power. After all, what has led to diversification within Protestantism was the determination of believers to be so exclusively determined by God that even aspects of faith or doctrine which otherwise would seem to be of little significance might become the occasion for forming a new denomination. Whether or not Christ is present in the Eucharist in, with, and under the elements, or spiritually in the hearts of the believers, may seem to be an altogether unanswerable question, which reasonable people should rather drop. Yet for the Reformers and their followers the right answer mattered so exceedingly in their quest for certainty of salvation that Lutherans and Calvinists finally decided to proceed on separate roads rather than give their consent to a compromise. The historical fact is undeniable that the enormous influence the two denominations had, one in cultivating spiritual inwardness and the other in engendering a spirit of service and daring, was based on their respective views of the Lord's Supper.

If espoused by itself, this Protestant subjectivism would defeat the very purpose of religion, for man cannot be religiously concerned with himself or the divine without being convinced that both his own self and God matter for his life. This explains the otherwise paradoxical fact that modern Protestant subjectivism is never a purely autonomous attitude. Rather it is based upon certain metaphysical assumptions which transform faith either into mysticism or a philosophy of history. In the former case the inevitable uncertainty of subjectivism is combatted by the belief that human nature in one way or another partakes of the divine. The underlying assumption is a purely dogmatic one, for there is nothing in human nature and man's achievements that would justify such a view. The argument is borrowed from ancient philosophy and on the basis of paganism it had a certain validity. As long as the divine is thought of as being the most excellent reality in this world, man could in turn be conceived of as partaking of that "supreme being." However, with the Christian idea of a transcendental Creator of this world, the notion of the divine spark, the divine seed, or the divine energy in man betrays loose thinking.

Seemingly more consistent is the view that regards the believer as the supreme manifestation of a historical process in which God's purpose with this world is realized. If human history is conceived of as history of religion, and Protestantism as the climax of that development, then the individual Christian is the necessary outcome of that process. His judgment, though that of an individual, is conditioned by the divinely guided process of evolution and thus has objective validity. Seen in this light, the religious subjectivist would seem to stand high above the fundamentalist and the confessionalist. Do they not lack belief in the Holy Spirit? In their view, the history of the church seems to be a process in which God's Spirit is satisfied with repeating himself incessantly. Did not Jesus himself promise the coming of the Paraclete who would lead his church into all truth? Is there no room for novelty in the church? If it is granted that such is the function of the Holy Spirit we are driven to the conclusion that, compared with contemporary Christianity, the church of antiquity and the Middle Ages was still in a preliminary stage of spiritual life. Is it too much then to say that, compared with Rome's clinging to tradition, Protestantism has a right to consider itself the highest form of spiritual existence?

This argument deserves careful consideration. Can we still say with the conservative theologians of the last generation that the holy history which forms the subject matter of so many biblical books came to an end with the death of the apostles, and that the history of the church is a purely human continuation of their work? Is it not obvious that the Reformation itself is anything but a repetition or imitation of the Primitive church? And does not the very designation *reformatio*, i.e., restoration of the original condition or principle after an apostasy, point to a new stage of history? Yet when all this is granted, the embarrassing fact remains that the spirit which, according to Schleier-macher, Ritschl, and Troeltsch, operates in the history of Christianity is not the Holy Spirit Jesus brought but rather the mind of mankind found at work in all branches of history.

Of course, there is such a thing as holy or redemptive history which, like the work of the Holy Spirit, has gone on in the past and still continues in church history. But its development differs specifically from that process which is described by Troeltsch as Neo-Protestantism. While it is obvious that this modern religious attitude could have originated only on Protestant soil, the specific features of the Reformation have been lost completely or reduced to insignificance in the developments of the eighteenth and nineteenth centuries. Their place has been occupied by secular accomplishments and a philosophical view of man. The question then is whether this type of religion can be measured at all by the Christianity of the churches. As Ernst Cassirer has rightly stated, the receptivity of faith which presupposes God's redemptive work has been replaced here by the activity of the human mind.[1] It is to be granted that this trend started as an attempt to deliver Protestantism from the fetters of a theological orthodoxy which, no matter how well-intentioned and necessary it may have been in its initial stage, had gradually paralyzed the Protestant movement. But during the last two centuries the basis imperceptibly shifted from the Bible, that is to say, God's revelation of his redemptive work, to the historical work of the mind.

As has been shown, such a shift could be performed only by means of a philosophy of history if the connection with Christianity was to be preserved at all. Those philosophers who abandoned the realm of history found themselves renewing a purely philosophical or "natural" religion. But the adoption of such a historical basis was insufficient to preserve for that religious subjectivism any specifically Christian character, because it failed to assign to the Jesus of history the central place in the historical

---

[1] *The Philosophy of the Enlightenment*, trans. Fritz C. A. Koelln and J. P. Pettegrove (Princeton: Princeton University Press, 1951).

picture. As Albert Schweitzer in his *The Quest of the Historical Jesus* has correctly observed, the numerous attempts to reconstruct the "historical Jesus" from the Gospel records all aimed in fact at invalidating the authority of the Jesus found in the Gospels and of substituting for him the portrait of the modern religious man.

Consequently their philosophy of history confronted the theologians with a painful dilemma. It mattered little whether (with Hegel and Schleiermacher) they considered the level to which Christianity had attained with their type of Protestantism as the absolute end, or whether they espoused Troeltsch's view that Protestantism itself was for the time being but the optimal manifestation of the mind's development. In the former case it would be hard to imagine a reason why the historical process should eventually have reached a terminus, since growth and evolution is of the very nature of life or the Spirit. Hence this view is defensible only when the Protestantism of these theologians is considered the absolute religion. Such an assumption is absurd, however. The only case in which something in this world can be termed "absolute" is when God takes upon himself a role in history and manifests the fact that in that event he has reached his goal with mankind. Traditional Christianity predicates this attainment of Jesus. Even so, however, the Christian faith is not rendered an absolute religion but only the religion of the absolute. Hence no form of Christianity may be called the best or the final one. The right of existence of each form of Christianity is derived from the fact that they are responses to the work of Christ, not from the theology they have made of it. While the Christian religion increases in insight and wisdom as the history of the church goes on, the advance is not to be credited to the people concerned but rather to the Holy Spirit who is leading them into all truth.

Of course, it is quite legitimate to assay the relative historical qualifications and attainments of the different groups of Christianity. In spite of the Great Schism and the Reformation, both the Eastern Orthodox and Roman Catholic churches continue to exist to the present day. This fact necessarily raises the question whether the Catholic form of Christianity, which has so marvelously withstood the impact of the ages, should not be regarded as better adjusted to historical conditions than Protestantism with its constant fluctuations and changes. In turn, when the view of Troeltsch is adopted, Protestantism is from the outset in a precarious situation. Its existence can be explained only as the religious adjustment of a sector of Western mankind to a given historical condition. Since religious subjectivism in its recent phase shows obvious signs of stagnation—if not of disintegration—one has a right to wonder whether it has not lost its adaptability. Might not its lack of vitality be a sign that the present spiritual situation can no longer be mastered by a religion that has its origins in Protestantism? Does not the fact that the dominant currents in contemporary literature and art are of a strictly "secular" character, whereas Christianity plays but a subordinate role, substantiate Troeltsch's apprehension that Neo-Protestantism would give way to a new "religion" determined by a radical shift of the historical situation? Perhaps then Tillich and others are right in telling us that we are already in the post-Protestant era.

2. Biblical Criticism

Protestant subjectivism is instinctively aware of its inconsistency. Christian faith cannot be entirely the offshoot of the human mind. If a religion is to be Christian it has to come to terms with the Bible. Yet seemingly it is the very message of the Bible which opposes the transformation of faith into subjective religion. For this reason, in addition to the recourse taken to the philosophy of history, Protestant subjectivism has looked to biblical criticism for support of its view. We do not contend that the critical treatment of the Bible is incompatible with faith but rather that the appeal which religious subjectivism has made to biblical criticism has been detrimental to the latter without strengthening the position of subjectivism.

The origin of biblical criticism antedates not only the rise of Neo-Protestantism but also the Reformation. Without exception the great interpreters of the Scripture have employed the critical treatment of the biblical text as an indispensable tool of exegesis. The Reformers were not the first theologians to notice the fact that the books of the Bible originated in very different historical situations, that they bore the marks of their authors' personalities and that their interpretation required linguistic abilities. The Reformers were keenly aware of the help that the new rise of philology, which the humanists had initiated, was giving them in their study of the Bible. The rapid development of biblical philology and methods of criticism that characterized the sixteenth and seventeenth centuries is intimately connected with biblical studies, and in many instances it was the biblical scholar who led. The radical change in the critical approach to the biblical text which occurred in the eighteenth century, however, had nothing to do with the legitimacy of biblical criticism. Rather what was originally meant to be a tool for an adequate understanding of the inspired text of the Bible was changed into a tool for proving the truth of the critic's own theological position. There seemed to be good reason for such a revolution. It was introduced as a legitimate reaction to the way in which Protestant orthodoxy had used the Scripture. Soon after the death of the Reformers, their followers became anxious to galvanize the fruits of their scriptural studies. Very instructive in that respect was the conflict between Beza and Arminius. The latter insisted that Reformed theology could not be true to the spirit of Calvin unless it continued to be fed by further study of the Bible, whereas Beza was obsessed by the idea of systematizing the master's teaching. That tendency soon prevailed not only in the Lutheran and the Reformed camps but also among Mennonites, Schwenckfelders, and other splinter groups. As a result, the achievements of biblical philology and textual and historical criticism had virtually no influence upon doctrine.

Whereas in pietism the protest against ecclesiastical orthodoxy led to a new study of the Bible in which philological research helped to deepen the understanding of the Bible, and hence of the gospel (as is evidenced by the works of A. H. Francke and J. A. Bengel), the development in the rationalistic camp went in the opposite direction. In pietism, biblical criticism respected the authority of the Scripture as divinely given revelation and aimed merely at an appropriate understanding of its text. Rationalism, however, postulated that the Bible had to be treated and interpreted in every respect like the rest of literature. The exegete was thereby given unlimited freedom of interpretation, which in actual practice meant that the exegete's own position would determine the outcome of his critical studies. If one knew a particular exegete's position, one would also know how much of the biblical text he would accept as "genuine" or "religiously relevant." No wonder that in this camp biblical criticism became a powerful tool for the disintegration of the biblical message.

Nevertheless, the real significance of this process was not clearly seen. Polemics between critical and "conservative" scholars indicated that Neo-Protestantism was opposed because of its disagreement in doctrine only, whereas in fact it had become the representative of an entirely new kind of faith. Significantly it was the Roman Catholic church which stated the nature of the conflict correctly when eventually, at the end of the nineteenth century, Protestant biblical criticism had made dangerous inroads into the Catholic theological faculties. In its fight against modernism the Holy Office correctly and sagaciously formulated the basic principles of the modernists in the Decretum *Lamentabili* (1907). Three of these principles may be mentioned as being particularly characteristic: (1) "To believe that God is in fact the author of the Scripture is evidence of excessive naivete or ignorance"; (2) "Although the ecclesiastical interpretation of the sacred books should not be despised, it must nevertheless be subjected to the more accurate judgment and correction of the exegetes"; (3) "The deity of Christ cannot be proved from the Gospels because it is a dogma which the Christian consciousness has deduced from the notion of Messiah." [2]

Significantly the condemnation of modernism on the part of the Curia was not directed against the use of the critical method as such. Anyone familiar with recent Catholic publications in the field of biblical scholarship will have noticed the extent and thoroughness with which this method is handled by the leading Catholic scholars. Nor does Rome think that these men thereby violate the anti-modernism oath which they took when the theological doctoral degree was conferred upon them. What the Catholic church saw, more clearly than many Protestants, was the fact that the theological principles underlying Neo-Protestantism were incompatible with the very nature of Christian faith. Its subjectivism and historicism did more than undermine the authority of the Bible. It denied the necessity of the redemptive ministry of Jesus.

Protestant modernists have occasionally claimed that all they wanted to accomplish was to deliver the believer from the slavery into which they had been brought by the alleged authority of the Scripture. They wished to meet God with the same freedom with which Jesus and his disciples did. However, in this argument the fact is completely overlooked that Jesus constantly referred to the Old Testament as the God-given root and basis of his own mission and ministry. And while it is true that there was a time when the New Testament books were not yet in existence, the Primitive Church nevertheless proclaimed its message of Jesus the Messiah not as its own production but rather as the divine kerygma. The modern exegete therefore does violence to the text of the New Testament when he interprets its

---

[2] Decretum *Lamentabili* (July 3, 1907), nos. 9, 2, 27, quoted in H. Denzinger and C. Bannwart, *op. cit.*, nos. 2009, 2002, 2027.

content as deliberate fabrication of the Primitive Church. Even when he studies the Bible as a historical critic, and especially in this capacity, the theologian must start from the way the New Testament writers and their readers understood their message. If he feels unable to believe in the kerygma in its historical sense he is free to disagree. But he dare not say that he speaks in the name of Protestantism when he substitutes his own religious ideas for those of the Bible.

3. FUNDAMENTALISM

Of course, it would be ridiculous to consider the whole of Protestantism since the eighteenth century as having espoused the subjectivism of Neo-Protestantism. While subjectivism was rampant in wide circles, violently declining to be called rationalistic, liberal, or modernistic, it was tempered sufficiently with traditional elements to safeguard the continuity with the Reformation. Notwithstanding the fact that the actual use of Holy Scripture was often an eclectic one, the authority of the Bible was upheld in these circles. Nevertheless, it can be stated without being unfair to evangelicalism and related movements that they were never really aware of the problem of Protestantism's place in the church of Christ. It was taken for granted that having the Bible and acknowledging its divine authority were tantamount to being with Christ. That is the reason why in these circles the problem of the church was never seriously raised. It seems that until recently the British Free Churches, for instance, never quite grasped the theological significance of their dealings with the Church of England. Similarly the Methodists, Baptists, Quakers, and other Anglo-Saxon people who tried to establish groups of their own on German soil were regarded by the German Protestant churches until 1918 as criminal invaders and their associations as sects, who in a damnable way would make proselytes from the established churches. In Sweden one was not allowed to be a Methodist without at the same time being a member of the state church. In other words, sociological and legal considerations completely obscured the theological nature of the church.

It would appear, however, that fundamentalism and confessionalism had a firmer grasp of the problem, because their opposition to religious subjectivism was a matter of principle; confessionalism in particular presupposes a definite view of the church. Fundamentalism, with its emphasis on the *sola Scriptura* and the belief in the Bible's infallibility, contends that it is the legitimate heir of the Reformation. Bitterly opposed to liberal theology and the exegesis that had undermined the authority of the Bible, fundamentalism attempted to restore the Bible's place in modern Protestantism. There are two features in the exegesis of the advocates of this position, however, that are disquieting. One is the relative scarcity of exegetical results. Where other students of the Bible, including Luther and Calvin, were overwhelmed by the inexhaustible wealth of ideas found in the Bible and taught that there never could be an end to exegetical discoveries, fundamentalism seems to be satisfied with those few ideas which had been the stock-in-trade of the revivals of the nineteenth century. Little interest is shown, for instance, in the ethics of the Bible, in the rich Christology of the New Testament, and in its eschatology; the biblical references to Satan and angels are brazenly ignored. This eclectic use of the Bible practically identified the word of God with the theologians' narrow scope of spiritual interest. Such an attitude is hardly in agreement with the Scripture's supreme authority.

No less bewildering have been recent tendencies to couple fundamentalism with apocalypticism by means of "prophetic" interpretation or dispensationalism. The development started as a legitimate protest against the static outlook of conservative theology in which eschatology had been practically eclipsed by the prevailing interest in Christ's accomplished work of redemption. Unfortunately, however, this rediscovery of biblical eschatology has resulted in an exegesis in which one aspect of the Bible's teaching has so completely lost focus that the Scripture's central message has been practically blotted out. Just as in the case of liberal theology, the exegete's idiosyncrasies here dictate the use he makes of the biblical proclamation.

Nor are things better in non-eschatological or amillennial fundamentalism. This group pretends to excel over all other Christians by the fact that it is guided exclusively by the word of God, and it engages therefore(!) in vicious attacks on other Christians. These people assert that they are the only Christians who believe in the Bible. We ask, with what right can one group in Protestantism set itself up as the infallible judge of all others? How does one know that the others tell lies when they affirm their allegiance to Christ and their strict acknowledgment of the Bible's authority? And how is it that this group's attack on the "unbelief" of other Christians is directed against their political and social views and their participation in the work of the World Council of Churches? This attitude is perhaps the worst perversion of the Protestant principle because in it the underlying subjectivism is disguised by its alleged adherence to the truth of the Bible. However, the truth in which they seek unity is identical with the opinions held by the leaders. Fatal to their claim to speak exclusively in the name of God or in obedience to the Bible is the conspicuous lack of theological agreement found among these preachers. In their desire to prove their zeal for God's truth over against the "infidels" numerous little popes have arisen in that camp, each one condemning the unbelief and the heresies of his closest associates.

This whole development indicates the fallacy of the orthodox axiom that valid theological doctrines can be derived from the Bible by means of purely logical procedures, and that such inferences possess the same authority as the biblical text itself. In actual practice such an axiom means that the theological conclusions predominate, so that it is theology rather than the Bible that forms the basis of faith. Far from adopting the approach to the Bible used by the Reformers, this view comes close to that of the Roman Catholic church, without, however, being acceptable to Rome. For Rome teaches that on account of the inevitable plurality of biblical interpretations, the supreme judgment in exegetical matters must belong to the ecclesiastical authorities. Otherwise the believers would be deprived of the certainty of faith or would be rendered dependent on a single exegete. Paradoxically, subjectivism is as powerful a factor in the fundamentalist camp as in Neo-Protestantism. Here too what is implied in the Protestant principle is not clearly seen. Thus the disagreements between liberal or modernist and conservative theologians concern only the quantity of the propositions in which one believes.

4. Confessionalism

One turns hopefully then to confessionalism because the confessionalists are a group in Protestantism which takes the church seriously. Will it have an answer for our quest of a Protestant church? Confessionalism is a small but vociferous section of Protestantism, especially in the Lutheran and Reformed churches. It originated from the realization that Protestantism's right of existence depends on preserving the continuity with its beginning. The Protestant churches, particularly in the sixteenth and seventeenth centuries, have held that in order to guarantee that continuity, a church or denomination must have a confession of faith. Unlike the dogmas of the Catholic church, which fix doctrines once and for all time and are entirely immutable, the confessions of faith were primarily concerned with the church's life of faith. This explains why the same denomination may possess a whole series of confessions, differing in certain respects from each other (as the Lutheran *Book of Concord*), or why after some time it may have felt the need for a new and revised confession (as some of the Reformed churches did). Furthermore, practically all of them are expressly placed under the authority of the Bible, thus leaving room for revisions whenever new biblical insights should demand them.

Protestant confessions of faith, in the absence of an absolute teaching authority, must give expression to the consent of all those members of a denomination who are responsible for teaching. Hence confessions more often than not are the result of a doctrinal compromise, as for instance the Lutheran *Formula of Concord* or the Reformed *Westminster Confession*. But it is easy to see how after the adoption of a confession of faith those in control of a denomination may be carried away by their zeal for its continuity and for pure doctrine. Confessional controversies have therefore been frequent in Protestant bodies, and it often happened that the group or faction in power used its political position to cause its specific understanding of the confession to prevail. Accordingly a dissension would be interpreted as caused by the minority's spiritual weakness and mental limitations in its understanding of God's word, or by the vicious machination of the devil. In the former case the controversies were resolved by eventually adopting a middle course between the extremes. In other instances, however, the powers that be and their theologians would decree what was to be taught as the truth, a procedure that is conspicuous, for instance, in the condemnation of Zwingli and the Anabaptists as incorporated in the Augsburg Confession.

Since Protestantism has never developed a theological doctrine of the teaching office and its relation to biblical revelation, the formulation of a confession of faith was probably the only way open for the preservation of historical continuity. The rigidity with which some people have insisted on a narrow interpretation of their denomination's confession of faith has called forth attempts to substitute more flexible standards, for instance, confessions composed of biblical passages, or to replace the confessions of faith by the teachings of the young Luther or of Calvin. But these experiments, which were the work of scholars, could hardly meet with the denomination's general approval. For, unlike the denominational confessions, these standards lacked even the authority resulting from the *consensus ecclesiae*. But quite apart from these innovations, the Protestant confessions of faith could by the nature of the case never enjoy the absolute authority ascribed to the dogmas and doctrines of the Roman church. Since Protestant confessions are the work of theologians they can be adopted only as a means of church discipline but can never be used to bind one's conscience, whereas the Catholic church claims the support of a divine institution and the direct and manifest participation of the Holy Spirit for its doctrinal statements.

Here we have reached the point at which the precarious situation of modern confessionalism is most obvious. In its attempt to establish Protestantism onesidedly on the doctrinal continuity between its present state and its beginnings, it is bound to emphasize the human origin of its denomination. That raises a very pertinent question. What actually is gained by this kind of historical continuity? While it is an effective means of keeping the theologian within the fellowship of the teaching congregation and thus effectively curbs subjectivism, does it not fall into the opposite extreme by ascribing absolute authority to the Fathers of one's denomination and thus finally to the Reformers? Surely even their enemies must admit their historical greatness. But does that fact suffice to assign them authority over the church's spiritual life? Does not rather the recourse to a historical standard imply that the Reformation or the emergence of one's denomination was merely a historical phenomenon, that is to say, the outcome of a particular combination of human urges and historical circumstances—for instance, a by-product of the Renaissance or of the social and political unrest of England in the sixteenth and seventeenth centuries? Understood in this way, however, the question must be posed to Protestants, as it was to Troeltsch, whether the Reformation had more than a temporary historical significance. That the Reformation of the sixteenth century was a historical necessity, no one who has studied the condition of the church in the late Middle Ages will deny. The radical revamping of doctrine and the completely new attitude toward the world to which the Roman church subjected itself at the Council of Trent was a manifest admission of the necessity of Luther's protest. But was there any cogent reason why, after Trent, and to the present day, Protestantism has insisted on perpetuating the schism?

Martin Chemnitz, in his critical survey of the decrees of Trent (*Examen Concilii Tridentium* 1565-73), had to admit that the Council had removed many of the obstacles and errors that had marred the medieval church. The anti-Catholic polemics of the Protestant theologians, fierce as it has been at times, has, nevertheless, not been able to assume a new position beyond the stance taken by the Reformers, and in a number of issues has had to drop its criticisms because Rome met its opponents half way. The question whether after the Council of Trent the opponents of Rome should continue to form a separate body has vexed both Protestants and Catholics alike. Is there nothing more we can say than that after a movement has assumed a specific form of organization, it is reluctant to admit that its purpose has been fulfilled? Yet with such a purely historical view of continuity the Protestant churches would not be able to provide spiritual blessings for their members. A denomination which lacks a spiritual necessity for its existence is a mere scandal. Rome, on the other hand, still contends that on account of her spiritual origin she is able to offer man deliverance from the cosmic forces, peace with God, and eternal bliss.

This question confronts us with increased intensity when we remember that, notwithstanding their authoritative claims, the Protestant confessions of faith are also marks of the divisions in Protestantism. Who then are the true Protestants? And what actually do we mean when we speak of Protestantism? Is there a Protestant church in the way in which there are the Eastern Orthodox and the Roman churches? Or is Protestantism a mere agglomeration of denominations like Lutheranism, Calvinism, Methodism, and so on? And again when we say Lutheranism, for instance, would we identify it with the Lutheran Church in America or with the Lutheran Church—Missouri Synod, seeing that their theological and ecclesiastical positions are so far apart? Yet the Synodical Conference, that stalwart champion of Lutheran orthodoxy, to which the Missouri Synod belongs, is on the verge of disintegration because its members condemn each other for adopting intolerable heresies. Is not Rome right in interpreting the divisions of Protestantism as clear evidence of its lack of spiritual truth and as proof of its utterly heretical character? Can it be denied that, unlike the Roman Catholic church, Protestantism lacks a world-wide authoritative organization and that it is unable to point to a set of dogmas adopted as supreme authority by all the denominations and churches which call themselves Protestant? If Protestantism were a church would it not possess a form of worship or devotion held by all its members?

It is hard not to become cynical when we listen to the way in which Protestant churchmen and theologians in our days pretend to speak in the name of Protestantism, while in fact asserting their own subjective views. Is not such an attitude a clear proof of the fact that these people regard Protestantism as a merely historical phenomenon to which they happen to belong? One can sympathize with the Reformers and their early followers, for they could no longer stand the tyranny and greed of the popes and their perversion of the Christian faith. But in our day that protest lingers on without aim and direction and for no good reason except that modern Protestants are people who like to protest. That is not to say that Protestantism is inescapably doomed and a lost cause; but if in spite of the distressing facts mentioned above and Rome's vigorous advance we still want to assert Protestantism's right of existence, we must look for a more substantial basis than that adopted by modern Protestantism.

B. THE TRUE BASIS FOR UNITY

1. SPIRITUAL VISION

Christ taught his disciples that the principal issue in history is truth. Power, success, glory, or wealth may seem to be desirable, and undoubtedly people who possess any of these are thereby placed in the limelight for a while. But one will not be able to leave his permanent mark on the world unless he performs works which are true, that is to say, in agreement with human nature and man's destination. This basic law of history applies to the history of Protestantism too. Protestantism set the ecumenical movement in motion out of a quest for the unity of the church. No one should therefore be surprised that once the ecumenical movement was under way, Protestantism found itself confronted with the question: Is there indeed such a thing as a Protestant church?

Our survey has brought to light the organizational vitality of modern Protestantism, its cultural attainments and its remarkable record of social services, but also the inner tensions and intrinsic contradictions of its history. But the problem that confronts us is not a sociological one. We are not interested in comparing the relative merits and attainments of Protestantism with those of other social organizations such as lodges and service clubs, nor are we concerned with the place of the Protestant denominations in the framework of national life and its political organization. Important as such issues are by virtue of the fact that the denominations are affected by social and political life and in turn affect it, the specific merits and shortcomings which the Protestant bodies have in those areas do not contribute to answering our basic question. For when we ask whether there is a Protestant church, we inquire not into the sociological aspect of the church but rather into its spiritual nature. By church we mean the church of Christ, that is to say, a corporate entity in this world which owes its existence and strength to the fact that it is under the permanent influence of the Spirit which comes from Christ. The ecumenical movement would be devoid of real significance if it were but a colossal organization of ecclesiastical administration. The achievement of the unity of the church assigned to the Protestant churches must be unity in the Spirit and in truth.

For this reason we discounted the attempts to find that unity in the field of theology. While it is quite legitimate to strive for a clear awareness of the nature of the church, such endeavor fails to reach its goal as long as the spiritual oneness of the church has not yet been envisaged, experienced, apprehended, and comprehended. Thus far so-called "ecumenical theology" has started from the idea of a desirable goal fixed by men, and the results were therefore doomed to remain vague and sentimental. Yet we also keep in mind that the Spirit of God is not a purely transcendental entity. Rather he reveals himself to us here on earth in events of redemptive significance. Statements concerning spiritual realities are therefore convincing only when one is able to point to facts in this world in which the operation of the Spirit manifests itself. Purely mental constructions and imaginary ideas of what the church and its unity might be are bound to lead people away from the real problem and its appropriate solution, even if they are based on biblical passages. Rather the problem of church unity is concerned with the extant bodies which call themselves Christian, and their unity must therefore be a basis of action upon which they agree. Yet since the quest for unity is motivated by the religious ends they pursue, the unity concerns their organizational character only inasmuch as the Holy Spirit manifests himself in them, and the will to unity must be wrought by God's Spirit.

A further consideration is in order. When we speak of Protestantism, we do not confine our reflection to those bodies which at present are counted as such. Rather we have to deal with the whole historical process that was initiated by the Reformation, and with all the religious bodies which sprang into being as a result of that event. The name that a group gives itself is of subordinate significance, for nobody can make himself Protestant merely by calling himself so. Rather it is the historical process that determines the present age and gives it its character. We cannot therefore make a selection and say, for instance, that the Presbyterians of the seventeenth century were true Presbyterians but those of the eighteenth century were not, or that we see the Spirit at work in confessional Lutheranism while it is absent in Lutheran subjectivism. The result of such a procedure would be an ideal type of Protestantism composed of all the "good" or "positive" elements, something that has never existed and never will.

By Protestantism we mean rather the sum total of all the churches and denominations that have received their inspiration from the Reformation, and the whole process of that history from the sixteenth century down to the present day. Such a view includes the ups and downs of that history, its accomplishments as well as its shortcomings, and its apostasies no less than its moments of faithful witness. However, Protestantism so conceived is not confined to what the people concerned in that historical process have done but includes also what the Holy Spirit has accomplished in their midst, what opportunities and resources he has offered them, and the manner in which he has kept them related to their spiritual origin. That is to say, the history of Protestantism, like the rest of church history, can be adequately evaluated only when seen as a segment of holy history or *Heilsgeschichte* (redemptive or holy history). We deny the power of God's Spirit when we hold that he was at work in the spiritual history of Israel and of the Primitive Church but discontinued his work when the last of the apostles died. As a matter of fact all the changes which occurred in the life of the church since the days of the apostles, including the formation of the canon of the New Testament, would be apostasy if it were not for the fact that the Holy Spirit continued to guide the church through the ages and never ceased to call it back from error and unbelief.

This perspective is obviously the only appropriate way of discussing the place which Protestantism occupies in the history of the church. Protestantism must regard itself as the outcome of the Reformation understood as a divinely wrought event. From the Roman Catholic viewpoint Luther was guilty of destroying the age-old unity of the church. This is a very serious charge, for oneness is unquestionably one of the outstanding marks of the church as the Body of Christ. A schism can be defended only if it is the outcome of Christ's own work. Protestants have too often been tempted by political and cultural circumstances to view the existence of Protestantism polemically as a defense of sacred rights threatened by Rome, or as a belated criticism of misuses that arose in the medieval church. Of course the Inquisition and the Roman hierarchy threatened sacred rights, of course much was wrong in the medieval church, and nobody should be reprehended for fighting these ills. But for such a fight no church is required, and in turn such conflict remains in the realm of secular history. Hence it cannot form the basis on which the question of Protestantism's right of existence can be settled. We hold that this right is exclusively established upon the work of Christ, by whose Spirit Luther was granted his understanding of faith, and it is lost wherever Protestants disregard this fact.

Viewed as a spiritual phenomenon the Reformation was the discovery of a new understanding of faith, namely, as the experience of God's call. The Reformation regarded itself as an event within the church; it never pretended to be an entirely new beginning. But over against the way in which faith was tied in with the institutional and sacramental life of the church in the Middle Ages, the Reformers pointed to a faith which was a personal response to the personal way in which God disclosed his gracious will to the individual through the Bible. The results of this discovery were three features through which the Reformation engendered Protestantism as a historical movement: (1) belief in the church as the place of God's present work here on earth; (2) belief in God's self-revelation to man through the word of the Bible; and (3) belief in Luther's vocation. Inasmuch as all three of them point back to the Reformation and its new understanding of faith, they form the legitimate basis for the continued existence of Protestantism. Wherever one of these characteristics is missing, the work of the Reformation has been slighted.

2. The Church

While Protestant individualism is unable to disregard completely the role which the Scripture plays in the genesis of faith, it nevertheless grossly misinterprets the way in which Luther discovered its authority and sufficiency. For it creates the impression that Luther was completely ignorant of true religion when he unexpectedly found that famous chained Bible. Yet the Reformer neither then nor at any other time lived in a religious vacuum and in spiritual isolation. Rather it was within the church's teaching and spiritual practice, and as a result of them, that Luther felt driven to his pangs of perplexity; it was within this church and from the resources it provided for the believer that he looked for a way to certainty. Thus it was in his capacity as a duly appointed professor of Sacred Scripture—that is to say, as a person who was familiar with the teachings and practices of the Catholic church and who voluntarily identified himself with them—that he received the illumination by which the Reformation began. Nor would it be in accord with the records of history to hold that once the light had come to him, he repudiated everything Catholic.

On the contrary, Luther continued to acknowledge the decisive role which the Catholic church had for his spiritual life by calling it the "Mother Church." Luther did not break loose from Rome out of a desire to have an independent church; it was the Pope who excommunicated him. Even so, Luther insisted that all the Pope could do to him was to sever his outward connection with the Curia, while spiritually he remained a member of the church of Christ. It is a well-known fact that shortly before his death, in the Smalcald Articles, Luther laid down the conditions under which the Protestants were willing to resume contacts with Rome, and he entertained the hope that a council of the church would be in a position to remedy the rift in the unity of the church. Far from advocating religious individualism the Reformers insisted on the fact that, notwithstanding its personal character, faith had its necessary place in the fellowship of the believers. Church and Bible cannot therefore be separated. Luther would have shown little understanding for the modern belief that in order to make people Christians it is sufficient to distribute Bibles to them. Where people interested in the gospel lack the common life of the church they will interpret faith and redemption as their own work.

For the Reformers the Bible was the word of God addressed to his people, and the gathering of that people is the very purpose for which the Bible is given. Faith is not an end in itself; it is engendered by God as a means by which individuals are made ready for his service. Luther as well as Calvin emphasized the centrality of vocation implied in God's speaking. The divine calling, in turn, implies both the assurance of one's election and the divine appeal to join God's people and serve their Lord. The fellowship of the church is required in order to make sure that salvation is continuously offered to mankind. By means of the church, God's people are both separated from the world and equipped for their mission to impart God's benefits to the world. This view differs characteristically both from the Jewish view, according to which Israel is an end in herself, and from that of the church of Rome, where it is held that the church is destined to rule over the world. Thus it is as recipient and mediator of the word of God, and as the place where God is worshipped and served in this world, that the fellowship of believers partakes of the church as a spiritual entity. When we realize this fact we are driven to a new understanding and evaluation of Protestantism. The glaring weaknesses which we pointed out, its subjectivism and its narrowminded objectivism, may constitute a real denial of the faith whenever they are coupled with a refusal to participate in the spiritual function of the church. When people are willing to share in the spiritual work of the church, however, these same attitudes are but deplorable shortcomings by which the spiritual function of the church and the believer's participation in it are more or less impeded. As a result the church is incapacitated in the service it is destined to render to the world, but it functions nevertheless.

With its new concept of faith and its spiritual view of the church, Protestantism completely modified the idea of heresy. According to the Roman Catholic definition, a heresy is a doctrine which pretends to be Christian and to have its origin in Christ, yet is in contradiction with the doctrine taught definitively by the teaching office of the church. Since they had rejected the teaching authority of the Roman Catholic church the Reformers could no longer start from a fixed set of propositions that would be binding on all. Their criterion of truth was the spiritual attitude underlying a man's teaching. To be sure, this view was not consistently held by the Reformers, and particularly the Protestant orthodoxy of the seventeenth century relapsed into a pseudo-Catholic understanding of heresy. That was the more deplorable because the standard employed was not the official teaching of the whole church but rather the dogmatic opinion of a theological school or even that of a single theologian. Of course, in its pursuit of truth a denomination and its teachers must strive after a clear apprehension of the significance and the implications of the gospel. But since the gospel is a message of facts, namely, the redemptive ministry of Jesus, its correct apprehension is dependent on the spiritual attitude one takes toward these facts. Where such an attitude is missing, a person is a heretic even when he gives his full assent to every proposition of the Bible. In turn, modern Protestantism is more consistent than it was in the age of controversies in that it applies the designation "heretical" only sparingly and never exclusively on the basis of propositions taught.

The spiritual view of the church held by the Reformers has subsequently been understood as meaning that the true church was invisible and that the term "church" designated the sum total of the true believers held together invisibly by the love of

Christ. The counterpart of such a view was a purely sociological understanding of the institutional churches and their organization. This was a distortion, however, of the view and practice of the Reformers. To them there could be no church except in its historical manifestations. What separated them from Rome was merely their refusal to derive the spiritual nature of the church from the activities of the ecclesiastical hierarchy rather than from the work of the Holy Spirit working alike in the faith of the believers and in the ministerial activities of the clergy. In this respect too the one-sidedness of the sixteenth century has been overcome gradually as the Holy Spirit has brought together antagonistic factions in Protestantism. The Reformers fought those Anabaptists who denied the necessity of an ecclesiastical ministry and wanted to establish the spiritual character of the church exclusively upon the work of the Spirit in the hearts of the believers. Yet the Anabaptists did not dispense with the regular preaching of the gospel, and they too insisted upon the necessity of baptism as a sacramental rite. The Protestant churches in turn have come to understand by now that their institutional ministries will be seriously handicapped if the minister has no spiritual experience, and that it was a gross mistake to make the effective performance of the ministry dependent primarily on the regularity of the call extended to the minister. Equally important was the realization, provided mainly by the revival movements, that helpful as the institutional ministry is for the continuity and methodical expansion of the church's work, its functions may and must be shared by the laity. Without their devotional life and witness the church withers away.

The strong emphasis placed upon the work which the Holy Spirit performs in the hearts of the believers explains why Protestantism has never created a culture of its own. The principal contribution which Protestantism has made to the history of the Western world lies in molding a new attitude toward oneself and the world. In this respect one notices certain characteristic differences between the various Protestant denominations, but it is nevertheless possible without much difficulty to tell a Protestant from a Roman Catholic or a non-believer. The direct confrontation of the individual with God has engendered a sense of personal responsibility and service which is unique. It is through this attitude that Protestantism has given impetus to cultural developments, particularly in Lutheranism and Puritanism. In turn, it is the slackening of the spiritual emphasis in modern Protestantism that accounts for the remarkable shift of perspective that has occurred in the cultural life of the West. Where idealism took the place of Protestantism, culture became increasingly subjective; whereas under the spell of materialism, culture degenerated into a source of entertainment or of gain.

3. The Bible

Over against the prevalence of subjectivism in modern Protestantism, it was necessary to remind ourselves of the fact that in the thinking of the Reformers the church and faith were found in close correlation. The church, nevertheless, is but the prerequisite of certainty of salvation; the Bible is its foundation. As has been shown, the significance which the Scripture has for faith is derived from the fact that God brought the Bible into being as the means through which he wants to communicate to man his gracious will of redemption. This view accounts for the fundamental difference between the Reformer's use of the Bible and that of the nominalistic medieval theologians, notwithstanding their formal agreements. Both hold that the Bible is infallible. But, whereas for the Catholic theologians the Bible is a repository of theological propositions whose understanding surpasses the power of human reason, the Reformers discovered in the Bible the revelation of redemptive facts otherwise unavailable to the human mind. Since the purpose for which that revelation is given is redemption rather than mere illumination of the human mind, the Bible in its totality is seen as related to the believer's quest for certainty. When the Bible is read for the purpose of developing a theological system, everything written in it must be considered as lying on the same level and as being of equal importance. The Reformers, however, adopted a Christocentric view of Scripture because for them the overwhelming significance of the Bible lay not in its being an infallible document but in the purpose for which God gave it, namely, to make man sure of his salvation.

This view enabled the Reformers to differentiate in their appreciation of the biblical books without thereby questioning their inspiration or their function as means of grace. God speaks through all the books of the canon, but he does not make known his saving will through each of them to everyone with equal distinctness and directness. It is a well-known fact that Luther held such books as James, Hebrews, and the Apocalypse in lower esteem than the letters of Paul or the Gospel of John. But far from excluding those other books from his canon he admonished people to be ready to hear God speaking through them. This is the point where the rationalistic theologians and later on some of the biblical critics were led astray. Starting from those passages of the Bible which had spoken most directly and clearly to them they sought to discredit the rest on allegedly historical and literary grounds. But there is no good theological reason, for instance, why one should assume that the sources underlying the Synoptic Gospels were closer to the truth than the Gospels in their final formulation, or that Paul has less to say to our generation in those letters in which he evidences familiarity with gnostic ideas than in those where such allusions are missing.

Likewise, while fundamentalists are to be commended for their determination to take the whole Bible seriously as the word of God, they also must learn from the Reformers. It is unfortunate that among fundamentalists the criterion of true faith is found in the absolute infallibility of the Bible. In their eyes a theologian is heretical when he does not define the divine authority of Scripture in terms of infallibility, even though he might share all their dogmatic views. Thus a purely formal aspect is assigned a central position. The most detrimental consequence of that view is the ensuing belief that the content of the Bible is evident for everybody who believes in its infallibility. Yet not only the Reformers but also many earnest students of the Bible have borne witness to the fact that the true meaning of the Bible can be apprehended only where the exegete is guided by the Spirit of God. They have warned the believers against the fallacy of identifying the plain meaning of the biblical text with its spiritual meaning. Luther and the other Reformers would never have advanced in their study of the Scripture beyond the position of the most enlightened of the Catholic scholars such as Faber Stapulensis or Erasmus except for the fact that they started from the realization of their spiritual ignorance. Since they were ready to enroll in the school of the Holy Spirit and to be taught by him they gradually advanced in their understanding of God's redemptive message.

In turn, where people lack this willingness to listen to God speaking they are confounded by the text of the Bible. In its light, God seems to be incomprehensible and inaccessible. In order to escape this frightening conclusion the same people who had so strongly advocated a literal exegesis then resort to what the Reformers called "allegorical interpretation," which they regarded as the main source of delusion. In order to find meaning and comfort in the Bible, the exegete then in an arbitrary manner makes the text of the Bible say what he wishes to find there. By doing so he actually derives his comfort from his own ideas. It seems to us that a good deal of fundamentalistic exegesis is vitiated by this method. There is no substitute for God speaking through the Scripture.

The Protestant belief in the sufficiency of the Bible has often been interpreted as an unhistorical disregard of tradition. This is not correct, however. The Reformers rejected a view of tradition according to which it yielded saving knowledge independent of, and above, that provided by the Bible. They pointed out that by doing so, the church substituted human opinions for God's own speaking. But they did not deny the fact that time and again church history had provided genuine insights into the meaning of biblical revelation which preceding generations had not yet possessed. Hence their aim was not to jump back over the centuries and rebuild again the Apostolic Church, which the Waldensians attempted to do. Rather they quoted frequently and with approval passages from the Fathers. But, unlike the Catholic church, the Reformers understood tradition in its relation to the Scripture, regarding it merely as an increased deepening of spiritual insight.

From this viewpoint Luther considered the Reformation an eschatological sign. The execution of the plan God has for his people has entered into its final stage of growth. Furthermore, it is possible in the light of this correlation between Bible and tradition to distinguish between genuine growth of tradition on the one hand, and human error and presumptuousness in the doctrines and practices of the past on the other. Bultmann is therefore right in pointing out that our interpretation of the Bible starts from a *Vorverständnis* (preliminary knowledge). It is as Christians that we read the Bible. But we would miss God's speaking if we expected the Scripture to confirm our religious views or at the worst to correct them in details only. In deference to the God who wants to reveal himself to us, we must be willing to be taught by him concerning the Bible's spiritual meaning, or, to use Calvin's phrase, the understanding of the Scripture is dependent on the *analogia fidei*. This does not mean that the exegesis of the Bible must be correlated with one's theological views. On the contrary, the "proof text" method has proved to be the most sterile approach to the Bible because the exegete, far from being taught by the Spirit of God, only had his own views confirmed by the appropriate selection of passages he made from the Bible. Rather the "analogy of faith" designates the reciprocal relationship between the propositional truths found in Scripture on the one hand, and the corresponding attitude of faith on the other. For instance, only when in reading it we acknowledge that that we have no goodness of our own can we understand what God offers in sanctification; only when through the Bible we are made aware of the power which sin holds over us can its offer of divine liberation become a reality in our lives. In turn, the fatherly love of God offered to us in the gospel cannot be experienced except by those who believe in his grace. Of course, the acceptance of the biblical message requires familiarity with its text and the assurance that it is true. But exegesis is not a purely scholarly activity. Luther's and Calvin's commentaries are the works of men who were anxious, both for the sake of their own lives and for the benefit of those entrusted to their care, to discover that comfort in the midst of life's perplexity and hopelessness which no man is able to give, but which God is willing to disclose in the Scriptures. Such interpretation requires no less scholarship than is demanded for "scientific" exegesis, and in addition requires spiritual effort and humble receptivity.

4. LUTHER'S VOCATION

Many Protestants would probably agree with those who define Protestantism as the religion of the Bible. But when we remember that the Ancient Church too never had any authoritative document but the Scripture, and that in the course of its history the church has never deliberately and consciously deviated from the Bible, it should be evident that such a definition requires some further qualification. For it is obvious that Protestantism differs considerably from those earlier stages of Christianity. Some are inclined to find the differentia in the Christ-centeredness of Protestant faith; yet neither Bernard of Clairvaux nor Saint Francis were Protestants! Others adopted Twesten's definition, according to which Protestantism has the Bible as the formal principle of faith and justification by faith as the material principle.[3] But even when this definition is accepted as an accurate description of Luther's spiritual attitude, the question still remains: By what right did the Protestant theologians and the

---

[3] August Twesten, *Vorlesungen über die Dogmatik der evangelisch-lutherischen Kirche* (1828), Vol. I.

Protestant churches in general follow Luther? The mere fact that one man had found in that way the solution of his problem does not imply that his was a normative solution of Christian perplexity, nor would the fact that Luther was personally right automatically mean that his way could be considered as appropriate for others.

The point is that Protestantism has a theological ground for existence only when it can be taken for granted that Luther played an extraordinary and unique role in the redemptive work of the risen Christ (i.e., holy history). A purely historical evaluation of the Reformer would signify the doom of Protestantism. For, although everybody is free to form a religious organization if he is able to enlist people for it, no man is capable of establishing a church in the New Testament sense, since the church is a spiritual entity which has its origin in the ministry of Jesus and derives its life and strength from the Spirit who continues the ministry of the risen Lord on earth. Hence the only ones who could deny that the Roman Catholic church is the church of Christ are those who also deny that the church had anything to do with the Jesus of history (as is held by Bultmann[4]), and even in that case they must postulate a spiritual origin of the church, if their own faith is to be not only psychologically but also metaphysically relevant. Few, of course, would deny that Luther was one of the outstanding men both in the history of Germany and also of mankind. His work left its lasting imprint upon the German language and German civilization, and his fight for the freedom of conscience is one of the most important landmarks in the genesis of modern man. Nevertheless, all the historical achievements of the Wittenberg Reformer would not suffice to support Protestantism's right of continued existence; on the contrary, Troeltsch and his followers, who took a purely historical view of Luther, were quite consistent in their

---

[4] Rudolf Bultmann, *Jesus Christ and Mythology* (New York: Charles Scribner's Sons, 1958); *Das Verhältnis der urchristlichen Christusbotschaft zum historischen Jesus* (2nd ed.; Heidelberg, 1961).

contention that, understood thus, the Protestantism of the Reformation had to outgrow itself in order to become modern man's religion.

Neither is Luther's real contribution to Christianity to be sought in the field of theological scholarship. Historians who compare Luther with Augustine have difficulty finding analogies in Luther's writings to the penetrating and inquisitive mind of the Bishop of Hippo—his wonderful diction, his subtle distinctions, and the breadth of his historical and philosophical perspective. This is not to minimize Luther's greatness as a theological thinker. While he never intended to write a systematic presentation of his thought comparable to the *Summa* of Thomas Aquinas, he excels over many others by the depth of his probing mind and the boldness with which he faces the perplexities of this world. Nevertheless, even if one of the highest places of honor were assigned to "Brother Martin," this distinction would not suffice to justify the separate existence of Protestantism. No theology, no matter how great or sublime it may be, is by itself a sufficient reason for destroying the unity of the church.

Still others hold that it is the depth and boldness of Luther's spiritual experience that has set an example which Protestants have deemed worthy of adoption. Here lies the answer to our problem, provided the meaning of his experience is rightly understood. Like the great thinkers of the Renaissance, Luther, the Reformer, was in quest of himself. But he had his own way of asking the question. Other seekers have been vexed by the conflict between human spontaneity and the constraining influence of the cosmic powers: How is man ever able to live his own life when he finds himself hemmed in on all sides and conditioned by material factors and social pressure? For others it is the question of man's ability to transcend his congenital nature and to raise himself above all other creatures. Luther's problem is neither that of freedom of action nor of self-transcendence, but that of man's divine destination. How shall a person ever be able to live in communion with God when God himself seems to be the cause which prevents him from attaining the destination which God has chosen for him? For is it not true that man has been placed by God into a world in which everything seems to move him away from God?

The boldness of Luther's question has been matched by very few thinkers. Gautama Buddha might be mentioned in this connection, and Paul, of course; perhaps Nietzsche. But what made Luther a reformer is not the excessive boldness of his question but his determination to endure the despair of his perplexity and to wait for that solution which would bring him full certainty. A comparison of Luther and Nietzsche is very rewarding in this respect. Nietzsche too is concerned with the quest for his true self and he is finally driven to the daring question: If there is a God how can I endure life without being God? [5] However, instead of waiting for the answer, which would probably have rendered him the greatest of all philosophers, he rushed in his impatience to the naive postulate: God is dead. On this basis he philosophized, unable ever to transcend the realm of his own mind. One admires and enjoys the play of his genial imagination and the cultivated beauty of his style. But his fantasies prevent him from ever seeing his own predicament.

Luther overcomes the temptation to which so many moderns succumb: to find satisfaction in the uncertainty and frustration of his perplexity. Is not this the plight of so many artists and thinkers in our time? They are properly disillusioned after probing the hollow claims of present-day leaders, their superficial questions and the cheap satisfaction with which they indulge themselves. In angry reply these younger contemporaries tell us in their works what this world looks like to them: dissonance instead of harmony, dismemberment instead of unity, chaos instead of order, worthlessness beneath a deceptive surface of brilliance and glamor, ignorance covered by pretense, hopeless-

---

[5] *Nietzsches Werke, Klassiker Ausgabe,* Vol. VI, *Also Sprach Zarathustra,* Vorrede 3; Teil II, p. 130; Teil IV, p. 148. Cf. *Thus Spake Zarathustra,* trans. A. Tille (New York, 1906).

ness and impotence concealed by an armor of newspaper. Inasmuch as this picture of perplexity is motivated by a quest for truth and a radical refusal to accept any substitute, it is all for the good. But there is this difference. Luther considered his crisis as an unbearable condition under which he was sighing and suffering, and in which he was longing for the true reality, whereas the modern artist seems to find satisfaction in his negativism, particularly in his radical denunciation of those who pretend not to have lost their belief in life. Beatniks and others apparently make a virtue of being unhappy and living in utter uncertainty. As a result the new quest ends in an utterly subjective existentialism which pretends to be superior to any objective truth.

Luther, in turn, was determined to endure the agony of his uncertainty because it resulted from his belief in God. He finally heard God speaking to him through the Scriptures and thus he learned that the solution to his problem was to be found in the grace of God as it condescends to man in Jesus Christ. The power of God that frightened him, because the Legislator had his omnipotence at hand to punish the transgressor, paradoxically revealed its overwhelming might in forgiving love. Luther's experience would be misinterpreted, however, if it were described as a passing period of crisis which was part of his monastic life and was definitely overcome in about 1517. Having once for all refused to be comforted by the theological and devotional devices which his church had at its disposal, he could not fail to be aware of the danger of objectivizing the word that God had spoken to him. The difficulty one has in characterizing Luther's theology has its roots in his willingness time and again to be thrown back into doubt and perplexity. For the rest of his life he was distrustful both of his own nature and of the wisdom of men who were looking for an easy or effective solution of the problems which the Reformation had engendered. Instead he would turn to the Bible and wait again and again for new light coming from God. While it is true that Luther constantly quotes certain verses of the Bible which had become especially dear to him, he is not a Biblicist in the sense that from a single biblical passage he infers what ought to be done or taught in a given situation. He is aware of his constant need of direct divine guidance, although it comes to him through the Scripture.

This is the reason why his disagreement with the church of Rome grew in the course of the years. He was not the first to be frightened by the weight of sin, the horror of death, the incomprehensible disorder of this world. But he was unable to follow his predecessors because, in his opinion, they sought for the solution in the wrong place. They took their condition as their starting point and hence would find satisfaction in anything that would alleviate their burden. Luther, however, insists that it is God's inescapable will which has brought us into this predicament. Thus no relative improvement of the human condition can be considered a way out of the damnation in which man finds himself. God alone can help.

The assurance that man's predicament is rendered tolerable and meaningful by the fact that God himself is speaking through the Bible to those who wait for him was understood by Luther as implying a divine commission. Unlike the mystics, he realized that when God assures us of his grace he thereby puts the individual under obligation to serve him with the divine gift. This sense of commission explains the boldness and the unwavering straightforwardness with which Luther then entered into the general affairs of the church and public life, and thus became the Reformer. Because he sought no self-chosen comfort for himself, as most of the medieval saints had done, but rather God's own light, he could not keep the word of God for himself once it had come to him. This final illumination Luther understood as a divine call. As soon as the opportunity arose—when Tetzel sold indulgences—Luther raised his voice in protest, not so much against the Curia, from which Tetzel had received his commission, as against the underlying erroneous concept of man's relation to God. Luther never entertained any doubt concerning the purely spiritual character of his vocation. He was greatly interested in the political and social problems of his age, but he steadfastly declined offers from various political groups to become their banner carrier. Luther's urgent admonitions for radical changes reveal him as a German patriot, but he was primarily a leader who insisted that the spiritual reform must come first.

In this divine call and commission of Luther we see the root of the Reformation. If he had surpassed his predecessors merely by the depth of his spiritual experience, the church would have had good reason for worshiping him as a saint; instead he stands condemned in the eyes of Rome for having broken the unity of the church. But Luther knew that the irresistible "madness" that made him bear his witness before the emperor at the Diet of Worms was a divine imperative which he had no right to disobey, irrespective of what the consequences might be for himself. This assurance of his calling led him through the rest of his life. Had it not been for his determination to rely exclusively upon God's bidding, Luther would probably have ended in megalomania. His faith, however, kept him humble and saved him from claiming any credit for himself. Luther placed himself completely under the word that had disclosed itself to him. He had no ambition to match Thomas Aquinas or Duns Scotus, nor did he boast that he was offering a new and superior theology. All he wanted to accomplish was to make the word of God generally recognized. He did not pretend to have ecstasies or mystical insights or to hear angelic voices. In that respect he differed significantly from Swedenborg, who could boast to have been "constantly and continuously in the company of spirits and of angels, hearing them speak and speaking with them in turn." [6] Nor could he match Joseph Smith to whom God spoke personally in a pillar of light and sent the angel Moroni, who showed him the golden plates upon which the Book of Mormon was written. But the apparent advantage which these men have over Luther has an-

---

[6] Emanuel Swedenborg, *Arcana Coelestia*, Vol. I, 4 (Standard ed.; New York, 1933) p. 2.

other side. In order to become a Swedenborgian or Mormon, one has to accept as truthful the otherwise unverifiable reports of the extraordinary experiences of their founders.

In turn, what made Luther popular so rapidly, and what resulted eventually in the coming into existence of Protestantism, was the fact that Luther did not make any special claim for himself personally. Rather he contended that anybody who would adopt his understanding of faith, the act of waiting for God's speaking to him, would share his experience. Approached in this manner the word of God would authenticate its truthfulness and power to every believer. Thus Luther's significance for the life of the church, far from lying in his remarkable experience, is in his ability to convey to others his encounter with the word of God as a typical implication of faith. It was this God-given ability which made him a reformer, and Protestantism's right of existence rests on his calling for this task. His life work proves that, like those of apostles, prophets, evangelists, and teachers, the office of the reformer is instituted by Christ. The event of the Reformation is evidence of the fact that Christ himself cares for the continuing purity and efficacy of his church.

When we consider that Luther thought of himself in terms of mission and commission rather than in terms of personal attainment, there is little sense in raising the question: Who was greater, Luther or Calvin? Neither of the two sought his own honor, and both realized that whatever they contributed to the life of the church was the work of God, who used them as servants. Nevertheless, inasmuch as holy history is history too, the fact cannot be overlooked that the divine call came to Luther first. There would have been no Zwingli or Calvin or the two dozen other men who stood in the center of the Reformation movement, had not Luther patiently endured the agony of his perplexity until God finally rewarded his faithfulness. Because his position was not based upon mere theory but rather upon factual truth, its proclamation stirred the masses over the whole of Europe and made of them a new type of men. So evident was that truth of God that even Rome felt compelled to undergo a radical transformation. There is a wide hiatus between the church of the Middle Ages and the church of Rome after the Council of Trent, one which continues to grow. Whereas Rome has paid little attention to developments in the Eastern Orthodox churches, she has been constantly disturbed and challenged by her coexistence with Protestantism. History confirms our view that Protestantism is a process which not only takes place within the church, but is also a decisive event in God's redemptive history.

The momentous significance of Luther's witness does not blind us to the merits of those who even before him had insisted upon the necessity of a radical change in the church. Others before him had pointed warningly to moral laxity in clergy and laity, to lust for power and greed in the hierarchy, to routine in spiritual life, and to the church's encroachment on political life. But all the reforms advocated or accomplished in the Middle Ages from Bernard of Clairvaux down to Luther's own age were planned on the basis of the Catholic system. They merely envisaged stricter discipline and deeper spirituality. None of these pre-Reformation reformers thought of searching for a remedy that God himself would offer to his church. Very significantly both the Waldensian church and the Hussite movement were originally intra-Catholic developments. They realized the necessity of a radical transformation when they were confronted with Luther's Reformation.

The early Protestant movement was fully aware of Luther's providential role, and they extolled him as the "Man of God." In turn, the fact that his opponents not only vilified his conduct but saw in him a messenger of the devil indicates their awareness that the Reformation could not be explained in purely historical terms. It is hardly by chance that a Catholic scholar, Ernst Walter Zeeden, has called our attention to this forgotten fact.[7]

---

[7] *Martin Luther und die Reformation im Urteil des deutschen Luthertums* (2 vols.; Freiburg, 1950-52), II, 1-18.

When Luther's friend and colleague Bugenhagen preached the funeral service for Luther he reminded his audience that through the work of the Reformer Christ had triumphed. Similarly, Michael Coelius in another funeral sermon speaks of the *Amt*, the divine office of his master, and as late as October 30, 1617, the great theologian Johann Gerhard in a public disputation defended Luther's ministry and reformation as the outcome of a special divine vocation. This fact strikingly confirms our interpretation of the Reformation. The father of Lutheran orthodoxy was fully aware of the fact that Protestantism was to be seen in the framework of *Heilsgeschichte*.

For Luther and his immediate successors, the Reformation was a new beginning that Christ had made in his church. That explains the otherwise inconsistent manner in which they speak of the church from which they were expelled as the "Mother Church." Reformation was to them evidence of the interest the risen Lord took in his church. As a result of the way in which the church developed in the Middle Ages, the work of Christ had been reduced to an event of the past, whose continuation was entrusted to Christ's Vicar seated upon the chair of St. Peter in Rome. This does not mean that during those times the church had entirely lost its substance and had become a synagogue of Satan. It would be childish to interpret a thousand or more years of church history as a mere manifestation of unbelief and apostasy, or to explain the formation of the papal position as the outcome of lust for power only. It is the immemorial merit of the papal institution that over against all kinds of heresies and schismatic tendencies it has made a firm stand for the oneness of the church. Because Luther was aware of that role played by the medieval church, he did not lightheartedly accept the fact that the Reformation was rending the church in a seemingly irreparable way. Yet his awareness of the present Christ was the reason Luther was never encumbered with a sense of guilt when he thought of his work. It was Christ's will to manifest himself, and thus he could be trusted to care for those who followed him upon the new way he had opened; for the Christ who speaks directly to those who read the Bible, and who engenders faith in their hearts, is also the Christ who makes them strong and willing to fight Satan, who in his fury desires to destroy the church. It is this same Christ who so guides his church that his saving will finally triumphs in it. Applied to the historical circumstances, this assurance implied the conviction that, through Luther, Christ had added a new branch to his church.

CHAPTER V

PROTESTANTISM'S QUEST
AND LUTHER

A. PROTESTANTISM AND LUTHER

1. Holy History

We have now reached the point at which our opening question, Is there such an entity as the Protestant church? can be answered. Within the ecumenical movement a purely sociological or historical approach to the problem would make no sense because the churches with which union is sought, namely, the Eastern Orthodox and the Roman Catholic, consider themselves to be the work of the risen Lord. Thus the historical event of the origin of Protestantism must be envisaged from the vantage point of holy history. That is why Luther's basic spiritual experience has been discussed in such detail. As long as Luther's significance is seen only in the realm of politics, culture, or theology we may be able to understand why his followers organized themselves into religious groups, but these congregations would be incommensurable with the two ancient churches.

Yet even the fact that Luther believed God was speaking to him through the Bible would not be sufficient ground for considering the various groups of his followers as churches. All the founders of religions have claimed to be in touch with the divine. Only when it can be shown that Luther was God's instrument in the context of holy history can we expect the ancient churches to consider Protestants as their equals. For this reason we were concerned to show that the Reformation was an event originating in the midst of the medieval church and called forth not by a defection from it but out of a genuine understanding of its way of salvation. Luther's protest against the Curia was not raised at the beginning of the Reformation, nor did Luther intend to question the spiritual authority of the Pope. The protest became necessary, however, when Rome was unwilling to admit the genuineness of Luther's experience. Luther's eagerness in the early years of the Reformation to convince his adversaries that his understanding of the gospel was in full accord with the Christian principles invoked by them is well known. Their lack of understanding proved eventually, however, that with its message the Reformation had made a new departure in holy history. Eventually it became evident that there was no hope of finding a home for Protestantism within the framework of the Roman Catholic church.

Under such circumstances Luther was justified in interpreting the new basis of salvation which he had discovered as a manifestation of Christ's concern for his church. The time had come when, in addition to the two ancient churches, a new branch of Christ's church was to make its appearance in history. The specific role which Luther himself played in holy history was thereby manifested. Within the Reformation movement he was the originator, that is, one of those rare people through whom an entirely new process in history is begun. His work determined the whole subsequent development. The accomplishment of an originator can be continued, criticized, modified, altered, corrected, or improved, but it cannot be repeated. Once a discovery has been made and publicly announced, for instance, all subsequent activity in its specific field is dependent on it. Even those who disagree find themselves under obligation to express their own view in terms that refer to the new historical factor. Thus Roman Catholicism has found it necessary since the days of the Reformation to state its views explicitly or implicitly in contradistinction to those of Protestantism or in anticipation of possible Protestant criticism.

The originator differs from the innovator by the fact that the latter alters only the form or expression given to an established principle, whereas the originator activates a new principle. That Luther was a true originator is evidenced by the fact that Protestantism is not a mere imitation of what Luther has done; rather people are Protestants insofar as they have come under the influence of the new principle of Christian life enunciated by him. In Luther's case, however, the epoch-making achievement is not the product of his personality, no matter how powerfully it may have tinged his work, but rather the action Christ has performed through him. Had Christ not manifested his redemptive work through Luther's word, no such overwhelming change as the Reformation would have taken place. In turn, however, since no other originator has appeared yet in holy history, the people who want to be Christians have no choice except to join one of the two Catholic churches or Protestantism. There is no way of stopping the progress of the work of an originator, once it has been performed, though in secular history it is of limited duration only. No substitute or replacement is available for an originator either. Once he has opened the gate for a new process his work goes on. For that reason men like Calvin and Luther cannot be compared as far as their significance for holy history is concerned. We do not disparage Calvin's greatness as teacher, administrator, and statesman when we refuse him the title of originator. His work, for all its independence, was erected on the foundation Luther had laid.

2. THE PROTESTANT CHURCH

Seen as the manifestation of Christ's redemptive will, the Reformation implies an entirely new view of the church. But this fact would not by itself suffice to establish the existence of a Protestant church which would be on a par with that of Rome and Eastern Orthodoxy. The new view of the church might simply form the basis of an intrinsic development within the church as was the case with the Waldensians or the Franciscan *Spirituales* in the Middle Ages. Protestantism has always claimed to have an independent basis of existence; but too frequently the reasons given for its right of existence were unsatisfactory when measured by the idea of the church found in the New Testament.

For instance, Cyprian's pertinent statement that there can be no salvation apart from the church was interpreted by Protestant scholars as evidence of an early appearance of Roman Catholic heresy. Luther, however, was in agreement with the ancient Bishop of Carthage, as can be learned from the intimate way in which the presence of Christ is tied up in Luther's thought with the means of grace and the ministry. But in the eyes of later generations this connection seemed to be a residue of Luther's Catholicism that had to be eliminated in order to render Protestantism consistent and modern. Beginning in the second half of the eighteenth century Luther was praised primarily for advocating "freedom of conscience," meaning the unmediated, direct contact of the individual believer with God. Of course, passages abound in Luther's writings in which he extols the glorious freedom of the believer. But in his "On Christian Liberty" Luther also points out that true liberty implies bondage too.

The modern understanding of freedom of conscience omits the latter feature. It contends that a Christian's religious thinking, while beginning from Holy Scripture, is free to choose how much of the Bible the individual Christian accepts as binding, and the individual decides what course of action he adopts in order to give expression to his faith. But it is obvious that this advocacy of freedom, if it is not to degenerate into an uninhibited subjectivism, requires an authoritative principle by which the individual's choice is governed. It is equally obvious that rationalism was mistaken in seeking that principle in "natural religion" or "natural ethics," that is to say, in the guiding function of reason. But a mere appeal to the voice of the Holy Spirit speaking in and to the individual's heart is not satisfactory either. The *testimonium Spiritus Sancti internum* is a mere cloak of subjectivism unless we recognize a criterion by which the voice of the Holy

Spirit can be distinguished from the various voices of the individual's unconscious aspirations and desires.

Here we reach the crucial point of our investigation. What do we mean by the voice of the Spirit, or by Christ's speaking to the believer? Is it a mental sense of assurance which merely adds authority to our subjective opinions and sentiments? Or is it the disclosure of a hitherto unknown sphere of reality, the opening up of the significance of Christ's redemptive work for us, a fact made manifest for the benefit of those who had been unable to find the assurance of their salvation within the framework of the Catholic system? The former view would make the church superfluous, but in turn it raises the pertinent question, How relevant is such a mental sense of assurance for our salvation? Do we as Christians start from the assumption that life is characterized by wholeness, or at least that we may take our redemption for granted? Yet what right do we have to assume with modern sentimentalism that since God is good or God is love, he cannot or must not let any man perish? And how realistic is a view of God that sees him interested in our after-life only, while this world must take care of itself or is well taken care of by man? The freedom of the believer, as Luther understood it, is related to man's salvation. It designates the assurance that as far as the real meaning of my life is concerned I must not be deluded by the apparent superiority of the cosmic powers, nor worry about my own inadequacy or the lack of fitness of those who work in the service of Christ. For it is exclusively through his power that I am saved.

But thus understood as the means of salvation, the Christian faith implies the recognition of my spiritual dependence on the church. If my life is to have true meaning it is not enough for me to be a member of the church as an institution. Rather I must take part in her life. The only way a person can become aware of Christ's saving will is through the means of grace, for it is through them that Christ manifests himself. They do not save us, not even in an indirect way as the Catholic church teaches, but in their ministerial function they are indispensable for the individual's contact with Christ. In turn, however, the believer's salvation does not depend on the specific material which comprises the means of grace. For their specific efficacy, it makes no difference, for example, whether fermented or unleavened bread, wine or grape juice be employed in the Eucharist, or whether I read the Bible in the original languages or a translation. What makes them indispensable, however, is their function of mediating the grace of Christ. The only limit set in this respect is their appropriateness for their function. The elements of the sacraments and the sacramental rite must symbolize what is happening in them, and a translation of the Bible must faithfully follow the original languages. In this relationship between material substratum and form on the one hand, and redemptive function on the other, we discern the specific character of the new view of the church introduced by the Reformation. While no church can completely dispense with outward visible organization and activity, these nevertheless derive their necessity from their function as signs. They point to the saving work of Christ. The signs apply the work of Christ to the lives of the believers.

Protestant discussion of the church has often been confused because the function of the church as the sign of Christ's redemptive work was misunderstood. With one section of Protestantism this resulted in the dogma of the invisible church. At best the advocates of this view would ascribe a pedagogical function to the historical organized church: it must prepare children and immature believers for a full-fledged life of faith. Others in turn have made the means of grace in their material existence the essence of the church. While the church should be permanently anxious to use the means of grace in such a manner that through their celebration people would be led to Christ himself, their function as signs to redemption has occasionally been obscured. Protestants, too, have often held that the form in which the means of grace are offered is the thing that matters. As a result, people were more concerned with the theology of the efficacy of the

Eucharist than with its actual effects, or with the doctrine of biblical inspiration than with the inspired content of the Bible. It should be obvious that in the light of the New Testament view of the church many of the theological controversies in Protestantism have been pitifully irrelevant. Of course, investigating the most appropriate way of giving theological expression to God's redemptive work is important, since people might be misled into false religion as a result of inappropriate teaching. But so frequently the contending theologians would present their view as though it were itself the subject matter of faith, whereas it should serve as a sign pointing to Christ, in whom we believe.

Since the Lord acts through the means of grace directly upon those believers who are anxious to find him there, we have a right to speak of a Protestant church, because its activities and resources are derived from Christ as head. But unlike Eastern Orthodoxy which is held together by the common allegiance to the conciliar principle, or the church of Rome which has its bond of unity in the hierarchy and the Pope, Protestantism has no visible unity. The unifying function of the risen Christ is only indirectly recognized: all believers believe in his presence and his redemptive work, though each from his special position, and with a particular perspective. Thus the Protestant denominations are like so many points on the circumference of a circle, all of which look toward its center.

3. The Flexibility of the Church

The Protestant principle of church unity explains the historical flexibility of the Protestant church as compared with the rigidity with which the two Catholic churches treat matters of theology and church polity. While the Protestant church implies the necessity of organization, it allows for various forms of church polity provided they are in agreement with the two basic requirements of church life, namely, fellowship of the believers and a ministry. By means of them the church fulfills its obligation to take care of the spiritual needs of its members and to bear witness to Christ's saving message in the world. Similarly there is room in the Protestant church for both diversity in theology and for historical development of the doctrines taught. While human presumptuousness has contended from time to time that a certain type of theology was to be accepted as absolutely true, history has silenced such contentions. How fast even the most orthodox theology becomes obsolete and is finally forgotten! The fact that Lutheran and Reformed Orthodoxy were not identical with the teaching of the Reformers has, therefore, never shaken the Lutheran and Reformed belief in their ongoing identity in history and in their right of existence.

Such flexibility does not obliterate the distinction between truth and falsehood or sound and heretical doctrine. Since Protestant theology derives its flexibility from the fact that it is the human understanding and explanation of the work of the present Christ, any theological endeavor that loses sight of its objective forfeits its claim to be tolerated as Protestant theology. Inevitably also the theologian's historical and personal position enters into the making of theology. As a result man's basic perplexity and quest for certainty will not be described by all theologians in the manner Luther experienced it. In the history of Protestantism and in the development of the denominations this fact is particularly conspicuous in the role assigned to the awareness of one's sinfulness. While in some circles it forms the center of Christian concern, it plays but a subordinate role in others. But here again it is obvious that a theology in which the atoning work of Christ is completely ignored, places itself outside of the Protestant fold.

The same observation applies to the use made of the Bible. Belief in the Bible as a means of grace applies to the Bible in its totality rather than to any special book or passage in the Bible. The Protestant view of Scripture implies that there is a common message underlying the whole of Scripture. Yet, when God speaks to the believer through the words of the Bible, it is not the Bible in its totality which has such an effect, but a certain book, and at times a single verse, as did Romans 3:28 in the case of Luther. Thus it is not surprising that each believer might have his favorite book in the Bible, nor is any harm done thereby as long as this selectiveness gives expression to his experience of the Christ speaking to him. The fact that critical scholarship tends to reduce the area of relevant revelation to certain portions of the Bible is not by itself heretical. It becomes unbearable, however, when it is combined with the contention that Christ can be found only in those passages which have been left over after the critical reductions, e.g., in the earliest layers of the gospel tradition.

The diversity resulting from this flexibility is not to be identified with subjectivism; for the diversity is tolerable only when it is accompanied by a common awareness of belonging together. It is in the fellowship of dependence on and allegiance to Christ that the denominations support and supplement each other. The rejection of the sacraments, for instance, on the part of Quakerism, would seriously impair that denomination but for the fact that it is and wants to stay in the Protestant community. Thus it is constantly—though perhaps unconsciously—influenced by the faith of people who by the use of the sacraments are made sure of the grace of Christ. In general the specific work of the Holy Spirit performed in any one denomination will be felt in all the other denominations too because the Spirit is one. In our day, for instance, the renewed interest of many churches in the healing power of the Holy Spirit or in the gift of tongues may be a result of Pentecostalism. In turn, however, any denomination which pretends to stand on its own feet and to be the Christian church while contending to have nothing in common with other churches has thereby placed itself outside of Christ. It hopes to be saved on the basis of specific ideas accepted about Christ and the church rather than by Christ's grace.

However, since the limits within which flexibility may be safely practiced are not automatically recognized, it will be necessary within the Protestant church to differentiate between normative and irregular Protestantism. There are individuals and groups who except for their awareness of belonging to the Protestant church show little regard for the oneness of the Protestant church. In the course of history many features in Protestantism, whose importance were clearly recognized during the Reformation period, are now taken for granted. The shift from a religion of redemption to mere subjective religiosity is probably the most outstanding case in point. What was for the Reformers an evidence of the grace of Christ, is interpreted later on as being of the substance of human life or the necessary outcome of history. That is why it is so difficult to say, in certain cases, whether or not a religious group which calls itself Christian is entitled to do so. In turn, an attitude which is determined by the factors which the Reformers viewed as constituting the Protestant church is designated "normative Protestantism."

Nevertheless this distinction between normative and irregular Protestantism does not mean that a normative denomination has the infallibility claimed by the Roman church. Even such a denomination is likely to overrate its specific features or to fail to give full consideration to certain aspects of the Reformation which were originally constitutive of Protestantism. For this reason the emphasis we have placed upon the experience of Luther does not convey primacy to the Lutheran churches within Protestantism. Their historical nearness to Luther did not save them, for instance, from the deadening intellectualism of orthodox theology. Historically, Lutheranism is but one of the many offshoots of the Reformation and thus shares the onesidedness of all the Protestant denominations. This is not to deny the special significance Lutheranism has had for the development of the Protestant church. Together with Calvinism it has upheld the necessity of normative Protestantism against many centrifugal tendencies, particularly during the last two centuries. Nor could the importance of the Luther Renaissance for our age be overrated. The study of the earlier writings of the Reformer has served to bring to light both the basic significance Luther's perplexity and quest for certainty had for the genesis of the Reformation, and the specific emphasis and dynamic of the new movement. Luther's later writings often obscure these aspects because they are concerned with specific problems of contemporary theology and ethics. Next to Karl Barth's insistence on a theocentric faith it was the Luther Renaissance which finally stopped the spread of Protestant subjectivism.

It is a matter of record that neither Luther nor the other Reformers were from the outset aware of the fact that the Reformation had given birth to a new church. No wonder then that in their desire to become aware of the identity of their movement they spent a good deal of energy and time on attacks directed against the church of Rome. They believed it was their task to purify and improve that church. Even at present some Protestants seem to believe that the essence of Protestantism is the protest against Romanism. It is obvious that on such a basis there could be no hope at all for a united church which would include Rome. Yet through the ecumenical movement we learn that, in God's providence, Protestantism is not meant to be a corrective of the Catholic church but a new branch of the church of Christ which has its own formative principle.

B. THE QUEST FOR ONENESS

1. Self-Scrutiny

The ecumenical movement has created an unexpected problem for the Protestant denominations. Early in this century the first advocates of church unity were more or less agreed on the individualistic understanding of Protestantism. A concept of the church like that found in the Roman Catholic or the Eastern Orthodox churches seemed to contradict the Protestant notion of faith. As has been shown, churches and denominations were appreciated for the practical services they rendered to their members, yet no spiritual function was ascribed to them. It was not by chance that the first effective call for unity came from the mission field, and accordingly church unity was interpreted as comity coupled with a timid beginning of cooperation. The

Stockholm Conference of 1925 was devoted to problems of social ethics and did not transcend the aim of the first Edinburgh Mission conference of 1911. The churchmen assembled in the Swedish capital asked themselves what contribution their churches could make to public life and morals in a world which began to show serious symptoms of de-Christianization.

The Lausanne Conference on Faith and Order in 1927, however, confronted the Protestant denominations with a new problem. Is churchhood an essential element of saving faith? Few of those present at Lausanne were then aware of the seriousness this problem had for the Anglo-Catholic and Eastern Orthodox delegates. The concern which the conference felt over the "scandal of disunity" was, in the opinion of the majority of the delegates, a moral one. It had to do with the indifference which the denominations were showing for each other and the prevalent sense of self-complacency in the churches. But once the real theological problem had been raised, it was there to stay in the ecumenical movement. Of course, it is true that the slogan "Let the church be the church" was understood for quite some time in European churches as meaning merely that the church should resist the temptation, powerful particularly in America, to concentrate one-sidedly on social action and propaganda. Over against this attitude the churches admonished each other to focus their attention upon spiritual matters, in particular upon evangelism and a deepened understanding of worship. Such a view, however, bypasses the theological problems and thus has no direct bearing on ecumenical relations. It is compatible with a one-sided interest in merely practical cooperation. Characteristic of the continuance of this outlook was the unexpected suggestion made in 1961 by some Episcopalian and Presbyterian leaders in the United States of America to the effect that their denominations should consider union, although no rapprochement had taken place either in the spiritual or in the theological field.

However, if there is such a thing as a Protestant church, then the objective of the ecumenical movement, at least as far as

Protestantism is concerned, must undergo a radical change. First of all, each of the Protestant denominations has to ask itself what it means to be part of the Protestant church. This is not a purely theoretical problem that can be answered from an established theology. Rather it is a spiritual challenge which requires the willingness to raise the basic spiritual question with the same radicalism as did the Reformers. A further task will be to live with the vexing problem: How far can we claim to be a church without thereby denying the other ecumenical partners their right of existence?

Rome and Eastern Orthodoxy have rightly seen that continuity is an essential feature of the church. Yet continuity is more than merely an uninterrupted historical flow, as it has so often been interpreted in modern Protestantism. Rather it requires a permanent connection of a church in its present state with the formative principle by which it has been brought into being. That is the reason why the Roman Catholic church attempts to interpret its own history, which to the outsider seems to be merely a sequence of responses to outside stimuli, as the gradual emergence of latent elements which were there from the beginning. This interpretation obviously begs the question. Likewise, however, the recourse to the Scripture, while essential for the existence of the church of Christ here on earth, will not suffice to give to any of the three main churches their right of existence. Protestantism has its originating principle in Luther's experience as a Reformer.

Yet how can we be sure not only that the Reformers were in the unbroken continuity of the church, but that we too are in it? The Anglican church is quick to answer that its continuity is safeguarded by the uninterrupted apostolic succession. But even if we concede that it is possible for a denomination to give indisputable proof of the apostolic succession of its bishops, how would that fact guarantee the kind of continuity we are looking for? Suppose the succession is an established fact in terms of canon law, would the legal requirement carry with it an unadulterated spiritual continuity? The Danish bishop Grundtvig, who was also worried by the problem of continuity, believed that it was built upon *homologia* and sacramental practice.[1] But in view of the enormous changes that the Christian doctrines have undergone since the days of the apostles, what more does the continuity of *homologia* mean than a general belief in Jesus? Furthermore, since the sacraments have been interpreted differently in Jewish and Gentile Christianity, in Byzantium and Rome, in Wittenberg and Geneva, is sacramental continuity anything more than the preservation of certain rites whose meaning has changed constantly? It is obvious that continuity must be based upon something more spiritual than is sought in these attempts.

However, the permanent connection of a denomination with its basic principle, upon which we see the continuity of the church established, is not identical with a constant awareness of its historical root either. If there were a necessary prerequisite, the Protestant church would have vanished from history long ago, for there have been considerable periods of its history when obviously nobody cared what the origin of Protestantism had been, and whole denominations would even deny that they had anything to do with Luther's experience. Nevertheless, the Spirit operates in a church through its institutional life and the means of grace, and since the historical principle is embodied in them a denomination remains related to the Reformation even when its members are spiritually blind and unaware of their origin. This explains why reconsideration of a denomination's origin, at whatever moment of its history it may take place, does not so much establish contemporaneity with its historical root but makes it aware of what has been its operating principle all the time.

Luther himself stated the meaning of his experience in a number of different ways, placing the emphasis at times on the human side (How can I find a gracious God?) and sometimes on the

---

[1] Hal Koch, *Grundtvig*, trans. Llewellyn Jones (Yellow Springs, Ohio: Antioch Press, 1952).

divine side (How can God justify human existence?). However, as has been shown, it was Luther's growing awareness of the incomprehensibility of the relationship in which God stood to man that drove him to despair, and it was in turn Luther's experience of God speaking his word of comfort in that situation that formed the basis of the Reformation. The task that results from this originating experience for any Protestant denomination in the present ecumenical context is to scrutinize itself in order to find out to what extent its specific features are related to the basic principle of the Reformation. We have pointed out how in the history of Protestantism new denominations have sprung into being in which the grace of God and the sufficiency of human life were taken for granted. But in such a case people were not directly confronted with God but merely with the theology of the Lutheran or Reformed church, which they modified on the basis of rational considerations or emotional urges.

The scrutiny which is thus demanded must not necessarily lead to the conclusion that Methodism or dispensationalism or any other newer denomination must disappear. Without predicting what the exact change will be, we can state with certainty that all the Protestant denominations will look radically different after such self-scrutiny, because in its light their institutional and devotional life and their theology will tend to be seen as nothing but an expression of faith. But how can true faith be known? It has been said that the test of true faith is the willingness of the people concerned to fight and to die for it. Such criteria are misleading, however. How many people have fought for their own interests or defended delusions! It is more accurate to say that the true believer is a person who is willing to be different from all the rest of mankind because he is determined to forego all things that in the eyes of the world render life meaningful and to rely exclusively on the grace of God.

Yet the Protestant principle would be completely misunderstood if it led to the conclusion that denominations and theological propositions were worthless. Belief in the doctrine of the exclusive grace of God would still be far from a direct confrontation with God. On the contrary, a person holding such a belief would cling to a mental image of God that had been abstracted from the theology of the Reformation and thus would rest exclusively on a historical position. In turn, however, a radical self-scrutiny on the part of a denomination is likely to bring to light the fact that its emphasis has been concentrated on matters which should have been means for developing faith and Christian life, yet which in the traditions of that denomination came eventually to be considered basic requirements of faith. This is true even of the Bible. Not that the Protestant church could ever dispense with it. But even among those who hold that the Bible requires faith in order to be the word of God for us, how seldom is it that this requirement has been understood as referring to trust in God's grace alone? Instead the efficacy of the Bible has, by some, been made dependent on one's assent to certain statements found in the Bible, while others demand a certain level of spirituality or holiness. In such instances people try to erect obstacles to the free operation of God's grace and the work of his Spirit.

When, as a result of a thorough and radical scrutiny of one's way of religion, the grace of God is finally apprehended, the whole perspective of such a denomination will be changed. In some cases it will be seen that the coming into existence of one's group was the result of historical circumstances which may or may not continue to exist and which, in all circumstances, must be relegated to a subordinate position, as, for instance, the ethnic character of the various Lutheran groups who came to the United States in the middle of the nineteenth century. Because all their members are now using the English language, they are giving up their original organization and are merging into larger bodies in accordance with theological affinities. Similarly, such self-scrutiny may bring to light the fact that personal dissension among its members was often the reason behind a denomination's origin, as was the case in numerous Baptist groups. Self-examination then must lead to an attempt to find out whether, in the light of a deepened understanding of faith, the specific spiritual emphasis of one's group still requires the existence of a special denomination, or whether it should not rather make itself felt as an urge within a comprehensive denomination. Obviously the rationale for independent existence cannot be found in the members' desire to continue the status quo in an unchanged manner. Such subjective motivation would be an indication that the group had not yet been exposed to the necessary self-examination. The encounter with the living Christ is in every instance a challenge to the status quo of church and doctrine.

We have no doubt, however, that notwithstanding serious self-scrutiny there will be instances in which a denomination must reach the conclusion that the specific contribution it makes to the life of the Protestant church is sufficiently important to warrant its continued existence. The facile manner in which the termination of the Protestant denominations is advocated by some ecclesiastical leaders is a symptom of the modern belief in mammoth organizations rather than of a spiritual zeal for church unity. One criterion by which the right of existence of denominations is to be measured is the role they have played in holy history. Whenever it can be stated that the history of Protestantism would have been essentially different had it not been for the contribution made by a specific denomination, one is entitled to see in their role the work of the risen Lord. Such a denomination has a spiritual and historical right to independent existence and only two reasons could oblige it to terminate that existence: if that denomination repentantly realizes that it has irretrievably lost its original spiritual momentum and thus is no longer capable of making its specific contribution, or if it is obvious that the specific gift it has to impart has so completely become the common property of the whole Protestant church that no special denominational agency for its propagation is required.

Yet we have to reckon a priori with the likelihood that a number of denominations will feel bona fide entitled to continue their work because they bring out an aspect of the Christian faith which no other denomination represents, the complete absence of which would result in a serious impoverishment of Protestantism. Of course, such evaluation would apply to the present situation only and would not entail the necessity of a denomination's permanent existence. But in the light of contemporary experience one can safely state, for instance, that without the peace witness of Quakers, Mennonites, and Brethren, Protestantism would lack one of the essential marks of the gospel message. In turn, however, although the outcome of such self-examination may justify the continued existence of a denomination, it can never mean a continuation of what it was like prior to such scrutiny. Confrontation with the basic problem of faith will inevitably shake not only everything that was carried on merely by the momentum of tradition and in a purely conventional manner, but it will also question the understanding of the very authorities upon which the denomination had based its specific features.

A symptom of such scrutiny is the recent discussion of baptism. The real problem is no longer the question: Which mode of baptism is prescribed by the New Testament? It has been realized that the New Testament writers either were not troubled by that question or were not willing to make a general statement. What is really relevant is the question: What contribution is baptism intended to make to life under grace? The answer given to this question will determine the baptismal practice. In this connection one is reminded, for instance, of the foundational role which Luther in his spiritual afflictions ascribed to the fact that he had been baptized as an infant. He regarded the act of baptism as an evidence of the Spirit's calling and thus of the prevenient grace of God. In the light of past experiences, including those of the Reformers themselves, it is to be expected that every new self-examination will have revolutionary consequences. Many views and practices a denomination once deemed indispensable and once fiercely fought for will then appear to be of doubtful value, or even, though considered help-ful, be discarded as other alternatives present themselves.

Since in the past such self-examination took place within the confines of a denomination, the weight of historical tradition seemed to preclude any real change. Things appear different in the light of the ecumenical movement. The Anabaptist emphasis laid upon the Spirit, for instance, seemed to Luther to be incompatible with the sole authority of Holy Scripture. Closer contacts between the denominations have shown in the meantime, however, that the Mennonites are far from being *Schwärmer*, i.e., enthusiasts rejecting the authority of Scripture. Moreover, a deepened understanding of revelation has shown that the kerygma of the Primitive church not only antedates the New Testament chronologically but also forms its spiritual basis. Thus when Catholic theologians contend that it was the church that made the New Testament, we can confidently retort that the church would never have come into being apart from the organizing center it had in its kerygma, that is to say, in the God-given proclamation of Jesus as Lord or Messiah. Far less would the church have been in a position to form a canon, that is to say, an authoritative list of New Testament books, if it had not been guided by the kerygma. The kerygma, however, notwithstanding the fact that it is the work of the apostles, as far as its external form is concerned, is substantially the manifestation of God's redemptive will made known to men through the Holy Spirit. Thus in the final analysis the basis of every denomination is the kerygma, and not the Bible as such but the way in which the biblical revelation is apprehended in that denomination by means of God's Spirit. In turn, however, Lutheran and Reformed theology both realize that, as a result of an intellectualistic literalism, their exegesis has left untouched biblical treasures which the Spirit alone is able to grasp. Similarly, even those who were unwilling to adopt Barth as their guide in systematic theology have, after the study of his works, no longer been able to continue the anthropocentric trend so characteristic of the majority of Protestant theologians prior to World War I because they discovered that in his biblical exegesis Barth had penetrated into long neglected depths of God's dealing with man.

Paradoxically, one might say that notwithstanding the fact that he never viewed the ecumenical movement with much interest or sympathy, it was Barth who enabled Protestantism to react in an appropriate way to the ecumenical situation. Confronted with the institutional views of the church held by Rome and the Eastern Orthodox church, the Protestant denominations would have been able to react only on the organizational line, had not Barth's stress on the centrality of God delivered the Protestant concept of faith from the fetters of psychology and restored its objectivity. Likewise it was mainly through Barth that modern Protestantism has become a challenge to Rome and Orthodoxy, whereas formerly its theology appeared to them a mere heresy not worth being taken seriously.

When in its self-scrutiny a denomination realizes that in faith man is confronted by God himself, not merely by some notion about God, it also inevitably becomes aware of the limitations of the human mind. Although God can be apprehended by man as an object of faith, he can never fully be known. In the pre-ecumenical age this limitation of man's noetic faculty was usually interpreted as implying that all theological knowledge of God is by analogy or approximation only, and that awareness of this analogical character was sufficient to prevent the acceptance of inadequate notions of God. Kant's philosophy of religion is a typically Protestant way of dealing with man's knowledge of God. Since the idea of God in which we believe is present to all human beings and serves to guide our theological, ethical, and ecclesiastical thinking, the Kantian theologians argue that the noetic limitations in these areas do not impair the appropriateness and sufficiency of denominational thought because all denominations must accept their particular views as mere approximations to the transcendental idea of God. With the realization of diversity in oneness which the ecumenical situation intimates, however, the awareness of our denominational particularity points in a new direction. Should our particularity be interpreted as an inseparable limitation of spiritual understanding and not as genuine knowledge limited in scope only by the denomination's specific vantage point? Such a view would presuppose that by God's Spirit specific insights have been granted to the various denominations.

In the ecumenical situation a response to the latter view could be made in two different ways. Some might hold that true Protestantism should be a synthesis of all the denominations united in one Protestant church. Theoretically such a suggestion sounds wonderful. But unless the specific differences of the denominations are seen in notions only, religious experience will not be capable of integrating all the denominational approaches to God in one individual's heart. The other alternative would be to interpret the diversity according to I Corinthians 12. It would mean that through their very diversity the denominations give expression to the vitality of the Body of Christ. In that case it would not be necessary for each denomination to emulate and imitate all the others. Rather it would be by its willingness to live together and to acknowledge each other as members of the one Protestant church that each denomination would contribute to the full life of the whole church. Of course, people who are really devoted to their denomination will not find this an easy solution of Protestant perplexity. For while it would enable us to continue the way of our denomination as a genuine approach to faith, it would at the same time demand that we give up the belief that ours is the only possible way in which true faith can express itself. Consequently, our expression of Christianity could no longer pretend to be more adequate than those found in the other denominations. It would simply be different. Yet on account of this very difference it would be essential for the whole Protestant church.

Thus those denominations which, as a result of their participation in the ecumenical movement, have engaged afresh in self-

examination will be led to the awareness of their mutual relatedness in the Spirit. The polemical attitude which they formerly
showed toward each other inevitably called forth a dangerous
belief in their self-sufficiency and thus hardened those features
in which they differed from each other. Since those characteristics, in spite of the emphasis given to them, are not necessarily
the most important aspects of a denomination, the awareness of
their mutual relatedness should render the denominations ready
to learn from each other, and allow each to test its own characteristics and attainments in the light of other denominations.
The mere fact, for instance, that the Lutheran churches have a
doctrine of the Lord's Supper which differs from that of the
Reformed churches is not directly related to eucharistic piety.
A denomination might discover that, even with a doctrine that
is theologically more consistent than that of another denomination, it bears less spiritual fruit. The doctrine of the Holy Spirit
held in Pentecostal circles, for instance, is highly debatable from
an exegetical viewpoint. Yet there can be no doubt that the
Pentecostal groups show a greater joy of salvation and a livelier
spirit of service than many denominations who confidently attack
them because they stand on more solid exegetical ground than
the Pentecostals.

Another feature in which the relatedness of the denominations
might manifest itself is a new ecumenical attitude toward financial
and material support. Church World Service has made a wonderful beginning in this respect. How surprised the Lutheran
churches of Germany were, for instance, when they discovered
that a great deal of the relief brought to them after the last war
had been contributed by Methodists, Mennonites, Baptists, and
Quakers, that is to say, by denominations treated in their own
country as undesirable "sects." A test of the depth of ecumenical
solidarity will be the financing of the missionary work on the
foreign field and the support of the younger churches in the
future. The generosity with which American congregations have
identified themselves with the mission enterprise of their de-

nominations is most remarkable. But one wonders whether they have already sufficiently learned to transfer this loyalty to the Protestant church in its totality, to an entity which inevitably is far less concrete than one's denomination and its Foreign Mission Board. The transition will be facilitated when the congregations realize that the goal of our effort on the foreign field is not the expansion of our own denomination but the spread of the gospel in the whole world.

We must further realize that denominational giving in an ecumenical setup cannot concern itself with individual needs only. It must be done while bearing in mind the spiritual and social development of the churches to which the recipients of the gifts belong. Leaders of the younger churches remind us of the fact that beneficial as have been the services rendered by American hospitals, schools, and libraries, they have also stymied the sense of initiative and responsibility in the benefactors of these institutions. Since they are entirely an effort of Americans for the benefit of others, these institutions have often failed to become an integral part of the life of the younger churches and thus have bred a certain complacency and passivity in them. While financial support and the supply of trained personnel on the part of the home churches will be required for a long time to come, it will also be imperative to hand over to the younger churches the administration and principal responsibility for these institutions.

2. THE PROBLEM OF PROTESTANT UNITY

Since the problem of Protestant unity is that of understanding the Protestant church as the work of the risen Lord, any approach to it from a purely utilitarian viewpoint is bound to be unsatisfactory. The advantages of a unified administration and strategy, the resulting financial and political power, the elimination of overlapping activities, and the creation of an impressive image of Protestantism in public opinion would all prove eventually to be the undoing of Protestantism unless their pursuit were motivated by spiritual reasons and controlled by theological thought. However, the same consideration applies to the diversity of the Protestant denominations. Undoubtedly the discovery of the principle of diversity in unity is one of the great merits of the Reformation. Yet to say that Protestantism puts such a high premium on freedom that it is willing to sacrifice even unity on its behalf is tantamount to contending that subjectivism is of the very essence of Protestant life, and accordingly that the quest for truth is irrelevant. One wonders, however, how Protestantism would ever have come into existence on that basis. Would not the humanists of the sixteenth century have been far more consistent by simply disregarding the church and pursuing their own ideals and ideas!

Luther's awareness of the living Christ manifesting himself directly in his Body on earth was a radical departure from the Christology of the medieval church, notwithstanding the enormous debt Luther owed in many other respects to past generations, in particular to Augustine, the German mystics, the nominalism of Gabriel Biel, and the exegetical skill of Erasmus and Faber Stapulensis. First of all, Luther's view of Christ implied the necessity to differentiate between the manifestations of Christ on the one hand, and the human response on the other. Christ in his risen life does not change, and although he manifests himself in this world to successive generations, he preserves his identity in the process of revealing himself. But the people to whom he manifests himself belong to this world and share its diversity. However, Luther never thought of a diversity based upon different temperaments or races in the manner of Neo-Protestantism. The way in which Protestant churches were organized on a territorial basis was considered a matter of expediency rather than of principle. But Luther opposed Rome's unwillingness to give room to the Holy Spirit, who in a diversified manner is moving people so that they must live their life of faith in accordance with his work (cf. Augsburg Confession, Art. VII). Thus the splitting up of the Reformation movement into different denominations, while regretted by the Reformers, nevertheless never seemed to imply a scandal in their eyes. Although the believers' allegiance is Christ's own work and thus substantially common throughout Christianity, it is diversified in its manifestations. On this point Luther clashed with the Curia, which pretended that there could be only one way of giving expression to the Christian faith. Although the Roman church had never completely lost sight of the fact of diversity, as can be seen for instance in the multiplicity of its monastic orders and to a lesser extent in its various theological schools, their diversity is only tolerated. Ultimately they all are controlled by the Vatican. The Pope alone may determine how far their diversity may manifest itself within the church. That is to say, in Roman Catholicism the principle of unity resides in a historical institution rather than in Christ.

Conversely, the only way in which the coexistence of various denominations in Protestantism can be apprehended as a spiritual necessity is by seeing in that diversity a manifestation of the vitality of the Body of Christ. In order to perform its task in holy history the church must differentiate itself. This feature is common to all churches, except that the conciliar principle in Eastern Orthodoxy and the office of the hierarchy in Roman Catholicism renders the diversity directly subordinate to the life and purpose of the respective church. It is true that Luther was both vehement and intolerant in asserting his views against opponents. But the fact that he never challenged the right of existence of the church of Rome, no matter how fiercely he denounced the papacy, is evidence of his conviction that the oneness of the church is not dependent on a common organization. The problem that confronts Protestantism in the ecumenical age is not that of the right of diversity but the problem of how to give such an expression to Protestantism that its diversity is rendered subservient to the oneness of the Protestant church.

The fact cannot be denied that for not a few people in the Western world, and for many more in Asia and Africa, the "crude" diversity of pre-ecumenical Protestantism seemed to be a mark of hopeless confusion and of a lack of interest in objective truth. The way out of the dilemma is not, however, shame for the denominational character of Protestantism, for it is on denominational diversity that our spiritual freedom depends. While it is necessary for the Protestant church to differentiate itself into various denominations, this intrinsic necessity enables the individual believer to choose his own denomination. There is no divine necessity, as Rome contends, by which the individual is compelled to join one of them rather than another. The principle of established territorial churches, with a monopolistic position, which may have been justifiable in the age of the Reformation, has lost all meaning in our time with its rapid shifts of population. That this anachronism still persists in Britain, Germany, and the Scandinavian countries has rather unspiritual reasons.

But the more emphatically the right of diversity is stressed, the more imperative is the obligation of the denominations so to behave and so to think of their own peculiar nature, that the oneness of the Protestant church can also be clearly perceived. The above-mentioned steps which the ecumenical movement took toward practical cooperation represent one mode of expressing that oneness.[2] Though in many respects more pragmatic than spiritual, that mode of manifestation of solidarity is probably the most urgently needed step in view of the atomization of Protestantism. Experience has shown that it was also the most effective one from a practical viewpoint. The publicity given to the various ecumenical meetings by the world press proves that even outsiders are unable to overlook these evidences of Protestant unity.

Another attempt to make visible the unity of the Protestant church has now been started in theology. Both the World Council of Churches and various groups of denominations have convened leading theological scholars for conferences in which they explore the reasons for disagreement as well as the possibili-

---

[2] See above pp. 174-175.

ties of underlying oneness, especially in doctrinal areas which seem to be responsible for the present separation. These gatherings are of inestimable value in that they offer opportunities for learning what the driving motive is that has led to the doctrinal dissension. It is more than doubtful, however, whether the time has already arrived where the theological consensus can be expressed in a common confession of faith accepted by all the Protestant denominations. In the absence of an authoritative teaching office in Protestantism the only other way open would be a general council of all the member denominations. But since, in order to have binding authority, such a confession must have a spiritual origin, the question arises: How would one proceed to elect to a Protestant Council only such delegates as would give guarantee of purely spiritual motives? And since such a confession could not be voted by a numerical majority but must be adopted unanimously, how would the organizers escape the danger of having crackpots and stinkers delegated by splinter groups not in favor of Protestant unity? The time may come in the future when these obstacles can be successfully removed. But it seems to be a senseless waste of time and good will to consider the formulation of a common confession of faith the prerequisite of ecumenical cooperation.

There is greater promise in an ecumenical approach to the exchange of theological teachers between denominations. Whereas formerly the great and fertile epochs of denominational theology resulted from a critical reappraisal of a denomination's foundation, the new situation demands also a mutual confrontation of the theologies of different denominations. In the history of Protestant theology two trends have continuously evidenced special vitality and intellectual strength. They are found in the Lutheran and Reformed churches. It would be most natural, therefore, that the theological exchange should be started by them. Of course, it is true that there have been other original thinkers such as Schwenckfeld or Swedenborg, and stimulating leaders in spiritual life such as Zinzendorf and Wesley, but their thoughts were not followed up by other theologians. Notwithstanding the polemics of the sixteenth and seventeenth centuries, and in part because of them, theological developments in Lutheran and Reformed theology have influenced each other mutually. The very fact that both in Germany and in America the two denominations lived side by side, and that their theology was in certain places taught within the same university, helped greatly to keep the two theological traditions in touch with each other. Pietism, Schleiermacher, Barth, and Brunner are probably the most outstanding meeting points of the two theological tendencies. In Great Britain a similar process of theological reciprocity has taken place since the beginning of the nineteenth century between the Church of England and the Free Churches. In keeping with the general outlook of British theology this exchange occurred mainly in the biblical field, and it is not by chance that the resurgence of biblical theology, which is such a characteristic trait of modern Protestantism in the British Isles, shows Anglican and Free Church scholars working hand in hand.

It would seem, nevertheless, that with the advent of the ecumenical movement a remarkable change of scope was noticeable. Whereas the pre-ecumenical development resulted in a hardening of confessionalism on the one hand, and a subjective synthesis of theological notions on the other, the most recent stage shows a paradoxical combination of the two trends. This development is in keeping with a new resurgence of denominationalism in our time. Notwithstanding a number of ecclesiastical mergers which have been consummated in recent years, the general trend has been toward a new self-assertion of the various denominations as is evidenced by the fact that most of them have formed worldwide organizations. Yet, while this trend can safely be interpreted as expressing the determination of the denominations to stay in existence for the time being, a new tendency has developed within confessional theology. The theological confrontation is no longer understood as a quest for synthesis but as a challenge to self-transcendence. The very fact that within the Protestant church theologians arrive at conflicting conclusions is taken as an indication that they were satisfied with penultimate realities.

Very characteristic of this new approach is a new appreciation of eschatology. In the theology of the past centuries, eschatology had been treated as one theological topic among others, slighted by the majority of theologians, while granted excessive significance by some apocalyptic movements. In recent theology, however, thanks in part to biblical realism, eschatology denotes a specific outlook which dominates the whole field of theological thought.[3] When it is said, for instance, that the church is an eschatological reality, the statement does not mean that the church is to be thought of as coming into being in the Parousia only. Rather the church is understood as a manifestation of the redemptive will of Christ that operates in human history. As a result, each historical stage of Christendom has full meaning in itself; yet even the totality of church history will not exhaust the meaning of his presence because history is but the means by which the final stage is prepared. Instead of the contrast between now and the future, between the visible church as a human institution and the future church of the redeemed, which was characteristic of former theological thinking, the church is now interpreted as continually contributing to the realization of the purpose for which it was brought into being.

Lutheran and Reformed theology have always been divided on the topic of the church. For Lutheranism, which in this respect was close to the Roman Catholic view, the church is the place on earth where the redemptive work of Christ takes place. In the Calvinistic tradition, on the other hand, the church is the place where the believing people give visible expression to their love of, and allegiance to, the risen Lord. The new eschatological view does not lead to a synthesis of these two traditions; nevertheless both of them are deepened and spiritualized by the ecumenical confrontation.

The Lutheran view had always been endangered by conserva-

[3] See above pp. 50-51.

tive tendencies, in which the form that the church had at a not-too-well-defined moment of the past was regarded as the realization of the ideal church, and the salvation of people seemed to depend on the old time-honored confession of faith (with or without the Formula of Concord?) and its sixteenth-century liturgy. Over against these temptations, the new eschatological view emphasizes the ministerial character of the church, which demands that its forms be adjusted to the needs of the people concerned and that the laity be activated. For the eschatological dynamic of the church rests upon the faith of its members no less than on its institutional character.

In the Reformed tradition, on the other hand, the eschatological understanding of the church underscores its institutional character. The people who are gathered as a congregation do not thereby found the church. Rather by gathering together they give expression to the fact that the Lord has called them into the fellowship of his people. The word of God as well as baptism and the Lord's Supper had been in existence prior to the church, and thus the significance of the church is not confined to the satisfaction of the spiritual interests of the congregation. The Reformed tradition has always been tempted to consider the life of the elect an end in itself, whereas it is meant to be the witness which Christ bears to himself in this world. In turn, this eschatological outlook makes obvious that the former inter-Protestant polemics concerning the nature of the sacraments missed the point. The sacraments were treated as though they were entities existing by themselves. Now it becomes evident that these disagreements between Lutheran and Reformed theologies were rooted in different views of the church. The result is not a theology of the sacraments which from now on may be held in common by two branches of the Protestant church. They are most likely to continue along traditional lines. Nevertheless, certain types of polemics will be ruled out. It can now be seen that the Lutheran view is not a relapse into Roman Catholic thought, for the Lutheran church does not pretend to represent

Christ but believes that the church is used by him. Likewise it cannot be denied that the Reformed churches are far from holding a merely anthropocentric view, for what the believers are doing is done in obedience to Christ and for the manifestation of his glory. Both denominations are agreed on God's presence in his church, yet the Lutheran view interprets it primarily as the "bodily" presence of the risen Christ, whereas the Reformed tradition lays the stress on the work of the Holy Spirit. Hence there is no reason for merging the confessional theologies, let alone for abrogating the denominations. But being confronted with each other in the ecumenical situation they must learn to consider themselves as jointly pursuing the goal which Christ wants to reach through his church rather than as redemptive ultimates. Thus they can patiently wait for the moment when, through the operation of the Holy Spirit, their specific differences have become so minimal that the fusion will come by itself.

As a result of the ecumenical situation, Protestant theology is prompted to move vertically toward a more radical encounter with God but also horizontally toward a better understanding of other denominations and of the function which God has assigned to the world outside of the church. It was particularly the vertical movement, becoming articulate in the Luther Renaissance and in Karl Barth, which enabled Protestant theology to eliminate the pseudo-problems which had vexed the churches in the past. We are referring to such a hoary problem as: visible church or invisible church? The truth is that both the Lutheran emphasis upon the institutional character of the church and the Reformed emphasis on the congregation as the nucleus of the church have encouraged the rise of Protestant subjectivism. The Lutheran institutionalism obviously clashed with the demand of personal faith. In view of its historical priority, the principle of *sola fide* seemed to imply complete rejection of the church as an institution. The Reformed view, in turn, had at times laid so much stress upon the social aspects of the church, that the practice of the spiritual life seemed to be relegated to the sphere of private devotions. With the eschatological view of the church the error of such an alternative is evident. The organized church is not a self-sufficient entity and an end in itself, but neither is it true that people may find Christ in this world apart from the assistance given by the church.

What has been said about the new eschatological understanding of the church could easily be applied to all the other points that are controversial between Lutheran and Reformed churches, and it could be shown how, in consideration of the ecumenical situation on the one hand, and a new self-scrutiny of confessional theology on the other, the theological perspective of the denominations is undergoing a radical change.

In the relationship between the Church of England and the Free Churches the specifically theological issues have not yet emerged with equal clarity for several reasons. First of all, the Church of England is itself a church in transition. For political and social reasons the great theological issue of the sixteenth century has never been faced squarely by the Anglican church as a whole, with the result that some of its members feel free to assert that their church is part of the Roman Catholic church, though without the Pope, whereas others contend that it is a Protestant denomination in every respect. In fact it is both and neither. Yet as long as the Church of England, and thus the Anglican Communion, has not yet fully discovered its identity, the British Free Churches will be determined in their relations with the Church of England by the theological opinions of individual Anglican scholars and prelates rather than by the theology of the Church of England. Another reason for the peculiar development of the ecumenical encounter in the British Isles is the nature of the Free Churches. In England and Wales the Free Churches belong mainly to the "practical" type, that is to say, they are more interested in personal devotion and ethics than in systematic theology. The Church of Scotland, in turn, with its strong Calvinistic tradition, has been so accustomed to living its own spiritual life irrespective of what is going on south of the border, that its theology has never felt decisively challenged by that of Anglicanism. This peculiar situation is probably the reason why the advent of the ecumenical movement was met in Great Britain by a resurgence of biblical rather than systematic theology.

The theological situation in the "younger churches" is still conditioned by the diversities and antagonisms of the pre-ecumenical age. In many places one notices a tenacious devotion to a brand of conservative theology of nineteenth-century vintage or to its modern substitute, namely fundamentalism. Similarly, however, members of the younger generation who have attended continental or American colleges and seminaries fight passionately for a liberal theology or advocate Protestant subjectivism. In a somewhat inconsistent and emotional way they raise the cry at the same time for a theology which has its roots in the soil of Asia or Africa. As mentioned above (see pp. 37-38, 68-69) it was impossible for the missionaries who brought Christianity to those two continents and Latin America to present the Christian message in any but the form which it had assumed in their respective denominations. Furthermore just as the nations of Europe had to adjust their thinking and ways of life to a Bible which came to them in the garb of the Near East, so the younger churches cannot be spared the wrestling with a gospel which in many respects must appear strange to them, but which nevertheless demands careful consideration on account of its intrinsic truthfulness.

In their case the appropriation of the gospel will be facilitated if they pass through the same process of self-scrutiny demanded of the sending churches. The younger churches must learn that the basic problem for which the gospel offers the solution is the relation of man to God, not of the American or German or Frenchman, not of the intellectual or the proletarian, but simply of man. Thus understood, it is the problem which concerns the Japanese, the Chinese, and the Indian with the same urgency and directness as it did the Jews of ancient Palestine, the Hellenists of

Alexandria, the burghers of Paris, or the Pilgrim Fathers. A mere adjustment of the gospel to the national traditions of the younger churches is most likely to blur the basic issue raised by the gospel. On the other hand, the greater the earnestness with which the younger churches ask themselves the basic question of the Reformation, the more it will be their own question, and the more directly will the answer they receive fit their specific predicament.

Denominations which understand their own existence in the light of the ecumenical situation, and engage in pursuit of knowledge of themselves in their relation to God's redemptive will, are essentially and actually one because they share a common problem and experience jointly the presence of Christ. Those who dream of a universal and united church in this generation will probably judge the kind of unity thus attained as a mere pittance. However, if the unity we seek is the unity of the Body of Christ, we must not start with the image of a church as we want it but with the unity that already has been brought about by Christ, now waiting for an opportunity to be given outward expression. On this basis only will it be possible to discover whether or not further progress is possible in our day; and if so, in what direction it is to be sought. Thus diversity is understood as a constitutive element of the Protestant church. The existence of the denominations is not the result of an unfortunate incidental break of Protestant unity but the work of the Holy Spirit within its bosom.

The constitutive role of Protestantism ascribed to Luther was intended in our analysis to indicate his providential place in holy history. It is not to be interpreted as though Lutheranism occupied a privileged position in the Protestant church. Although chronologically the first historical result of the Reformation, Lutheranism was never understood as having a monopoly. If Protestantism had remained coextensive with Lutheranism only, Rome would be right in calling Protestantism a Lutheran heresy. But Zwingli, Bucer, Calvin, and all the "minor" Reformers realized that the presentation of the gospel as proclaimed by Luther gave them a right to mold their response of faith in full accordance with their own spiritual understanding and experience of man's religious quest. Just as the Holy Spirit was instrumental in bringing about that diversity, so also the unity of the Protestant church is the work of the Spirit. Through him the various denominations are joined together with and in Christ. It is therefore wrong when, in support of the tendency of modern Protestantism to split up in innumerable denominations and sects, people appeal to the Protestant principle of diversity as if it implied an unrestricted right to separate. The mere fact that a person holds religious views that differ from those of fellow Christians does not give him the right to secession.

Notwithstanding human unbelief and discord the church's spiritual unity can never be lost. Thus it is a gross and dangerous misrepresentation of Christ's work here on earth when people, in an otherwise laudable zeal for the advance of the gospel, contend that the disunity of the denominations made it almost impossible for the churches to engage in the service of Christ and that their multiplicity has immobilized the gospel's mission to the world. Much as Protestant disunity and lack of regard for other denominations is to be deplored, Christ is never divided. Moreover, it can hardly be said that the Roman Catholic church, in spite of its unity, has accomplished greater spiritual feats than the Protestant denominations.

3. Searching the Scriptures

The ecumenical movement has reminded the Protestant denominations that having a doctrine of the *Una Sancta* and believing in the oneness of the church in Christ are not enough. If we really believe in the one church we have to make every effort also to give expression to its unity. We have just reached the conclusion that this goal cannot be reached without theological reflection. At first sight, to do so would seem to be the task of systematic theology because its very aim is oneness of thought.

Yet in view of the ecumenical challenge this goal could be accomplished only by means of an entirely new understanding of the method and task of systematic theology. It is a well-known fact that since the days of Protestant orthodoxy there has been a constant tension between the Bible and systematic theology. The latter started from certain axioms which were introduced as representing the essence of the Protestant faith, while the Bible served as a repository of proof texts. Notwithstanding the efforts of a few biblicists and evangelicals, this cleavage between systematic theology and biblical exegesis has grown from generation to generation. Yet it was not without good reason that such a profound and powerful thinker and voluminous writer as Luther was not engaged in composing tomes of systematic theology but instead emphasized the fact that he was a teacher of the Scripture. The genius of the Reformation is found in Luther's exposition of biblical books and his numerous sermons, all of which aim at nothing but proclaiming the message of the Bible. It is also well known that Calvin was not only the most skillful and many-sided exegete of the Bible but that his *Institutes* too, like Melanchthon's *Loci*, started as an exposition of the principal topics of Paul's letter to the Romans. Although none of the Reformers was adverse to theological thought, they realized its derivative character. Far from considering theology on a par with God's revelation, as does the Roman church, Protestantism regards it as the human attempt to give scientific expression to belief in the divine message.

Since systematic theology is a highly rational discipline, it is not surprising that the theologians should consider their disagreements mutually intolerable; hence theological controversies are notorious for being particularly bitter and venomous. But in view of the dominant role which the theologian's personality plays in his thinking, one should not marvel either at the fact that these polemics never lead to a real agreement or a cogent refutation of the opponent's view.

Considering the central role which the exegesis of the Bible has played in the Reformation, the most promising way of giving visible expression to Protestant unity would seem to lie in a joint exegetical enterprise. The reason many theologians look upon such an approach with misgivings is found in the Bible itself. Recent scholarly research in the Scriptures has disclosed an amazing diversity of viewpoints and beliefs found therein. While we speak of the Bible in the singular and confess its basic unity, the exegete who deals with the details of its text has the greatest difficulties pointing out in what this unity consists. Hence it would seem to be methodologically more advisable to start from the confession of faith which derives its validity from the fact that its statements have been gleaned from Holy Scripture as understood by faith. In the confession the diversity of the Bible has been integrated in a consistent set of propositions.

Beginning from a confession of faith complicates our task in two respects. First, the confessions, at least in the Lutheran and Reformed churches, were adopted several centuries ago. Thus it is legitimate to ask whether or not we can take it for granted that the basic problem of faith as it besets modern man was experienced in the same manner by the believers of the sixteenth and seventeenth centuries. Perhaps the child that memorizes the Heidelberg Catechism—and even his teacher—is not certain that the problem of consolation in life and death is for him the most urgent one. He is probably concerned with the quest for strength and success more than with meaning. This does not mean that the problem with which the Catechism starts may not eventually become relevant for him too. But it will probably be on a rather circuitous road that he will eventually find himself confronted by the problem with which the Catechism starts. When it is a matter of solving new issues of faith—and the modern problem of ecumenical unity is a brand new one—it is always necessary to go right to the source of revelation instead of attempting to solve the new problems by way of analogy, that is to say, on the basis of past insights. That is why all Protestant confessions of faith declare explicitly or implicitly that they themselves stand under the authority and judgment of the Scripture.

Second, each denomination is geared to a specific type of biblical teaching. While the attempt to identify each of the larger denominations with one of the leading apostles or New Testament writers may be a vain play of one's imagination, there can be no doubt that the denominations have come into being on account of various emphases found in the Bible and brought to light by biblical interpretation. Their understanding of faith is therefore inevitably one-sided, and that is another reason why, in our quest for an appropriate expression of Protestant unity, we maintained that a fresh exegesis of the Scriptures was indispensable (see pp. 48 ff., 138 ff.). In turn, the readiness of the Protestant churches to search the Scriptures in order to discover their unity is in itself evidence of unity. Nevertheless, if such an enterprise were performed by each denomination entirely by itself and without regard for the exegetical work going on in other denominations, the total picture would be disappointing because it would tell us that even though the Holy Spirit was guiding all of them in their search for a doctrine of church unity, none of them really cared for unity or was anxious to work for it.

Fortunately there has been and is a good deal of intensive cooperation and discussion going on in Protestant exegesis, notwithstanding the fact that a considerable part of that cooperation is concerned with historical and philological studies only. Furthermore, among those who strive after the theological content of the text, a certain number will content themselves with repeating or rejecting traditional views. Nevertheless, there are enough biblical scholars for whom the study of the Scriptures is a real quest for truth and who therefore derive new spiritual insights from the Bible. Especially gratifying in this respect is the intimate cooperation of Roman Catholic exegetes with non-Catholics, particularly in Belgium, France, and Germany.

However, in order to yield the results needed for unity, the Scriptures must be approached in the right way. Obviously the exchange of exegetical observations as it takes place at the meetings of biblical scholars, while creating a fellowship of research among them, will nevertheless be unsatisfactory for our purpose because there the notions and ideas of the Bible are dealt with in a purely pragmatic way, a result of individual reflection. Thus only indirectly can they be used to illumine the problem of faith. Yet not everyone who believes in the sole and infallible authority of the Bible is thereby enabled to make an exegetical contribution to the problem of church unity. His investigation may stop short of the spiritual realities to which the Bible points. The openness required of the interpreter presupposes not only familiarity with recent historical and philological studies pertinent to the study of the Bible but also, and above all, recognition of the Bible as God's word. This demands willingness to study the Bible without preconceived ideas, as though one had opened it for the first time and wanted to be taught by the Holy Spirit to discover its divine message. Such an approach is possible only when the exegete is certain that the Bible is the divine means by which he will find certainty concerning God's purpose with himself and the world. It is easy to ridicule a biblicism which ascribes inerrancy to the Bible as book rather than to the Holy Spirit who teaches us through it; but it is also ludicrous to misrepresent the hermeneutical principle "through Christ alone" as if it deprived us of any and all this-worldly security. Rather, what we said above about the self-transcendence of theological studies applies in particular to biblical exegesis. The very fact that one denomination does not understand the biblical texts as another should serve as an incentive for them to overcome the provisional understanding implied in each viewpoint.

It is not difficult, for instance, to discern the one-sidedness of Bultmann's existentialism and his method of demythologizing. Not quite as easy will be the refutation of his underlying theology, if the rebuttal is to have convincing power. But what actually is gained by mere refutation? Even granted that one had shown Bultmann to be on the wrong path in every respect, would that prove that my own interpretation was right? More useful certainly would be an exegetical method that realized that Bultmann had hit upon important problems of New Testament exegesis, even though he expressed them in an inappropriate way. The next and most important step in an ecumenical approach to biblical exegesis is to review one's own exegesis in the light of Bultmann's or any other critic's problems. Through Bultmann's insistence on the self-transcendence of the text, for instance, we will learn to understand how all biblical texts point beyond our level of understanding of the divine realities. Even if in a given case we are unable to state positively what that transcendence consists in, the very fact that we know it points beyond our actual representation will help us to come more closely to the reality thereby designated.

Exegesis thus understood will continue to yield new results through the ages. But the appearance of new spiritual insights does not mean that the former ones are obsolete. Since Christ has a purpose with his church, namely, to use it as his instrument in his redemptive work, there is an accumulation of spiritual wisdom in the church. In this sense we may unashamedly speak of tradition in the Protestant church, while at the same time rejecting the Roman Catholic view according to which tradition supplements the Scripture. Tradition implements the Scripture, tradition being the fruit of faith derived from listening to the Scripture. The Roman misunderstanding could originate because doctrines were considered ultimates in God's revelation. Protestantism holds that beyond its verbal revelations the Scripture leads us to the experience of Christ's presence and redemptive work and the operation of his Spirit. There is nothing beyond that experience that our faith needs. Tradition in the Protestant sense cannot be held to provide additional revelation above and beyond the Scriptures. Rather it enables the believer to grow in faith by describing the experiences of faith of past generations.

It is not only inevitable that in the exegetical approach to unity, as in all exegesis, the interpreter should be influenced by the tradition of his denomination; it is also good that this is the case. For it is not on account of his individual insights that his exegesis will make its contribution to exegetical cooperation. Other exegetes are listening to him as members of a denomination, and they want to hear the voice of the partner's denomination. While the exegetical tradition thus presented may be conditioned by the confession of faith of the exegete's denomination, its function is not primarily to preserve its specific teachings. They may change from epoch to epoch. Rather the tradition describes the denomination's way of faith, that is to say, its specific encounter with the risen Lord.

Yet the very fact that in the exegetical endeavor the interpreter is in search of the living Christ rather than of the teachings of the early church raises an important problem. What right do we have to confine the Protestant church to the traditional denominations? Should we not take into consideration the fact that side by side with a churchly Protestantism a new type of nonecclesiastical or secular Protestantism has developed? Is not perhaps Tillich a more reliable guide to religious realism than the denominational theologians when he redefines Protestantism as the radical protest against tradition and conventions in any religion? [4] May it not be that as a result of our view, Christ, though the Son of God, is hemmed in by the New Testament? How can he be the word through which all things are made when we make him the servant of the Christian religion?

These objections are legitimate inasmuch as they remind us that the living Christ surpasses the frame of any human image which faith will form of him. But it is equally erroneous to espouse radical skepticism for no better reason than that the substance of every fact invariably transcends the observer's factual knowledge and comprehension. In turn, we cannot infer from the universal function of the Son of God that he can be

---

[4] Paul Tillich, *The Protestant Era* (Chicago: University of Chicago Press, 1948).

known in his cosmic activities with the same clarity with which he reveals himself in the New Testament. Factual knowledge rests upon the ability of our mind to discern sense data by their specific appearance, even though their nature is not yet given. Hence we may say that the Son of God is known to us in his incarnate life. Beyond that we can only believe that he is at work in the universe too; but we are not able to identify that activity except by the analogies that work has with his ministry. In liberal theology and other peripheral types of Protestantism, notions of the world, man, history, and evil are held which are incompatible with those found in traditional Protestantism because they are derived from a non-Christian kind of experience. Inasmuch as they have a foundation in facts, their significance for faith is confined, nevertheless, to their ability to illumine our perplexity. In order to be realistic, the answer of faith must take these experiences and notions into consideration. But they do not contribute to the substance of the answer which our perplexity receives. The divine light comes exclusively from the Christ of the New Testament.

When we keep this fact in mind we will not be deluded by those who insist that in order to be ecumenical, that is to say, worldwide, modern Protestantism must heed the revelations implied in the great non-Christian religions. Of course, if this demand merely means that in those other religions statements are found of which the believer should take cognizance, we gladly agree. Just as in antiquity and the Middle Ages, Christian theology was stimulated by the contact with pagan philosophy, so it is likely to derive benefits from new contacts with Hinduism or Buddhism. But if the demand implies that the Christian faith must be supplemented by the truths found in those religions, we demur. For these religions will never be able to confront man with the finality implied in the redemptive reality of God in Christ. It would therefore be a fatal mistake if people would substitute the basic question of Hinduism or Buddhism for that of Christianity. While it is not unimportant to inquire into man's relation to the universe or into the way to true happiness and absence of suffering, these questions do not touch the real problem of human existence, which is man's strained relationship to the personal Creator of this world. For that reason not much help is to be expected in the theological realm from discussions with Hindu and Buddhist theologians, useful as such exchanges may prove to be for missionary strategy.

Yet, when we insist that in the present ecumenical situation the exegete should choose his place within his denomination, will not the result be a narrowed experience of the believer's perplexity? Will he not for the same reason arrive at an answer which is an encounter not with the living Christ but with the image of Christ as propagated by his denomination? If this were a correct description of our situation the search for Protestant unity would be a hopeless cause, because the result of our quest would consist in a mere juxtaposition of denominational views. Though held together by the adjective "Protestant," they would nevertheless lack intrinsic unity. But notwithstanding the influence our faith has upon our religious thinking—we all start with a provisional understanding or *Vorverständnis*—the radical urge of our questioning, which is the Spirit's work in us, will enable us to transcend our starting position.

In addition to the attempts to give expression to the unity of the Protestant church by means of a common exegetical and theological approach to man's religious predicament, common worship is a second opportunity. The significance of interdenominational prayer groups can hardly be overrated. By addressing themselves together to God, people confess the unity of the object of their worship. It should be kept in mind, however, that the sacraments still present a serious obstacle to a fully integrated life of common worship. Although it can hardly be assumed that the efficacy of the Lord's Supper depends on the doctrines held by the various denominations—it is the presence of the Lord by which it is made a means of grace—the celebration is nevertheless understood by the denominations as the apex of church life. The faith of the communicants is the Spirit's operation in their hearts. Thus intercommunion, while it is practicable among a considerable number of denominations, is not by itself an evidence of church unity. It merely indicates that, in the opinion of those participating, the sacramental rite is considered to be of subordinate significance in comparison with the Lord's real presence. For this reason, those who feel unable to participate in intercommunion because they are so strongly aware of the differences of spiritual life should not be scolded. They may work with no less fervor than others for the unity of the church, but they prefer to work in areas in which cooperation would not impair their particular ways and institutions of faith.

PART THREE

THE ECUMENICAL TASK
OF PROTESTANTISM

CHAPTER VI

SHOULD PROTESTANTISM CONTINUE TO EXIST?

A. NECESSITY OF PROTESTANTISM

In the first part of our study we surveyed the place of Protestantism in the modern world. From an analysis of the factors challenging Protestantism's existence we turned our attention to the basic problem now confronting Protestantism, namely, its quest for a place in ecumenical church life. The resources which are at its disposal, as well as those factors which might constrict its growth, were discussed. In this last section we propose to look at the ecumenical task of Protestantism, noting reasons why its existence should continue and attempting to suggest possible lines of future development.

The new situation of Christianity created by the ecumenical movement, and particularly by the formation of the World Council of Churches, has introduced a new dynamic into church history. The various churches and denominations united in the Council cannot accept this unexpected development in a purely passive way. Their very coexistence in a comprehensive organization confronts each member with the disquieting question of its own necessity. Could not Christianity do without just this church or denomination? The mere fact that a denomination is in existence is no proof that it is indispensable for the church today. Even if a denomination were able to show that its origin was necessitated by compelling circumstances—the degeneration of the Catholic church of the Middle Ages, for instance, which called forth the Reformation—this fact would not by itself justify the continued existence of a denomination or church. In the presence of Rome, for instance, Protestantism is asked if the Council of Trent has not sufficiently taken care of all the criticisms and complaints raised by the Reformers as to make the existence of Protestantism superfluous. Even if this question were answered in the negative nobody could ignore the mighty changes which Protestantism itself has undergone since the days of the Reformation. May we confidently say that all the Protestant denominations of our day still meet a real need in the life of the Church Universal?

Of course, once the question is asked in this way it cannot be confined to the Protestant denominations. Without denying, for instance, the providential role which Eastern Orthodoxy has played since antiquity, we have a right to inquire of that church, whether its faithful allegiance to tradition suffices to justify its continued existence in the ecumenical age. Even Rome, notwithstanding the reforms accomplished at Trent and subsequently, cannot dodge that question. For in their historical development all churches and denominations are constantly in danger of aberration from the right way. None of them can claim inerrancy or infallibility notwithstanding the fact that the Church Universal in its totality can never lose sight of Christ, and that the Lord of the church will provide whatever is necessary to bring an erring or apostate church back to its true function. But no particular church—and both Orthodoxy and Rome are particular churches— is safe from being spewed out by the Lord (Rev. 3:16).

The necessity for a church to exist depends on its relation to the goal which God has set for the Church Universal. The fellowship of faith, through the power of the Holy Spirit, enables its members to fulfill on earth the will of God in harmony with the Savior's work and thus to transform the earth into God's kingdom. As has been shown, however, fulfilling this task does not require the reduction of all the churches to numerical oneness. Diversity in unity is the way God has chosen to reach his redemptive goal here on earth. But there is no merit in mere multiplication either. A denomination or a whole church has the right to exist only insofar as it is able to make an essential contribution toward the goal which God has set for the Church Universal. Hence when a particular church or denomination contends that it is the only body on earth which is capable of offering salvation to mankind it attempts—fortunately in vain— to flout the plan of God. In turn, however, the providential role of diversified church life implies that a denomination, in order to give proof of its necessity, must offer evidence that its existence and peculiar understanding of the Christian message is compatible with the existence of other denominations. A denomination which would acquiesce in mere coexistence would thereby indicate its disregard for the presence of the Lord in his church. Unity in diversity means that the existence of the other churches is accepted as a reminder that our own church is threatened by the temptation of self-righteousness and one-sidedness. In turn, we may dislike eccentricities and unnecessary externalities in the life of a denomination and even disapprove of them; yet before we condemn them we have to find out whether or not these features are meant to give expression to the specific task assigned to that church. In that case we may hope for changes in its forms of expression, but we have no right to expect it to surrender its basic principles.

The formation of the World Council of Churches implies furthermore the recognition that the existence of the three great churches is not to be explained as the result of divisive tendencies but as a manifestation of the principle of diversity in holy history. The churches that form the World Council reject in fact, if not theologically, the Roman contention that the divine task assigned to the churches is their reunification in one homogeneous body with a common single head. If Rome were right, the kind of coexistence for which the ecumenical movement aspired would lead the church into an intolerable condition, even if it were meant as a transitional stage only. Since they believe in a spiritual reality underlying the ecumenical activities, the churches united in the World Council must regard themselves as branches of the Church Universal.

For Protestantism, proof of the necessity of its existence is a most urgent task in the ecumenical setup. Although theoretically Rome and Orthodoxy are confronted with the same task, their situation is different. True, they mutually consider each other as schismatic churches, yet in the course of the centuries they have acquiesced in their unrelated existence. They obviously respect each other's specific features, and in the minds of their leaders we look in vain for the hope that the two bodies might be unified in the foreseeable future. Rome's treatment of the Uniate churches indicates the direction in which the reunion with the Eastern churches would be sought by the Vatican. The main objective realistically pursued by the Roman Catholic church in ecumenical relations is a recognition of the Pope as supreme head of all the churches, which would make feasible an exchange of clergy and members. Protestantism, however, faces a different problem because it is a newcomer in church history. Thus, before any further step toward closer cooperation is taken by the elder churches, Protestantism is expected to prove that it is an integral part of the Church Universal and that it fulfills an essential function in ecumenical life.

This requirement cannot mean, of course, that the Protestant church should show reason why the Church Universal is unable to exist apart from Protestantism, for the other churches had been in existence for nearly fifteen hundred years before the Protestant church came into being. Rather the question addressed to the churches is in principle the same for all: do they constitute forms of human fellowship which, under present conditions and for the people of today, are essential as means through which redemption can be found? Protestantism in particular has to show how through its existence the Church Universal is enriched and stimulated beyond what it was until the Reformation. Since conditions of life and the mentality of people undergo constant changes in history, this problem is not an absolutely new one. It has confronted the churches time and again in past history. The coming into being of new ways of devotion, new monastic orders, new kinds of theology, new ecclesiastical institutions were all prompted by the fact that sections of the church had become aware of this problem. But as long as churches or denominations existed more or less by themselves, as was the case in the pre-ecumenical age, the problem was not as urgently felt. For in our day, when they are united in the World Council of Churches, the churches are compelled to live together and to cooperate with many apparent rivals. Even Rome is today under pressure to face the reason for her existence, notwithstanding her remaining apart from the World Council of Churches. She finds herself now in complete isolation, for since the Orthodox churches from behind the Iron Curtain have recently joined the World Council of Churches, the Roman Catholic church is practically the only major Christian body left which refuses to listen to the common call for unity. Her claim to be the only true church will therefore be without real weight unless she too gives proof of her being an essential part of the Church Universal.

But in what way are churches able to prove their right to exist? Negatively it can be said that the mere contention on the part of a church that it has this right constitutes no proof. It would seem that too often the Anglican and Lutheran churches in particular have presented themselves in this manner to the other churches in the ecumenical movement. But even if their common contention to be the "Church of the Middle Road" had a historical basis, this fact would not suffice to prove the necessity for existence of such intermediate bodies. Similarly, the historical proof that a denomination has been in continuity with the medieval and ancient church does not render its existence indispensable. We would, rather, like to know how far those churches which continue the ecclesiastical tradition are capable of coping with the radical change which both the ecumenical movement and the modern age have called forth in the Church Universal.

A truly satisfactory proof must be of a twofold character: spiritual and practical. First of all a denomination must show that it understands its particular nature and outlook in a truly spiritual way, not sociologically only. Beyond this, however, it has to give evidence that, as a basis of its practical life, it has elements which other churches too recognize as essential for the life of the Church Universal. This practical acknowledgement alone would not suffice, however, because the same forms of religious life may be interpreted theologically in different ways by different denominations, and they may be mere survivals of the vitality or of movements of a great past. The fact, for instance, that a denomination has the sacraments of baptism and the Lord's Supper in common with others does not necessarily and by itself prove that it is essentially at one with other denominations who also administer these sacraments.

As far as Protestantism is concerned, its spiritual contribution is to be sought in its original concept of faith. Yet what this means cannot be shown by means of a theological definition, but it has to be evidenced by a spiritual study of the Bible. While the Catholic church and Eastern Orthodoxy do not fully agree with Protestantism in the role it ascribes to the Bible, there is hope that such proof will be acceptable to them, because those churches too, even with their different doctrine of Scripture, nonetheless acknowledge the divine authority of the Scripture. The kind of scriptural proof that is required today, however, must differ greatly from that by which denominations formerly founded their claim for recognition upon the Bible. It is no longer sufficient that a denomination declare to its own satisfaction that every aspect of its work, thought, and church polity has the support of passages of the Bible. Unless the foundation it finds in Scripture has the power to convince other denominations of its validity, this denomination's presence in the ecu-

menical fellowship will be looked upon with distrust and suspicion.

B. ECUMENICAL STUDY OF THE BIBLE

Basically there are two methods of studying the Bible. The
first treats the Bible in a purely scientific way, that is to say,
detached from its message. In modern times this method has
been considered by many as the only adequate way, and its
advocates looked with disdain upon those who studied the Bible
because it was relevant for the life of faith and redemption. The
second method does not necessarily proceed in a less scholarly
manner than the first, but it considers the scientific study as a
preliminary approach only and adds a new dimension to the
understanding of the Bible.

As subjectivism prevailed in the pre-ecumenical age, theologians were of the opinion that they could dispense with the
"believing" study of the Bible because they trusted in their own
personal inspiration or relied on the power of their religious
faculty. But the new situation created by the formation of the
World Council of Churches addresses its question to denominations and churches rather than to individuals. Membership in
the Council does not depend on what religion Professor A. or
Dr. B. has, but whether or not a clearly circumscribed denomination accepts in earnest the Council's creedal "basis." According
to common agreement the spiritual life of a Protestant denomination is based upon its acceptance of the authority of the Bible
and manifests itself in the way its faith is nourished by the study
of the Bible. Thus adherence to the World Council of Churches'
basis must express itself in a return to the Bible.

The new situation created by the ecumenical movement
demands a shift of perspective. The goal of biblical study is no
longer confined to discovering the unshakable basis upon which
the faith of the individual or the church rests. The churches also
have to find out how their understanding of the faith must mani-

fest itself in order to make a relevant contribution to the life of the universal church. Far from precluding the former orientation of exegesis, this new perspective widens its horizon. Both individual believer and denomination are to see themselves in the context of the denominationally differentiated Body of Christ.

Such biblical study requires the interpreter to take a critical attitude toward his own denomination's traditional religion. He must be prepared to discover superficialities and weaknesses in its spiritual life, no less than misunderstandings of the Bible and of the Reformation. The result, however, will not be an alienation from his denomination but a deepened view of its faith. The more seriously one practices this critical attitude, the more effective will be the guidance which the student of the Bible offers to his denomination; and this result will again determine the contribution which this denomination is able to make toward the ecumenical movement. In turn, the cheaper and more superficial the arguments one draws from the Scripture in support of his own denomination, the smaller the regard other denominations will have for it. An equally critical attitude must be taken toward the Reformation. It may be that our image of the Reformation is a caricature of the actual historical events and the Reformers' understanding of Scripture. Nor must one be frightened when the biblical evidence seems to bring to light shortcomings and blind spots in the Reformers themselves, for instance, their neglect of biblical eschatology. Their authority will not be lessened thereby; for these men took a realistic view of themselves and regarded their own work as being in constant need of revision in the light of the authority on which they depended, the Bible.

Such self-criticism would not be ecumenical, however, if it were done in disregard of the Bible study in which other denominations are engaged. Characteristic of the pre-ecumenical situation was the fact that the representatives of "scientific" exegesis were engaged in a world-wide exchange of ideas and methods, but their fellowship lacked a spiritual basis; whereas "believing" exegesis indulged in a monolithic understanding of the biblical truth: "If I am sure that I have apprehended and comprehended the meaning of a biblical text, then it follows that those who disagree with me must be wrong." The arbitrariness of such opinions the theologian could conceal from himself as long as each denomination or school of theology disregarded and lived in isolation from the other denominations. In the ecumenical movement, however, a broader view of the word of God is required. If it is God himself who reveals his redemptive plan and work to man in and through the Bible, then it follows that he does not address himself to one denomination only, because the depth of his message transcends the human mind both individually and collectively. Hence no type of interpretation will be able to exhaust its meaning, no matter how much of the divine truth may have been grasped by a denomination.

In practice this means it will no longer be permissible to argue that ours is the only true understanding of justification in the Pauline letters, so the Roman Catholic or Baptist understanding would be utterly wrong. For a theologian who understands the ecumenical situation as God's work can no longer contend that the Catholic exegete is not capable of spiritual exegesis or that Catholic theology deliberately distorts the meaning of the text. One is obliged to grant them that they have reached their results by working as bona fide Christian theologians. In many instances exegetical differences are caused by the respective theological perspectives of the churches concerned. There is gain in such recognition. It makes us aware of the fact that we have been enabled to notice features in Paul's view of justification which had escaped the attention or understanding of the Catholic scholars and which, with their different perspective, they will have difficulty in reconciling with their exegesis. Yet their exegesis also discloses exegetical possibilities to us of which we were not aware. Thus there is a new element which enters into our Bible study through the ecumenical movement. It is the willingness and eagerness of the interpreter to understand the other denomination's position and thus to become aware of that aspect in his own understanding which is indicative of the fragmentariness of his denomination's spiritual understanding.

This new approach to the Scripture will prove to be difficult and even painful because it hurts the interpreter's pride. As a scholar he wants to proclaim the whole truth of his subject of study, and as a theologian he will be anxious to attain to certainty in his life of faith. The inevitable self-limitation that the ecumenical situation carries with it will make the student of the Bible aware of the fact that in dealing with the word of God he remains a creature who in this life is unable to see God face to face. It will, however, also teach him that as a member of the church of Christ he shares in the fullness of its life. Thus notwithstanding its limitations his knowledge of God is adequate. The Lutheran exegete, for instance, will not be under pressure to change his denomination and to become a Methodist or a Presbyterian; the Protestant has no reason to be converted to Roman Catholicism or Greek Orthodoxy in order to behave ecumenically. But by carrying out his work in the ecumenical fellowship, the biblical interpreter will be challenged by other views and enabled thereby to add to his exegesis a new accent which it formerly lacked. To mention one or two instances, Protestant exegesis of the Lord's Supper has learned from the Orthodox churches that references to the cosmic work of the Logos are to be found in the New Testament as surely as references to the historical work of Christ. Similarly in the interpretation of Romans 3:21-26 we have been made aware of the fact that in the personalistic nature of justifying faith an indirect reference to the church is also implied.

This practice of interrelation which is so characteristic and essential for ecumenical fellowship obviously precludes the patronizing attitude symptomatic of pre-ecumenical Christianity. Did not Luther, for instance, consider it his right to tell the Anabaptists that there could be no work of the Holy Spirit apart from the "outward" word and sacraments? Likewise, the

Augsburg Confession is amply spiked with *damnationes* of all those who disagree with it theologically. Yet, in order to be valid, such contentions would require not only infallibility of exegesis but also perfect and exhaustive knowledge of the divine plan of redemption such as only the Son of God could have. Since these attitudes linger on in the Protestant denominations, the ecumenical approach to Bible study is bound to create a terribly uneasy situation. The old type of polemical discussion is out of the question, while mere acquiescence in other views would be tantamount to disregarding their truthfulness. Of course, ecumenical exegesis must not indulge in relativism, which would compel it to accept every fancy of interpretation as legitimate. There are obvious limits to the right understanding of Scripture beyond which the exegete would place himself outside of the Christian pale. Yet it is hardly possible to draw this line of demarcation by way of a vote of the World Council of Churches. The only thing to be accomplished by a vote would be a statement of what all of its members consider the inalienable core of the Christian faith. But little would be gained thereby except perhaps that the Council could exclude plainly non-Christian views allegedly supported by the Scripture.

For the rest, however, the problems that will disturb the fellowship stem from exegetical discoveries whose relation to the core of the Christian faith is not obvious. Scientific methods alone have proved to be of little help in solving such problems because scholarly opinion has seldom been in agreement on what is to be considered authoritative in the Bible. It is well known, for instance, that Johannes Weiss drew attention to the eschatological meaning of the kingdom of God in the Gospels, yet he also felt free to dismiss eschatology altogether as irrelevant for the Christian faith. In his opinion it was but a residue of Jewish thought and lacked intrinsic connection with the ethical teaching of Jesus.[1] Yet later scholarship has completely reversed

---

[1] Johannes Weiss, *Die Predigt Jesu vom Reiche Gottes* (2nd rev. ed.; Göttingen, 1900).

this view and has pointed out that the eschatological context was the specific differentia of Jesus' ethics. Obviously the problem cannot be settled on historical or philological grounds only; it has to be seen in the light of spiritual experience.

The exegetical difficulty is further aggravated by two facts. First, there is no theologian in the Protestant church who can claim the right to speak in the name of the whole of Protestantism, nor even for his denomination. While his denomination may delegate him to attend a theological conference as its representative, his findings nevertheless will not bind it without its subsequent approval even though he would identify himself with its standards or traditions. In modern Catholic exegesis the situation is similar. While as a rule Catholic biblical scholars in our days are anxious to remain within the framework of the tradition and official doctrine of their church, they are considerably more daring than their predecessors of a hundred years ago. In their interpretation they uncover views which had formerly been ignored by Catholic exegetes or naively interpreted as supporting the church's tradition. The outspoken character of some biblical scholars is embarrassing to the Vatican; yet, since they are so obviously on sound exegetical ground, they cannot be charged with heresy, silenced though they may be. How utterly mistaken it would be, nevertheless, to interpret the rapprochement of Protestant and Catholic biblical scholarship as a sign that the church of Rome is moving into the Protestant camp!

Secondly, while teaching the unity of Scripture, Protestant theology has never been able on strictly exegetical grounds to point out wherein that unity consists. Luther had taught that it is to be found in *was Christum treibet,* that is, in the Christocentric concern of God's word. But the Bible is a library, a collection of many books, whose authors differ in outlook, aim, and method of presentation. How then do we state in theological terms and in an unmistakable manner what unites all these writers? The very fact that staunch supporters of orthodoxy, who believe in the verbal inerrancy of the Bible, are not able to agree among themselves on how to formulate the message of the Bible in such manner that it is comprehensive, definite, and consistent, would seem to be the surest indication that the unity of the Bible refuses to be fettered by theological formulae. As the Reformers had already seen clearly, it is not theological logic but the Holy Spirit working through its authors which holds the Bible together and gives it unity of outlook. In turn, then, what holds Protestants together is their spiritual approach to the Bible.

This fact has important consequences for the ecumenical movement. Necessary and useful as is the outward organizational oneness of the churches, that fellowship is not directly related to the life of faith and redemption. It is obvious that in order to be relevant to the Christian believers today, the ecumenical movement must also pursue a spiritual end. It is in this goal, however, that we find the real problem of ecumenical Bible study in our days. While the fact that all the churches have an organization has made possible their association in the World Council of Churches, it is their very institutional character that renders difficult, if not impossible, their spiritual cooperation. The perplexity of faith which besets ecumenical interpretation is not that of Luther; rather it is the question: How can the church be a spiritual factor in this world notwithstanding its institutional life and organization? As far as Protestantism is concerned the question had never really been raised in the pre-ecumenical age; it had been dodged. Most Protestants formulated the problem of faith so that the existence of the institutional church was ignored and the problem was understood in terms of individual existence. By those who interpreted it as the church's concern for this world, the problem was couched in terms of a philosophical or social function and not a spiritual one. Things were somewhat different in the Catholic church, which has over the years thought of its task as that of maintaining the primacy of the spiritual in this world. That church has nevertheless unduly narrowed the realm of the spiritual, not only by coupling it with ecclesiastical authority but also by interpreting its primacy as implying control of political and social life.

In the history of the Protestant denominations one notices in the nineteenth and particularly the twentieth centuries a growing self-assertion on the part of the institutional agencies of the church. As a result, those in control of the institutional life were able to direct the affairs of the church as though its energy resided in its elaborate organization, its numerical strength, and its finances. Paradoxically, however, all the conferences, training courses, syllabi, and symposium volumes dealing with this aspect of church life prove to be but so many evidences of an unconscious bewilderment.

This bewilderment is further increased by the fact that the aim of biblical study must be to ascertain the providential place which, by the will of God, the church occupies in this world. Yet the environment in which the church must live has radically changed its character during the last one hundred years or so. Hence whatever hint theological tradition was able to offer for the solution of this problem has practically lost its value in our days because it presupposed an image of this world which has but little resemblance with its actual conditions. It is now evident that the relative ease with which the philosophers and scientists of the seventeenth and eighteenth centuries handled our problems was rendered possible by the fact that their image of the world was but a modification of the biblical view. No wonder the theological understanding of the relationship between church and world presented no unsurmountable theoretical obstacles. For all of them the world was a spiritual universe.

Modern man has abandoned that belief, and the universe in which he lives is, in his eyes, so utterly a material one that even human relationships are interpreted in terms of the analogy afforded by mechanical processes. Nevertheless, for clarity's sake one must welcome this strange development. With the advance of science and technology man's horizon has been infinitely widened, yet from the image of this world thus engendered, all contact with God or a superior world has been deliberately and radically eliminated. This trend away not only from God but also from spiritual values has had its inevitable repercussions upon social life. No matter whence a principle of order is derived, it is certainly not sought in the will of God, and any connection between social life and a spiritual reality is categorically denied. This is particularly obvious in National Socialism, Russian communism, the anti-colonial movement, and modern imperialism. Yet by adopting such views modern man has created a serious dilemma for himself. The world in which man lives is not only no longer under his control but resists all attempts to accommodate to man's mind. Both in the cosmos and in social or international relations this incomprehensible independence frightens man no matter how boldly he pretends to accept it. Gone is the trust in a natural balance of nature or of historical life; gone is the hope for a steady progress in this world, as well as the expectation that, living in a rational world, man might be able to rule over it by means of his reason. This cosmic homelessness which permeates all modern life indirectly increases or radicalizes our spiritual perplexity too, for it deprives the theologian of all hope that he will ever find assistance or support in modern science or philosophy.

It should be obvious that in such a situation of radical aporia there is no point in calling for a theology "that will take this world seriously" or in looking for an "ecumenical" theology which would provide the answer to all the questions which assail us in our present bewilderment. Once one has admitted his nescience, every recourse to tradition appears unrealistic, and every theological synthesis is soon unmasked as wishful thinking. Throughout Christian history the spiritual leaders have learned that it is only by foregoing every claim of knowing the truth and by passing through the "dark night of faith" that the presence of Christ can be discovered. One would hope that the way out of this agony could be found in a concerted Bible study on the part of the churches affiliated with the World Council of

Churches. But the project proves to be unmanageable. This perplexity, while subconsciously haunting whole denominations at the present time, reaches the level of consciousness in strictly personal experience and thus by different roads in different interpreters. It is only when scholars emerge from the agony of their perplexity and discover the light in the Scriptures that they will be able to collaborate, because then only will they find a common foundation. This will not consist, however, in the smallest common denominator of their respective theologies but rather in the experience of the presence of Christ which transcends all possible theologies, because such experience is the ground upon which theology must rest.

In the age of subjectivism, people were reading the Scripture with an eye for what looked edifying to them. In the ecumenical situation, however, we are driven to the question: Where is the place at which Christ meets the church in such a way that it is able to emerge from its perplexity? In a general way we can say that it is not the notion or representation of God, be it naive or sophisticated, which will lift us out of the "miry pit," nor the mere assurance of his work in the past—for instance, in the creation, the sending of Christ, or the making of the Bible—but God's redemptive presence in Christ. This divine presence is apprehended by means of spiritual illumination. Those, in turn, who have reached this level of Spirit-guided understanding of the Bible will also be able to recognize it in other interpreters. Although differing from each other in their particular interpretations of a biblical passage or book, they will nevertheless be aware of the fact that their differing views are related to the same divine reality.

In the light of this experience, a denomination is enabled to restate its faith again in a relevant way because its interpretation of the Bible is related to that problem with which a denomination is wrestling at present and also enables that denomination to encounter Christ at the place where they need him. In this manner, Wesley rescued people's belief in God when they were bewildered by the impersonal sacramentalism of the Church of England on the one hand, and the dry moralism of the Puritans on the other. He was enabled to show them in the Scripture a Christ who sanctifies personal life. Similarly, George Fox could point to a Christ who through the light of his Spirit illumines and activates the hearts of all the believers no matter how low their social or mental condition might be; whereas they had been fettered by the dictates of man-made theologies.

We cannot overlook, however, the different situation which the ecumenical movement has brought about. How is a denomination's new understanding of itself to be related to the ecumenical organization? And what ways are open to the Church Universal to speak about its relation to God in this age with a united voice? Apparently the very readiness to face the problem adds to our perplexity. For we cannot say what ways God will choose to lead his church into the future, particularly since the search for the present Christ who speaks to us through the Bible has hardly begun in Protestantism. Few are those biblical interpreters who have become aware of the new demands which the ecumenical movement makes in this respect upon the denominations affiliated with it.

A consequence of the kind of biblical study described is respect for the particular position of other denominations which proceed in the same manner. On the basis of the older traditional type of theology, denominations can at best ignore those aspects of other denominations on which they disagree. In that case, the tolerance issues from indifference. One is prepared not to attack or criticize the other denomination because one has adopted a relativistic or skeptical view of theology. There lies one of the dangers besetting the ecumenical movement in our day. The new fellowship in which Protestant denominations find themselves seems to demand that ecclesiastical standards be abandoned and that we refrain from criticism of the other denomination's position. Yet obviously this is an utterly sterile attitude which is in no way able to contribute to real unity among the members of the World Council of Churches. Of course, a return to old time interdenominational polemics would be no less frustrating, and past experience has shown too clearly that no denomination has ever thereby been moved to change its position.

Viewed from an ecumenical vantage point, denominational differences will lead to mutual questioning. We have no right to assume from the outset that the other denomination must be wrong, merely because we are certain that our position is true; but ecumenicity does not require us, either, to regard other denominations as infallible in every respect. The bewilderment or amazement which the particularities of another denomination call forth in us entitles us to ask for an explanation why it was led from the common spiritual basis to a position differing from ours. Thereby the other denomination will be stimulated to engage in the same self-scrutiny which we have practiced, and the denominations concerned will assist each other spiritually. Even when the explanation given by another denomination does not convince us that we should adopt its position, it will hardly leave us unchanged. For by such an encounter we are enabled to enlarge our spiritual horizon, or we realize in the light of the unfamiliar position of the other denominations that our common problem has depths which we had not suspected. Protestants may see no reason, for instance, why they should understand the church as including the dead no less than the living, as do the Eastern Orthodox churches, but churches that have any experience of the Spirit's work at all will probably be stimulated by contacts with Orthodoxy to meditate upon the constitutive role which the spiritual past plays in the redemptive work of the church. Similarly, Methodists or Baptists may very well be overawed by the mystery of grace when their view of the "steadfast love" of God is confronted with the Lutheran understanding of God's groundless love shown in man's justification. In this way the ecumenical diversity in unity ceases to be mere coexistence. Although there is no theological or confessional unity, denominations discover their oneness in the common spiritual experience of the redemptive presence of Christ.

Since this process of mutual questioning and stimulation depends both on the awareness of a spiritual crisis and a subsequent spiritual experience called forth by the study of the Bible, it will not take place among all the churches simultaneously. Furthermore, it is bound to go on as long as the World Council of Churches is in existence. Ecumenical interrelation does not denote a form of organization but an ongoing process in the spiritual relations of the Christian churches. Its objective cannot be to heal the split in the church by undoing the Reformation and to return to the conditions or the faith of the Middle Ages, as Anglican theologians sometimes suggest, but rather to move onward towards the full realization of the common spiritual life of the churches.

The full appropriation of the truth in Christ must be the work of the Church Universal because each of the particular churches represents only that segment which is accessible from its viewpoint, and its complete apprehension is reserved for the life to come. Yet the spiritual understanding granted to each member of the Church Universal proves sufficient for an adequate apprehension of the redemptive presence of Christ. This diversification does not preclude the acknowledgement that some denominations have a more profound spiritual life than others, but it renders invalid the claim of any church that in its theology it possesses the full and absolute truth.

CHAPTER VII

THE FUTURE OF PROTESTANTISM

We have seen that the nature of Protestantism is such that each branch must answer the fundamental question about its right of existence, if with a good conscience before God it is to take its place in the company of the other churches. Mere organizational cooperation, as in the World Council of Churches, is at best an indication of intention to take the unity of the church seriously, in spite of the multiplicity of denominations. The first actual step toward unity, however, is taken in an inspired study of the Bible and common worship. Thereby the churches manifest their common allegiance to the Lord Jesus Christ, the Head of the church.

A. ACTUAL UNITY

As we look beyond these preliminary steps, the future course of Protestantism will surely be affected to some extent by the way in which the issue of church unity is resolved. Church unity, the need of which emanates from spiritual perplexity and which is accomplished through a study of the Bible which leads to spiritual experience, is the permanent task assigned to the denominations and churches engaged in the ecumenical movement. Obviously, however, there is no merit in the mere continuation of this process unless there is hope that some tangible unity can be obtained thereby. The churches cannot believe in their oneness unless there are visible manifestations of their common spiritual ground. These exist, indeed, and they give hope of further progress.

First to be mentioned is the ecumenical movement itself. The very fact that the age in which the churches and denominations treated each other with disdain, suspicion, and hostility has come to an end, is evidence that in some sense all the churches concerned have apprehended their common ground. This awareness has not only led to the official formation of the World Council of Churches, in which the churches are united as organizations, but also to an intensive exchange of people, ideas, and experiences. The interdenominational composition of the student body in the leading seminaries and theological faculties of the world is a good omen of intensified collaboration among the denominations. Of particular importance is the fact that in this way students acquire an intimate familiarity with the devotional life and worship of other denominations and thus enter most directly into spiritual fellowship with them.

A second tie that binds the churches together is a new evaluation of the Bible. It is read and understood again as the word of God, and people turn to it for guidance in spiritual perplexity. The widespread preoccupation with biblical theology is indicative of this new treatment of the Bible. Connected with this change are symptoms of a reappraisal of the sacraments in Protestantism. Characteristic for the pre-ecumenical view of the sacraments in wide Protestant circles was the subordination of the sacraments under the word. They were supposed to illustrate doctrine, and people who ascribed to them a specific spiritual function of their own were suspected of Catholicizing tendencies.

It is obvious now that there can be no spiritual fellowship with sacramental churches if the sacraments are held to have no spiritual function of their own. In this respect, too, unity will not require that all churches and denominations hold identical views of the sacraments, but the ecumenical situation will demand openness for the specific mode of divine activity which is tied up with the sacraments in the view of certain churches. In this respect, Luther's view of the "God who speaks," when applied to the sacraments too, will probably enable Protestants to adopt a deepened view of these means of grace. Just as the Bible was changed thereby from an infallible textbook of doctrine into a personal communication of divine comfort, so also through the sacraments Christ reveals himself in the life of the church as the source of true life and the support of that life. Although it is impossible to foretell in advance how such development will proceed, it will be good to remember how deep a unity can be experienced when people are willing to be guided by the Holy Spirit. Let me illustrate this statement by a half-forgotten episode that took place at the Faith and Order Conference at Lausanne.

On August 13, 1927, representatives of the Greek Orthodox, Congregationalist, Reformed, Anglican, Lutheran, Baptist, and Methodist churches, and a Quaker, read statements expressing the respective views of the sacraments held by their denominations. The immediate impression of this bewildering diversity of doctrines was devastating. The general feeling was that the theological differences among the churches represented were so great as to be insuperable, and this realization seemed to be evidence that the conference had tried the impossible. However, Bishop Charles Brent of New York, the President of the conference, suggested that the delegates stay together in a prolonged period of silent prayer for divine guidance. Then the delegates were asked to rise to their feet and to recite together, each one in his own language, the Lord's Prayer. This act of common worship saved not only the Lausanne Conference but also the ecumenical movement. The delegates were made aware of the stirring of the Holy Spirit, who was more powerful than the divisive forces. The next day, August 14, found all the delegates united in the Cathedral of Lausanne for a common worship of prayer and repentance. Subsequently, at the invitation of the local congregation, the sacrament of the Lord's Supper was most impressively celebrated in a ceremony in which ministers of the various Protestant denominations officiated and all the Protestant delegates communed. Although the members of the Orthodox churches were prohibited by ecclesiastical law to partake of the elements, many of them were present and joined spiritually in the ceremony. Under similar circumstances a communion service was celebrated at the Conference on Church, Community, and State at Oxford in 1937.

Pressure was brought to bear on the ecumenical movement, particularly on the part of certain Anglican circles, which has since rendered the problem of intercommunion less tractable, with the result that the Student Christian Movement too has become reluctant to continue its practice of unlimited intercommunion. Yet a precedent has been set by the Holy Spirit himself, and one hopes that he will show new ways to the churches concerned.

There is a great deal of fellowship and exchange on an un-official basis. Theological institutes and conferences bring pastors and laymen of different denominations together and foster the exchange of theological views and fellowship in prayer and worship. The same end is accomplished by various societies for evangelism and foreign missions, by numerous interest groups in the clergy which operate on an interdenominational basis, and by the nondenominational religious press. While all of them serve practical purposes, they have a religious inspiration, never-theless, and help to bring members of different denominations to common spiritual experience and thus to the realization of their common spiritual basis. The union services celebrated in many American towns and cities on Thanksgiving Day also point in that direction. A purely secular act of law passed by the Congress of the United States has become an occasion for the churches to become aware of their oneness in the Spirit and to worship together on the basis of full equality. Might it not be possible for the churches united in the World Council of Churches to set aside August 14 in commemoration of the miracle that happened in Lausanne and to urge the congregations to unite on that day in worshipful expectation of the next step the Holy Spirit will take? Is not perhaps the main reason why the ecumenical movement appears to many as a wish for unity, rather than its manifestation, to be found in the fact that the churches concerned expect so little of the Holy Spirit, and instead of being open to his urgings, prefer to follow their own ideas?

B. INTERDENOMINATIONAL RELATIONS

The majority of Protestant denominations have been brought to the recognition that as a result of their common origin in the Reformation they possess a basic unity. Thus there is a general desire to practice this unity and to give it such outward expression that even non-Christians will become aware of it. Our survey has shown, however, that this transcendental unity brought forth by the Spirit of the risen Lord goes hand in hand with differences in theology, church polity, and forms of worship. There would be no problem if a common spiritual experience had already been granted to all denominations. In fact, however, the waiting and striving for a common experience based upon a Spirit-guided study of the Bible does not do away with their differences. While the denominations are able to respect each other and to share their spiritual insights with each other, they feel, nevertheless, unable to yield to each other in those matters in which they have their own particular features.

This irreducible difference creates a thorny practical problem. Should denominations continue to evangelize in each other's domain? This tendency is less outspoken between Reformed and Lutheran churches than between the older Protestant denominations and the new ones. Baptists, Quakers, and Methodists have propagated their views in Puritan and Anglican circles; and in more recent times Holiness and other Revival groups, no less than Jehovah's Witnesses, have indiscriminately raided all Protestant denominations. But even the polemics between Lutheran and Reformed theologians were never meant to be of a purely theoretical character. They were aimed at swaying the denomination attacked so that it would give up its own independent existence and join the criticizing denomination, or at least so individual members would choose that course. The concept of comity, upon which the Protestant members of the World Council of Churches are agreed, should consistently apply to the domestic relations of these denominations no less than to the foreign mission field. Yet this tendency is obviated by the denominations' sense of mission. No matter what their original cause and reason may have been, the denominations consider their particular features as being rooted in their basic principles. Consequently they hold that another denomination which lacks them has missed something which is constitutive of the truth, or that it may even in that respect be on the wrong side. In recent times the issue has assumed especially painful consequences in Greece, where the Orthodox church contends that the work of Protestant evangelists is incompatible with their membership in the ecumenical movement. The evangelizing circles, in turn, retort that the Greek Orthodox church has not satisfied people's need for a strictly personal religion. Similarly, missionaries ask themselves in what respect the denominational rivalry on the foreign field will be influenced by the merger of the International Missionary Council with the World Council of Churches.

One thing is obvious. The churches united in the World Council of Churches are not able to regard their specific differences as irrelevant. In discussing the new approach to biblical study we pointed out that the spiritual understanding thus gained would serve as a challenge to other denominations to scrutinize their own position. Inasmuch as the other denomination fails to accept that challenge, members of the challenging denomination will feel free, and perhaps even spiritually constrained, to familiarize members of the nonresponsive denomination with their own views, to urge them to accept their spiritual insights, and perhaps even to join their denomination. It is hard to see how things could be otherwise. We may feel irritated and angered by the missionary zeal of Jehovah's Witnesses, for instance, but we must grant them the right of their viewpoint. They believe sincerely that they have a sacred right and duty to propagate their ideas in Christian circles, for failing to inform us of what they consider to be the victory of truth over error would be tantamount to abandoning us to inevitable damnation.

The situation is somewhat different in the ecumenical movement, at least as far as the Protestant churches are concerned. They would hardly have recognized each other as members of the Church Universal if they had held that some of them were engulfed by deadly error. But the Christian religion is concerned with man's salvation (*soteria*), that is to say, with his supreme good (*bene esse*), not merely with an indispensable minimum (*esse*). Thus Christians will instinctively feel that it would be a disservice to members of other denominations if they did not inform them about those elements in the Christian faith which in their view are essential for making the offered salvation the supreme good.

There is, nevertheless, a vast difference between the propagation of ideas on the one hand, and proselyting on the other. We should keep in mind the fact that membership in the World Council implies the recognition that all the churches so united belong to the Body of Christ. Hence a denomination has a moral right to seek converts from another denomination only in a case where it discovers a lack of spiritual insight which causes serious spiritual harm to its members and which that denomination is not willing to remedy. Whether or not that is the case can never be known except where a real exchange of spiritual views has taken place between the two denominations. This requirement should not prevent individual Christians from applying for membership in another denomination whenever, after careful examination, they feel they would be more at home in the other denomination. It seems that the methodical raids of other denominations are now limited to groups which refuse to join the World Council of Churches because they are not willing to undergo the mutual spiritual test and questioning. Their hope to win adherents is based upon denouncing the spiritual rights of the churches united in the World Council rather than upon the spiritual superiority of their own message.

While within the ecumenically-minded churches strict comity should be the rule, mutual questioning in the fields of theology and ethics will continue. As a result, adult baptism, for instance, will remain a hotly debated issue between Baptists and non-Baptists in the ecumenical movement. Similarly Lutherans will feel unable to keep silent on their view of justification by faith, and Anglicans will feel an urge to stress the importance of Apostolic Succession. However, with the denominations viewing each other within the Church Universal, they will no longer be able to see the speck in the brother's eye while unaware of the beam in their own. The pre-ecumenical approach treated the other denomination as lacking an essential feature while considering one's own denomination as being in need of nothing. In an ecumenical perspective it will be noticed that the newer Protestant denominations owe their origin to the fact that their founders thought they detected in the older denomination the absence of some elements which in their opinion could not be ignored without loss. Hence the Lutheran or Reformed theologians will no longer be able to dismiss the Baptist view with the contention that they have evidence for infant baptism in the New Testament. Rather they will humbly ask themselves whether there is not some important element lacking in their concept of faith which is duly emphasized by the Baptist insistence on the necessity of believers' baptism. The outcome might be the conviction that there is no harm in either infant or adult baptism, but that the work of the Holy Spirit is stultified in an adolescent who pays no attention to the Spirit's urge manifested in his baptism.

The ecumenical movement is strained more seriously by differences in ethics, however, than by differences of theology, church polity, and worship. This problem was highlighted when the Russian Orthodox church applied for membership in the World Council of Churches. Opponents to her admission at the New Delhi meeting in 1961 contended that the Russian church was under pressure of the Communist government. The real problem, of course, was whether a church which did not in principle categorically reject a socialist order of economic life could be expected to live in harmony with the churches of the West. The problem raised at New Delhi was not an absolutely new one; it had been referred to already at Evanston by some representatives of churches living behind the Iron Curtain. It gained greater urgency, however, at New Delhi because the Russian Orthodox church was believed to play a more or less official role in Communist Russia. Nevertheless, the problem appears only in a new form, for its roots reach back into the nineteenth century, and in a certain way even into the sixteenth.

Medieval devotion had sought a way by which the believer could detach himself completely from the world in which he lived. However, the Reformers reminded people that faith had to be applied to, and tested by, one's life in this world. Necessarily this would imply one's attitude to state and government, culture and economic life. Epoch-making as this principle was, its application was not an easy one. It is well known that the Reformers rejected the *apolitie*, i.e., civic indifference, of the Anabaptists[1] as well as the economic and social claims of the German peasants in 1525 as incompatible with their understanding of the gospel and Christian faith. Justified as may have been the Reformers' objection in given circumstances, the fact is undeniable that their principle led eventually to compliance with the status quo in the Lutheran countries and Switzerland. Christian reasons for opposition to the government were proffered by other Protestant groups, however, for instance, the Huguenots, the Dutch patriots, and the Dissenters. In the nineteenth century the general preoccupation with social problems made Christians ask whether support of the existing conditions was compatible with Christian charity and love of one's neighbor. This feeling

---

[1] See Hans J. Hillerbrand, *Die politische Ethik des . . . Täufertums* (Leiden/Köln: E. J. Brill, 1962).

gave rise to various reform movements but also strained seriously the inner unity of the denominations.

The advance of Marxist socialism has considerably sharpened the issue. The question now is no longer whether certain social evils ought to be fought by Christians but whether or not the present economico-political order of capitalism or free enterprise will ever be able to satisfy the divine demand for justice. Formulated in this way, the issue concerns each member of the Christian church personally: some because they are to gain economically or socially from the adoption of a Socialistic or Communistic regime, others because they are likely to suffer loss of property and status. Unfortunately, however, this preponderance of economic and social interests is bound to blur considerably the ethical issue. No wonder that there should be utter confusion in the evaluation of communism. The United States government, for instance, has declared the Communist party illegal because it is supposed to teach the violent overthrow of the government; the Roman Catholic church invokes in a rather inconsistent way— for many of its monks and nuns live under a collectivistic regime —the sanctity of private property, as it calls for a crusade against Russia. In turn, those Protestant pastors living behind the Iron Curtain who have espoused communism support its social reforms while rejecting its theoretical atheism and materialism.

This confusing diversity of attitudes and viewpoints is an indication that the problem has not yet reached the depth of a spiritual issue. What separates Christians at the present moment in this respect are political and economic interests and convictions rather than spiritual differences. The controversy concerns the appropriate means by which the Christian faith is to be implemented while the basic question is dodged, namely, in what respect and for what end is faith related to the believer's economic and political situation.

Things are not much different with reference to the problem of war. Here too the dividing line between those who accept war as an unavoidable necessity, or perhaps even as a moral obligation in international life, and those who want to abolish war altogether, runs right across the denominations; and the differences seem to stem from emotional rather than ethical reasons. In view of that situation it is hardly legitimate to deny membership in the World Council of Churches to denominations which refuse on principle to condemn communism as such or which are radically opposed to war. But it is not desirable either in an indifferent mood to let things stand at that. Just as in theological matters, so in ethics; nothing is gained spiritually by merely opposing conflicting views. The viewpoints from which communism and war are to be judged can be reached only by those who make their participation in economic and international life a matter of Spirit-guided faith. Until light on these issues has been gained, the members of the ecumenical movement must realize that secular disagreements cannot serve as a pretext for severing ecumenical fellowship; but they must also admit that such far-reaching dissensions concerning the mode of implementing the faith in practical life must be understood as a concrete and urgent challenge to discover an appropriate spiritual perspective in which they are to be judged.

C. THE ECUMENICAL MOVEMENT AND ROME

We began with the historical fact that the ecumenical movement is the outcome of Protestant theology. The participation of the Eastern Orthodox churches does not mean that they regard Protestantism as a genuine church in the spiritual sense. Rome finally has chosen to stand altogether outside of not only the World Council of Churches but the whole ecumenical movement, and to set up an ecumenical organization of its own. But behind the ecumenical movement we discern the belief that the unity of the church exists because it is both the Body and the Bride of Christ. That belief is the reason why the ecumenical interest issued in a dynamic movement. The people who are engaged in it can neither acquiesce in their past accomplishments nor be satisfied with the formation of an international organization. They recognize that ecumenicity requires further organizational efforts but also, and above all, that a spiritual advance toward the experiential apprehension of the present Christ must accompany such efforts. The final goal must be visible manifestation of the unity which all three churches, Eastern Orthodox, Catholic, and Protestant, have in the present operation of their work.

At first sight it would seem to be most appropriate that in the next step Protestantism and Orthodoxy should come to terms, because they are already collaborating in the World Council of Churches. However, historical and geographical reasons seem to demand that the rapprochement of Protestantism and Rome should take precedence. Both occupy the same geographic area and, as has been shown, Protestantism has its roots in the Roman Catholic rather than the Greek Orthodox church. While Protestants disagree with Catholicism on a number of doctrines and practices, they cannot assert their right of existence without at the same time confirming the priority of the older church out of whose midst Christ called Luther and then rendered possible the Reformation. Even if, with the Reformers, we take a very serious view of the abuses which had besmirched the face of the church in the late Middle Ages, it remains the church of Christ in which Satan wrought havoc. Constructive relations between the two churches have been rendered difficult by the fact that in the course of the heated controversy that raged in the sixteenth and seventeenth centuries, both churches tended to give extreme expressions to their views. Thereby the impression could be created that the points most vigorously debated were also the central ones. In fact, however, there is full agreement on the doctrines of God, Christ, redemption, and eschatology; and even in the doctrine of man, the divergences concern only some of its aspects.

With the fallibility of human nature it is inevitable that those who are responsible for the preservation of the revealed truth will tend to overemphasize what they consider especially important in church life. Rome has laid all stress on the unity of the church and its doctrine as well as on the necessary place the church occupies in God's redemptive plan, the providential function of the episcopacy, and the active character of faith. The Reformation, in turn, has emphasized the transempirical nature of the church and of revelation, God's personal dealing with the chosen ones, and the receptive aspect of faith. The fact that Rome is at the present moment mainly interested in improved relations with the Eastern churches, and regards Protestantism as a heresy to be healed, does not compel us to take the same view of Rome. On the contrary, it would seem that there is no better way of manifesting our superior spiritual insight than by recognizing that the church of Christ is and always remains one and cannot be split by man's sin. But such recognition does not demand that Protestants return to Rome and undo the Reformation. Rather we are able to acknowledge Rome as a true church because we consider Christ himself the agent of redemptive history, and thus in the existence of three churches we find evidence that the Lord himself has introduced diversity into his one church. Nor does our recognition imply approval of, or acquiescence in, the political activities of the Vatican; rather we watch them with grave misgivings. But we cannot become aware of them without realizing that Protestant churches and denominations too have often been engaged in political activities.

To some the very idea of dealing with the Catholic church in terms of ecumenicity will seem unrealistic and utopian. We cannot deny the fact that after the Council of Trent any ecumenical approach to Rome has been rendered almost impossible. While that assembly was, in a way, an admission that the medieval church needed the radical shake-up applied by the Reformation, it also, in a seemingly final way, closed the door to reconciliation with Protestantism. Rome is hardly able to make any concession to Protestantism on the three points which are beyond discussion for us, namely, (1) that the risen Christ rather than the vicar of Christ is the head of the church; (2) that God speaks to the believer directly through the Scriptures, and not through the teaching office of the church only; and (3) that Luther was called by God to reform the church and was not a rebellious and heretical disrupter of the church's unity.

In view of the stubbornness with which Rome contends that she is right in all spiritual matters and Protestantism in its very essence is wrong, it is hard for Protestants to overcome their suspicion and distrust of the Pope and the Catholic hierarchy. One thing is certain. The naive way in which some Protestants hope to build bridges to Rome by way of theological and ecclesiastical concessions is merely evidence of their superficial understanding of the treasures they have in Protestantism. The problem is so enormous that one wonders whether it can ever be solved by human means. The divine origin of the Catholic church does not preclude the eschatological interpretation which the Reformers gave to the conditions prevailing in their days. They saw rightly that Antichrist was almost completely in control of the church. Nietzsche very sagaciously perceived that except for Luther's Reformation, Christianity would have ceased to be a power in the Western world.[1] In turn, Luther was aware of how ludicrous were the attempts of the humanists to restore the integrity of the church by means of loftier ethics and increased erudition. Had he not expected support from Christ, Luther would have given up the hopeless fight. The mood of despair that dominates the preface to the Smalcald Articles and leads to the anguished cry, "O dear Lord Jesus Christ, hold yourself a Council and deliver thine own through thy glorious Parousia!" even to the present day fills the heart of many a Protestant who thinks of the unity of Christ's church.

We have to ask ourselves seriously, however, whether in the light of the subsequent history of the Catholic church we still have a right to repeat the severe verdict pronounced by the Reformers. Would it not be more correct to say that the continued existence of that church is an indication that it repented

---

[1] Friedrich Nietzsche, V, 8, *Antichrist*, Section 61.

of its faults, and that we should consider the fact that it has been preserved and has continued to grow for an additional four hundred years as a divine sign that it was deemed necessary for the growth of the Church Universal and worthy of the Spirit's continued blessing?

If we are to take the Catholic church seriously within the Church Universal, it will not do to concede that insofar as it has certain doctrines and practices in common with the Reformation, or Protestantism, it is in the truth, but that in all its particular features it is completely mistaken. Such an attitude would be tantamount to asserting that the Protestant church is the only true church. Rather it will be necessary to regard Roman Catholicism in its totality as a true church, that is to say, as an organization which, though subject to human aberrations and weaknesses, will also time and again be purged by the Spirit of Christ. We cannot see much point, either, in speaking of "essential catholicism" (Wilfred Monod) which is found in all churches,[2] as distinct from ecclesiastical catholicism. Quite apart from the methodological weakness of thinking of the church in idealistic rather than historical and theological terms, who would be the man of God capable of discerning that essence in all the historical churches and denominations? This whole approach attempts to solve the problem of church unity according to the pattern found in Eastern Orthodoxy and Rome, that is to say, by means of a commonly accepted theology or confession of faith. This view starts from the axiom that basically only one type of church is possible, whereas Protestantism is in an indissoluble way established upon the principle of diversity in unity.

The only legitimate way in which we can hope to make a positive approach toward the Catholic church consists in obediently following the Holy Spirit as he is at work in church history through the ages. Since the medieval church, far from being annihilated, was restored to new life after Trent, the pos-

---

[2] Monod, *Du Protestantisme* (Paris, 1928).

sibility of an encounter with the Catholic church must be sought in spiritual activities. There would be little value in dealing with it from a purely historical or organizational angle. The fact that it has adjusted its form of government and view of doctrine to its mediterranean background is as much an unalterable historical fact as is the nordic character of the Reformation. We are not holding that fact against the Catholic church, although we deplore that the sociological element was often allowed to hold sway over its spiritual function.

We do not deny that Rome is a true church and that it needs nothing from outside of itself to be a church. But we consider it a serious error that it should interpret its wholeness and inner oneness as implying uniqueness (encyclical *Satis Cognitum* of 1896).[3] The only way the churches can manifest their unity is by jointly recognizing in every respect Christ as their head. For that purpose it is not sufficient that all should hold the same belief in Jesus Christ. Rather the fact that he alone is our Savior must become manifest in the way in which we act in the church and are prepared to serve him obediently as our Lord. By making this spiritual worship its supreme concern, the Catholic church would recognize its interrelation with the other two churches. That this kind of truly Catholic ecumenicity is not unknown in the Catholic church is evident in much that goes on today in its theology and biblical research. For instance, Catholic scholars are engaged in an intensive study of Protestant research. However, such activity should not be done *sub rosa* but should be acknowledged as essential for the well-being of Catholicism, just as Protestantism has to receive a deepened understanding of the nature and the ministry of the church by studying the life and doctrine of the Catholic church. In particular, modern Protestantism is challenged by her to come to terms with the problem of teaching authority. The mere fact that we reject the privilege of the bishops to interpret Scripture authoritatively is not enough to satisfy the believer's demand for assurance of faith.

---

[3] Denzinger and Bannwart, *Enchiridion Symbolorum,* II, nos. 1954-62.

Similarly we can hardly ignore the radical change that has taken place in the evaluation of the Scriptures on the part of the Catholic church. Three or four decades ago it was customary in Catholic circles to dissuade people from reading even annotated Catholic Bibles, and the few devout priests who dared propagate the study of the Bible were officially discouraged. Today, modern readable translations of the Catholic Bible are available in many languages, and in the English-speaking parts of the Catholic church, the Protestant Revised Version has recently been adopted as replacement for the Catholic Rheims-Douai Version. Catholic scholars are studying the Bible intently, and theological thought is receiving its inspiration from the Bible. Of special interest to Protestants is the fact that Catholic scholarship no longer treats the Bible as though it had fallen from heaven or were relevant only on account of its miraculous inspiration, but it has become aware of the fact that the Bible is the book of the church and can be truly understood only in the context of the church and its worship. While the way Canon Law defines the right of the episcopacy to control the exegete must be considered an attempt to muzzle the Spirit, we should in turn be reminded by Rome that biblical interpretation practiced on the basis of modern Protestant subjectivism is tantamount to denying the divine origin of Scripture.

The Roman understanding of faith has often been presented as constituting the most radical difference between the two churches. Reviewing in retrospect the polemics on this issue, however, one easily discovers that both sides have built up a straw man. While Protestants have stressed the element of trust and confidence as the core of faith, and thus have singled out the personal relationship between God and the believer, in contrast with the Catholic emphasis placed upon assent, neither side considers its perspective to involve a comprising of the whole of faith. The *Catechismus Romanus*[4] expressly mentions the fact

---

[4] *Catechismus ex decreto Concilii Tridentium sed parochos . . . editus* (Rome, 1566) II. 9. iv.

that the assent of faith is not given to ecclesiastical propositions
but to the divine act of self-disclosure, and the Council of Trent
(*Decretum de Justificatione*, Sessio VI, c. 8)[5] characterized faith
as "the beginning, foundation and root of the whole justification,
so that apart from it, it is impossible to be acceptable to God."
To be sure, that is not exactly the Protestant view of faith. The
Council does not state that it is by faith alone that people are
justified, and the justifying faith is the *fides caritate formata*,
that is to say, faith manifesting itself in good works rather than
the surrender of the self to the forgiving grace of God. It would
be grossly unfair, however, to contend that the post-Tridentine
Catholicism, while making verbal concessions to the Reformation,
retained all the features of the medieval doctrine. It is too obvious
that in connection with the Counter-Reformation, Catholic piety
has undergone a radical change and has little in common with
the forms of piety so often associated with the Reformers. This
new life of faith is indebted not only to the *via moderna* but also
to Protestantism. The crisis of perplexity and the agony of
doubt, so eloquently described by Pascal and John of the Cross,
have their roots not only in Augustine but also in the renewed
understanding of Augustine that characterizes the Reformation.

On the other hand, the Catholic contention that for Protestants
faith is merely subjective trust in an otherwise unknown God
may refer to some tendencies in nineteenth-century Protestantism, but it has no basis in the writings of the Reformers or in
the Protestant confessions of faith, and hardly describes the way
faith is handled in modern Protestant theology. If nothing else,
the heated theological debates which characterized the history
of Protestantism in the nineteenth century would refute the
charges of subjectivism and sentimentalism brought up by
Catholic polemicists. The correlation of faith and the Bible, so
characteristic of Protestantism, assures that faith has a well-
defined subject matter and presupposes a clear view of the work
of Him in whom the trust is put.

---

[5] Denzinger and Bannwart, *op. cit.*, no. 801.

Certainly the concepts of faith taught in the two churches are much more alike than polemicists have admitted. Thereby we do not mean that the remaining differences are trivial and insignificant. The Catholic view does not stress the fact that faith is ultimately an attitude of the self, not an act of the mind and the will only. Above all, the grace of which the Catholic church speaks in connection with faith is the grace by which one is enabled to become acceptable to God; whereas in Protestantism the grace which people apprehend by faith designates the act of God by which people have been made acceptable to him. In turn, Catholic theology has rightly seen that the traditional Protestant view of faith has great difficulty making the transition from faith as an attitude of the self to the daily life of the believer which should be a manifestation of his faith. In view of certain intrinsic tensions and obscurities in the traditional Protestant notion of faith, it might be a wholesome experience for Protestantism if we took a positive and open-minded attitude toward some of the aspects of faith as held in the Catholic church.

Finally, we mention the role of tradition which has been a bone of contention between the two churches ever since the days of the Reformers. By "tradition," Rome understands those doctrines and practices which the apostles either received orally from the Lord, or which were disclosed to them by the Holy Spirit and were, so to speak, passed on from hand to hand or mouth to mouth. Concerning traditions, the Council of Trent asserted that they are received by the church "with the same devotion and reverence as the Bible" (*Decretum de canonicis scriptures*, Sessio IV, c. 8). This statement clashes head-on with the Protestant principle of the Scripture alone. Nevertheless there is more agreement between the two churches than immediately strikes the eye. The Reformers were fully aware of the operation of the Holy Spirit which had constantly gone on in the life of the church. Consequently in their writings they quite frequently referred to the teaching of the Church Fathers of both antiquity and the Middle Ages. Yet they did not quote in the indiscriminate way in which the schoolmen appropriated the whole teaching of the past in support of their theology. Proceeding in such a manner would have been tantamount to equating the human factor in the history of doctrine with the work of the Holy Spirit. By means of their selective method, the Reformers wanted to show that their message was not an absolutely new beginning but that they were backed by the Spirit's continual work, as a result of which the substance of the gospel had been manifest in the church throughout the ages.

On the subject of tradition there remains a very wide divergence of views, for the Reformers appealed to tradition only when they were convinced that it was in agreement with Holy Scripture. Thus they safeguarded the sole and supreme authority of the Bible, whereas in the Catholic church, as a perusal of Denzinger's *Enchiridion* will show, all those teachings of the past which are not obviously incompatible with the Bible can be considered as binding traditions. Furthermore, it is the ecclesiastical hierarchy which, in the exercise of its teaching office, actually decides whether or not a teaching is compatible with the revealed truth. Although this role of the episcopacy introduces a certain element of flexibility into the notion of tradition, which is often overlooked by Protestant critics, the two churches are still far from seeing eye to eye on this matter. Yet here again we must admit that the absence of a contemporary teaching authority in Protestantism makes it difficult to develop criteria by which the agreement of tradition and Scripture is to be measured. The striking differences in the Protestant evaluation of the theological significance of Ignatius of Antioch or Bonaventura, for instance, form interesting cases in point.

Some Protestant theologians, realizing the wide agreement between Protestantism and Catholicism, are gradually giving up their purely polemical attitude toward Rome. It would seem to us, however, as though some of these men are going too far in their desire to deal fairly with the Catholic church. Above all, the agreement reached thus far is prevented from having extensive practical consequences because the two churches hold different views concerning the work of the Spirit. In the Protestant faith spiritual experience based upon the Scripture is paramount. As a result, specific doctrines are relevant for the life of faith only to the extent that they interpret and illuminate it in the light of biblical insights. The official Catholic view, however, is that the Holy Spirit has manifested himself in the formulation of dogmatic propositions promulgated by the ecclesiastical authorities. Such statements are therefore the primary object of faith. Furthermore, people should be reminded that unless one has first attained to a full appreciation of the specific spiritual treasures which the Protestant church offers, he is apt to lose doubly in joining the Catholic church. His gain will lie in the psychological rather than the spiritual sphere. We expect even less gain from attempts made in Anglican and Lutheran circles which adopt certain Catholic doctrines and practices, while continuing as members of separate denominations.

The Second Vatican Council is most instructive in accentuating the differences between Protestantism and Catholicism. We would certainly be unfair to a pope like John XXIII, or Paul VI, if we minimized the kindness and consideration shown to their Protestant guests during the illustrious assembly in Rome, or by questioning their remarkable zeal for the unity of the church. But the significance of the Council would be completely misunderstood if the fact were overlooked that its agenda dealt exclusively with problems that have arisen within the work of the Catholic church, partly through new emphases and methods in theology, and partly through the necessity to adjust herself to the conditions of the modern world. But future historians will look in vain for signs that the Council regarded any aspect of Protestantism as a challenge to her position, notwithstanding the fact that she was living side by side with the Protestant denominations in the modern world. This aloofness which is so evident in the Fathers, or at least the officers of the Council, would indicate that the spiritual image Rome has of itself makes it deal with the Protestants in a purely pragmatic way.

It is for this reason that any agreement which Protestant groups reach with friends in the Catholic church, enriching as it may be for them personally, can at the best be interpreted as an indication that striving for ecumenical encounter between Protestantism and the Catholic church is not utopian. But it is equally important to keep in mind that such an omen is not identical with the reality which it forebodes.

Roman Catholicism is a whole. Those who want to embrace it must embrace it in its totality, including the primacy of the Pope. The Protestant church, as has been shown, has its own right of existence. But understanding itself in the light of the ecumenical movement, Protestantism must realize that the Reformation must go on indefinitely.

This does not simply mean that the Protestant church and its constitutive denominations must alter their positions and forms of organization all the time. If there is a lesson to be drawn from the history of Orthodoxy and Rome, it is the realization that there is no evil in change as such. If the *ecclesia reformata* is *semper reformanda,* this can only mean that it has its formative principle in the Reformation. It is by its willingness, in its changing historical circumstances, to be constantly challenged by that principle, that Protestantism preserves its identity and thus has a permanent right of existence.

In turn, however, the Reformation must not be detached from the life of the Spirit as he operates in the history of the church. Since, like Rome, it has its roots in the church of the Middle Ages, the Protestant church must constantly ask itself how far that common heritage has been preserved in its own midst as well as in the Catholic church of today. Thus the present position of the church of Rome must appear to Protestants not only as a challenge to their own doctrine and practice but also as an innovation which is repulsive to Protestant faith. We do not therefore entertain the hope of an eventual merger of the Protestant church and the Catholic church. But we are nevertheless looking forward to an age of peaceful and positive relations between the two churches for their mutual benefit and as a sign to the world that, being manifestly united in Christ, his people have a providential mission in this world.

D. ON THE WAY

Being a venture of faith inspired by the Lord of the church, the ecumenical movement has labored from its very beginning under the fact that it must pursue a practical goal, namely, effective cooperation of the churches and denominations as an outward expression of the unity of the church. In the World Council of Churches the movement has created for itself an appropriate tool for the attainment of this end. Yet, since the Council represents primarily the administrative heads of these bodies, it is inevitably limited in scope and accomplishment. It must necessarily confine its work to actions in the practical field. Even the adoption of a theological "basis," no matter how simple and brief it may be, is subject to question within this body. It would be fatal if the theological statement which forms the basis of the World Council of Churches were considered a legal document rather than a common confession of faith. But who then is able and competent to decide whether or not a member faithfully adheres to the common formula of admission? Can matters of orthodoxy and heresy be decided by a majority vote?

It is to the credit of its outstanding leadership that the World Council of Churches has established, or at least initiated, all that can be done for the manifestation of church unity by means of organizational measures. Shifts in the international situation, especially the growth of the "younger" churches, may require it to place increased emphasis upon activities which receive minor attention at the present moment; but in the foreseeable future no radical steps toward organizational or organic union are to be expected, such as intercommunion or even a merger of the Anglican Communion and the Presbyterian Alliance. Such developments presuppose spiritual experience and growth which cannot be brought about by means of organizational measures, and which, except for the coming of a new reformer, will demand considerable time. This difficulty does not preclude an increase in familiarity between individual members of different denominations. But the time is gone when kings and princes could decide what confession should be adopted by their subjects. Manipulated mergers, even when cleverly contrived by ecclesiastical leaders, are bound to disintegrate again.

In turn, notwithstanding all the publicity given to the organizational aspects of the ecumenical movement, its strength resides in its spiritual energy, and this is hidden from the eyes of the general public and the journalists. The old saying *Ecclesia orans ecclesia docens* (through its worship the church prepares new theological insights) applies in a broader sense to all the ecumenical activities. Of course the fact cannot be denied that a good deal of so-called ecumenicity lacks a real inspiration—the local pastoral associations, for instance, are in many places merely clerical service clubs—but it is equally true to say that work for spiritual unity requires an outward organization, in and through which it can operate. It is only through such contacts and by working for common causes that members of the various denominations get to learn what is the genius of Protestantism.

There can be no doubt that common worship of different congregations on a local basis is proving to be the surest way to a deepened understanding of what the unity of the church is like, provided it is real worship and not a mere opportunity for one denomination to learn "how things are being done" in another denomination. Since outside the specifically political field there are large areas in which Protestants and Catholics can and should cooperate in a world that rapidly moves toward complete secularization, there is also hope that closer familiarity between the two leading churches of the West will be initiated and intensified. The prerequisite in all these instances is, however, that the spiritual aspect of the common activity should not be neglected. The field of ecumenicity has unfortunately become a happy hunting ground for activists, status seekers, and would-be leaders. Common theological study is neither the first nor the most effective step in a spiritual rapprochement, but it has its legitimate and necessary place in ecumenical activities. We emphasized that the prerequisite of an ecumenical encounter in theology was a deepened study of the Bible. The value of interdenominational theological conferences lies in the opportunity they provide for the individual theologian to familiarize himself with the specific emphases and the spiritual motivation of the theology of other denominations. The fact should be kept in mind, however, that until recently, in practically all the Protestant denominations, the work of the theologians has been carried on in isolation from the spiritual life of the congregations. As a result, the individual theologian, even when appointed by the supreme judicatory of his denomination, performs his work more or less as a private theologian. Some theologians consider themselves therefore completely free to disregard the confessional basis of their denominations; others who feel an urge to return to the traditional outlook of their denomination discover to their dismay that in recent times their congregations have abandoned their traditions and adopted entirely different views. Lutheran congregations in the Middle West for instance have often espoused dispensationalist fundamentalism; Mennonite congregations may be found practicing a rigid legalism that has no connection with the spiritual basis upon which their sixteenth-century forefathers built.

The lack of representative denominational theologians renders the pursuit of an "ecumenical theology" utopian. Even if a group of theologians should succeed in stating their agreement on certain topics, their findings would represent their personal views only. None of them would have a right to speak in the name and on behalf of his denomination. In our opinion, opportunities for theological exchange should be vastly multiplied, but not in the hope gradually to reach theological agreement thereby but rather as an opportunity for the participants to develop a truly ecumenical outlook in themselves. They will learn thereby that the topics which they expound have other relevant aspects in addition to those cherished by them personally or found in the confession of their denomination. Through the contact with other denominations they may also become aware that, more than they realized, their personal spiritual outlook has been tinged by the traditions of their denomination. Thus the denominations will be enabled to transform traditional positions into spiritual attitudes. This should be the principal end for which theological conferences are convened in our age.

Paradoxically, and yet in a way quite logically, this renewed understanding of their own nature which the denominations experience through their ecumenical contacts will result in a disintegration of their traditional forms of worship and church polity. The Protestant denominations are beginning to comprehend what the Reformers meant by the invisibility of the church. The nineteenth century understood that term as a synonym of religious subjectivism. No wonder that the excesses of such an attitude called forth a reaction which considered a return to the sixteenth-century forms of church worship, liturgy, and hymns essential for the preservation of the church. Gradually, however, this antiquarian outlook is fading away. The denominations understand that, in the view of the Reformers, the gospel is not tied to any specific form of church polity or worship. Such forms must be understood functionally, that is to say, as satisfying the spiritual needs of the followers of Christ in ever-changing circumstances. Thus various forms of polity and worship can and must be adopted in the course of time. No specific form of ecclesiastical life is necessary for redemption. Through the form they adopt in response to the specific demands of an age, the denominations make manifest that they are the people of the risen Lord. Hence, although they do not contribute to our redemption, the ecclesiastical forms have an important historical function in indicating the localities in which holy history takes place. Yet for that reason the underlying spiritual principle will now determine the form to be adopted.

The disintegration of the traditional modes of worship and church polity is most evident in the churches behind the Iron Curtain. There people discovered, under the pressure of adverse circumstances, that a great many of a denomination's traditional forms had been preserved because they were dear to past generations or because they facilitated or embellished the church's life. For instance, whereas the privileged position formerly enjoyed by the church had allowed a separation of instruction and devotion, under political coercion both had to be combined. A similar process is going on in the younger churches. The more they become aware of the centrality of spiritual life, the more outmoded the imitation of forms which originated in the entirely different environment of the sending churches will appear to them.

Increasingly it becomes obvious that a purely functional understanding of ecclesiastical forms is inappropriate. In order to be legitimate, the differences between denominations must have spiritual reasons, and their outward manifestations cannot be guided by practical programs only but must depend in the first place on the progress and maturity of spiritual life. By accentuating the differences, the contact with other denominations also raises the question why they have been adopted, and thus serves to emphasize the primacy of the spiritual. No wonder that the ecumenical age should be ushered in by radical changes in methods of evangelism, forms of liturgy, and styles of church architecture.

It must be kept in mind, however, that no more than a beginning has been made towards the consolidation of the Protestant position. As noted above, the diversity which is so characteristic of Protestantism, must not be understood in a purely functional way, because that would lead to relativism and thus to the loss of the unity we seek. Paradoxically, that unity is menaced by two developments, both of which ostensibly aim at unity. It is threatened on the one hand by the formation of international denominational organizations, such as the Lutheran World Federation, the World Alliance of Reformed Churches, the Lambeth Conference, and the World Methodist Conference. On the other hand, it is threatened by the new course taken by biblical theology.

Both trends are geared to overcoming the fragmentation of Protestantism. But the former, by emphasizing the denomination's heritage, takes back with one hand what it has granted to the World Council of Churches with the other. The inner contradiction of such policies should be obvious. It is not possible to form such international organization except on an historical basis. The various members are held together by what they are accustomed to do, or to believe, that is, by a common confession of faith, a common sacramental practice, or a common polity. But on such a basis, it is difficult, indeed impossible, for such a denominational body to do justice to the ongoing work of the Holy Spirit as he manifests himself in the life and growth of a denomination.

Any student interested in the work of international denominational meetings will notice that such gatherings are torn between two incompatible tendencies. There is the desire to stick to the "faith of the fathers," on the one hand, a desire which will eventually end either in an antiquarian dogmatism or in a formal traditionalism. In the opposite camp, one encounters the wish of individual theologians or groups to sell their respective concepts of a "modern" or modernized church to a reluctant denomination. In that case, the vagueness of what is to be considered modern, will serve to increase the intrinsic disintegration of that denomination without making a positive contribution to the life of the Church Universal. The solution of the problem of Protestant unity is to be sought in a completely different direction.

What is basically wrong in the manner Protestant denominations handle the present ecumenical problem, is not their effort to consolidate the denominations, but rather their failure to notice the alienation of denominational theology from the Scripture. While in international and interconfessional debates *sola scriptura* is emphasized,[6] the respective theologians seem to identify Scripture with the interpretation of the Bible handed down from the fathers, which most frequently turns out to be that of the orthodox theologians of the seventeenth century. The new biblicism is a welcome antidote for that tendency. During the nineteenth century, biblical theology was increasingly understood in a purely historical sense. Scholars wanted to know how the ideas held by the biblical writers were related to the thought of their period, and how their views grew and changed in the historical process. Underlying that approach was the axiom that the Bible lacked authority for our times because it contained the religious literature of a distant past.

The newer method of biblical study, inaugurated by men like Adolf Schlatter, Julius Schniewind, Karl Barth, Ernst Lohmeyer, and Gerhard von Rad, starts with the recognition of the authority of the Bible. Scholars were no longer preoccupied only with the historical growth of the biblical ideas, but rather turned in the first place to the question of the true meaning of the biblical texts. As a result, biblical theology has gradually replaced systematic theology in the thinking and preaching of many ministers and professors of theology. This tendency would be wholly laudatory if it did not result in a new subjective dogmatism. It appears that the individual scholar's research now decides whether or not we must espouse realized rather than futuristic eschatology, belief in a history of redemption rather than religious existentialism, faith as a collective attitude rather than personal trust, etc. What is to be deplored is not the inevitable diversity of interpretations of the Bible in the development of a new biblicism, but the failure to use the new views brought to

---

[6] See, for instance, Regin Prenter's article "Protestantismus" in *Lexikon für Theologie und Kirche,* 2nd ed., Vol. VIII, cols. 816-820.

light by biblical theology in a way that will truly restore the theological authority in Protestantism.

As has been pointed out, there never has been a Bible per se. The Bible which forms the basis of our faith exists only in the church, that is to say, as recognized, interpreted, and believed in by the church and passed on to subsequent generations in conjunction with the witness the church bears to its truthfulness. This correlation between the Bible on the one hand, and the faith and witness of the church on the other, has an important implication. Although remaining substantially the same throughout the ages, the church nevertheless passes through an historical process, because it exists in a changing world. Consequently, the Bible, in which the church believes and to which it bears witness, is not a static unit either. New experiences will lead to new perspectives and new emphases in the use and study of the Bible. That is all for the good since it helps to discover new facets of the wealth and depth of the biblical message. Inevitably, however, these changes carry with them the danger of overlooking other aspects of the biblical truth, of which past generations have been aware, and they may even imply those wrong who originally formed the foundation of the denomination, or of Protestantism in general.

For that reason, theology must be carried on as a confrontation of contemporary experience with one's denominational past, and in particular, its exegesis of the Bible. While its present experiences and insights have their legitimate place because they are evidences that the Lord's Spirit is at work in the church, disregarding the past interpretation of the Bible would be tantamount to denying that the same Spirit had been at work in the church's history. The purpose of such study of the history of exegesis should not be to add past theological insights to those of our age, but rather to deepen the insights gained by our generation. We have to ask ourselves why it was that the fathers adopted different emphases and were led to different interpretations of that Bible which we have in common with them. The difference between our exegesis and that of former generations can never be explained exclusively as originating in the differences of historical circumstance. We have above all to take into consideration the fact that the Spirit had led them to insights which in their phase of church history were necessary. The question which thus confronts us is not whether or not those emphases and insights have lost their significance for us, but rather how the spiritual "concern" of the past is related to the total message of the Bible, and in particular to our own interpretation.

It is obvious, for instance, that the sixteenth century's interest in justification resulted from the development of theological thought and spiritual life in the two preceding centuries. Since that situation has given way to an entirely new one in our day, it is not surprising that the orthodox understanding of justification no longer plays the same central role in modern biblical theology that it did in the lives of the Reformers and their pupils. But may it not be that we are in danger of losing sight of an important aspect of Paul's message by failing to ask ourselves what spiritual reality did the Reformers find in Paul's insistence on justification by faith? Our new experiences may lead to distortions of the biblical message, unless the spiritual history of the past is integrated in our faith. In turn, it seems that the spiritual authority, apart from which Protestantism would lose its right of existence, can be re-established and rendered articulate only in such a spiritual confrontation of our understanding of the Bible with the spiritual history of the church. In that way, theological individualism is led back into the fellowship of the believing church, and the antiquarian interest in the traditional views is revived by its contact with living faith.

The ecumenical movement is a phase of holy history. Under the guidance of the Holy Spirit the churches of Christendom have realized the need to give outward and effective expression to the unity of the Church Universal. In this process the Protestant church, brought into being by the divine calling of Luther, has its legitimate place. What can be accomplished by way of organization in the main has been done by the World Council of Churches. The powerful spiritual process that God has thereby set in motion is still in its initial stage. We can predict with certainty that the extensive organization of the World Council will become an intolerable burden rather than a blessing to Christianity if we fail the Spirit of God. What will emerge in the arena of close spiritual cooperation no one can foretell; but surely it will be a miracle in the eyes of those who see it.

INDEX

KANSAS SCHOOL OF RELIGION
University of Kansas
1300 Oread Avenue
LAWRENCE, KANSAS